Paris

A LITERARY COMPANION

Ian Littlewood

John Murray

First published 1987
by John Murray (Publishers) Ltd
50 Albemarle Street, London W1X 4BD

Typeset by Fakenham Photosetting Ltd
Fakenham, Norfolk

Printed and bound in Great Britain
at The Bath Press, Avon

British Library Cataloguing in Publication Data

Littlewood, Ian
Paris: a literary companion.
1. Literary landmarks—France—Paris
2. Paris (France)—Description—1975–
—Guide-books
I. Title
914.4'3604838   PQ148
ISBN 0-7195-4387-8

Contents

Illustrations

BN: Bibliothèque Nationale, Paris
MC: Musée Carnavalet. Photothèque des Musées de la Ville de
Paris

Introduction

Ah! la charmante chose
Quitter un pays morose
Pour Paris...
(Guillaume Apollinaire, 1880–1918)

'Was it fun in Paris?' asks Zelda Fitzgerald in a letter to Scott. 'Who did you see there and was the Madeleine pink at five o'clock and did the fountains fall with hollow delicacy into the framing of space in the Place de la Concorde, and did the blue creep out from behind the Colonades in the rue de Rivoli through the grill of the Tuileries and was the Louvre gray and metallic in the sun and did the trees hang brooding over the cafés and were there lights at night and the click of saucers and the auto horns that play de Bussey...?'[1] It scarcely matters whether we have noticed these things before—or whether they are still there to be noticed; Zelda's words are not intended to describe a place but to cast a spell. And the spell is stronger than the reality. Even the dismal changes of the past half-century make curiously little difference to our vision of the city. Choking on exhaust fumes at the edge of the place de la Concorde, we are still more likely to see it with Zelda's eyes than our own.

Paris comes to us second-hand. Our imagination has been there first, worked upon by the imagination of others. It is through the filter of their memories, desires, dreams, descriptions, lies, gossip that we experience the city. What we respond to is an imagined place. The dull reality of the boulevard Montparnasse will never be quite enough to triumph over the romantic associations of its name. In *À la recherche du temps perdu* Proust's narrator, Marcel, tells how as a child he was obliged to play in the Champs-Elysées—but there was nothing in this public garden that attached itself to his dreams: 'Going there I found unendurable. If only Bergotte had described the place in one of his books, I should, no doubt, have longed to see and to know it, like so many things else of which a simulacrum had first found its way into my imagination. That kept things warm, made them live, gave them personality, and I sought then to find their counterpart in reality...'[2]

For anyone who has known a similar feeling there is scarcely a corner of Paris that does not awaken imaginative echoes of one sort or another. This book is an attempt to capture some of them. It can at best offer only a personal selection. What Balzac alone wrote about the streets of Paris would fill a volume larger than this. Montmartre, les Halles, Montparnasse, Saint-Germain-des-Prés—all of them have whole books devoted to their history and mythology. The haunting images of Paris created by French film-makers are unrepresented here. So, too, are a number of appealing novels and poems which do not lend themselves to brief quotation. A fondly remembered scene often yields no more than a few scattered phrases, vivid in context but lifeless in isolation. No one, I suppose, will read the book without regretting some one or other absent writer or unmentioned place. My own regrets are many.

This is not a guide that takes the reader through Paris street by street, but it does focus in some detail on particular areas of the city. Within obvious geographical limits I have tried to arrange these areas according to the prevailing tone of a given district—the faubourg Saint-Germain, for example, seemed in better company with the residential quarters of western Paris than with the intellectual centres of the left bank. The book is designed, as its title indicates, to be a literary companion rather than just an anthology—a book for the departure lounge or the Channel ferry, but also, more precisely, for the café in the place de la Contrescarpe or the bench in the Luxembourg Gardens. With this in mind I have included a map at the start of each section which should enable readers to get their bearings.

For those inclined to track down some of the addresses mentioned in the text it might be worth noting that street numbers in Paris are determined by the street's relation to the river. Those streets which are roughly parallel to the Seine are numbered from east to west, following the current of the river; those which are roughly perpendicular are numbered from the river outwards. Odd numbers are on the left.

Not everyone will feel an impulse to tramp the streets. For many it is enough just to be in Paris ... to open the long windows onto the balcony, to watch the faces in the café mirror, to tread the white-tiled corridors of the métro stations. The place is kind to idlers. As Bertie Wooster once remarked, in a phrase which offers itself as a genial epigraph to guides to the city of every sort, 'There's something about Paris that always makes me feel fairly full of *espièglerie* and *joie de vivre*.'[3]

CHAPTER 1

The Islands, the Seine and its Bridges

The Ile de la Cité

Lutetia—the beginnings

'Paris is a beast of a city to be in,' declared the essayist William Hazlitt when he visited it in 1824:

> Fancy yourself in London with the footpath taken away, so that you are forced to walk along the middle of the streets with a dirty gutter running through them, fighting your way through coaches, waggons, and hand-carts trundled along by large mastiff-dogs, with the houses twice as high, greasy holes for shop-windows, and piles of wood, green-stalls, and wheelbarrows placed at the doors, and the contents of wash-hand basins pouring out of a dozen stories—fancy all this and worse, and, with a change of scene, you are in Paris.[1]

Hazlitt might almost have been describing a town from the Middle Ages—as in some ways he was. This was the old Paris, poised on the brink of dissolution. Its nucleus was the ancient quarter of the Ile de la Cité. Whatever was cramped and dark and dangerous in the rest of the city was worse on the island. To Eugène Sue when he wrote the opening scenes of *Les mystères de Paris* (1842–3) it was like some grimy region of the underworld: 'The mud-coloured houses were pierced by occasional windows with worm-eaten frames and practically

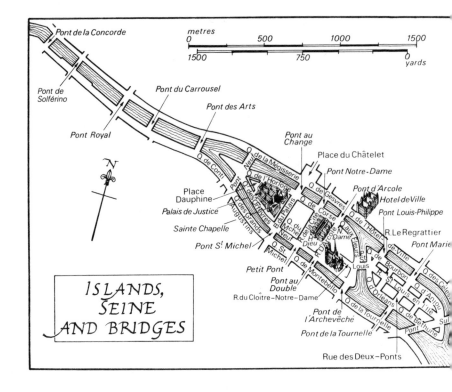

Pont de la Concorde

metres
0   500   1000   1500

1500   750   0
yards

Pont de Solférino

Pont du Carrousel

Pont des Arts

Pont Royal

N

Pont au Change

Place du Châtelet

Pont Notre-Dame

Pont d'Arcole

Hôtel-de-Ville

Pont Louis-Philippe

Place Dauphine

Palais de Justice

Sainte Chapelle

Pont S.¹ Michel

Q. de Conti

Pont Neuf

Q. des Grands Augustins

Q. de l'Horloge

Q. de la Mégisserie

du Palais

de l'Horloge

Q. de Gesvres

R. de la Cité

de Corse

Q. aux Fleurs

Q. de l'Hôtel de Ville

R. Le Regrattier

Pont Marie

Q. du Marché Neuf

St Michel

Dieu

N.-Dame

Petit Pont

Pont au Double

R. du Cloître-Notre-Dame

Q. de Montebello

St Louis

Q. de la Tournelle

Pont de l'Archevêché

Pont de la Tournelle

Rue des Deux-Ponts

Q. de Bourbon

St Louis en l'Île

Q. d'Orléans

Q. d'Anjou

Q. des Célestins

Q. de Béthune

Sully

ISLANDS, SEINE AND BRIDGES

no panes. Dark, noisome alleys led to stairways still darker and more noisome, so steep that they could only be climbed with the aid of a well-rope fastened by grappling-irons into the damp, high walls.'[2] Then, in the middle of the 19th century, came Baron Georges Eugène Haussmann, Prefect of the Seine under Napoleon III. Within a few years everything had changed. Haussmann was not given to half measures; he evacuated a large part of the island's population and swept away the network of stifling old streets. In their place he laid the dead hand of official architecture. Of the Ile de la Cité as it used to be, Notre-Dame, Sainte-Chapelle and the old prison of the Conciergerie are more or less all that is left; these buildings, and the intimate little triangle of trees and houses that forms the place Dauphine, adjoining the Pont Neuf. This too escaped the most drastic of Haussmann's plans. Modestly tucked in beside the bridge, it has a singular charm which the leader of the Surrealist Movement, André Breton, set out to analyse:

I have been moved to say, in the past, that the place Dauphine 'is truly one of the most secluded places I know ... Every time I've been there, I added, I have felt gradually slipping away from me any desire to go elsewhere; I have had to struggle to disengage myself from a very soft embrace which is too pleasantly insistent and, in the last analysis, destructive' (Nadja). It was only later that, with the force of a revelation, the significance of this impression became clear to me. Now it seems difficult to believe that others before me, venturing into the place Dauphine from the Pont Neuf, should not have been overwhelmed at the sight of its triangular formation, with slightly curved lines, and of the slit which bisects it into two wooded spaces. It is, without any doubt, the sex of Paris which is outlined in this shade ...[3]

Not, after all, such an outlandish fancy, since it was on the Ile de la Cité that Paris came into being. Two thousand years ago, when the island was a desolate patch of marshland dotted with huts, the tribe of the Parisii selected it for their stronghold. The decision was essentially a military one, and it is in a military context that we first find mention of the place that was then called Lutetia. In 52 BC, at a time when Julius Caesar was hard-pressed by a coalition of Gallic tribes, the settlement enjoyed a brief but spectacular moment of importance. It was here, in an intricate series of moves and counter-moves, that Labienus succeeded in out-manoeuvring the aged Gallic chieftain Camulogenus. On the site of what is now the faubourg Saint-Germain he defeated the Gauls in a battle which had a decisive influence on Caesar's campaign. And so, in Book VII of De Bello Gallico, Paris made its first, troubled appearance in literature.

In Roman hands the island prospered. Four centuries later, Julian, the apostate emperor who had abandoned Christianity for older and more congenial gods, found it a pleasing site for his headquarters. He writes affectionately of his 'dear Lutetia', and it was from Julian's own description[4] that Gibbon later drew his sketch of 4th-century Paris in The Decline and Fall of the Roman Empire:

A mind like that of Julian must have felt the general happiness of which he was the author; but he viewed with peculiar satisfaction and complacency the city of Paris, the seat of his winter residence, and the object of his partial affection. That splendid capital, which now embraces an ample territory on either side of the Seine, was originally confined to the small island in the midst of the river, from whence the inhabitants derived a supply of pure and salubrious water. The river bathed the foot of the walls; and the town was accessible only by two wooden bridges. A forest overspread the northern side of the Seine, but on the south, the ground which now bears the name of the University was insensibly covered with houses, and adorned with a palace and amphitheatre, baths, an aqueduct, and a field of Mars for the exercise of the Roman troops. The severity of the climate was tempered by the neighbourhood of the ocean; and with some precautions, which experience had taught, the vine and fig-tree were successfully cultivated. But in remarkable winters the Seine was deeply frozen; and the huge pieces of ice that floated down the stream might be compared, by an Asiatic, to the blocks of white marble which were extracted from the quarries of Phrygia. The licentiousness and corruption of Antioch recalled to the memory of Julian the severe and simple manners of his beloved Lutetia, where the amusements of the theatre were unknown or despised. He indignantly contrasted the effeminate Syrians with the brave and honest simplicity of the Gauls, and almost forgave the intemperance which was the only stain of the Celtic character.[5]

Sainte-Chapelle

According to one tradition, it was on the site of the modern Palais de Justice that in AD 360 Julian's troops proclaimed him emperor. Any remnants of the Roman fortification have long since disappeared. Today the oldest survival within the precincts of the Palace is the church of Sainte-Chapelle. It was built at great speed (33 weeks) in the middle of the 13th century to house the crown of thorns and a selection of other relics which Saint Louis had purchased at an exorbitant price from the Emperor of Constantinople. When she visited the church in 1835, Frances Trollope, mother of the author of *Barchester Towers* and the Palliser novels, recorded with punctilious disdain a list of the relics originally lodged there. Amongst them were the rod of Moses, a sample of the Virgin's milk, Christ's swaddling clothes, some of his blood, and some more blood miraculously distilled from a statue of him which had been struck by an infidel. Mrs Trollope clearly felt that Saint Louis had been taken advantage of. 'Is it not wonderful', she asks, 'that the Emperor of Constantinople could consent to part with such precious treasures for the lucre of gain?'[6]

Although the spire of the chapel has three times burned down—the present one dates from the mid-19th century—the building has in other respects fared better than its relics, which were dispersed at the time of the Revolution. Its chief memorial in literature is Nicolas Boileau's satirical poem *Le lutrin* (1674), which announces its subject with a mocking echo of Virgil's 'Arms and the man I sing...' at the start of the *Aeneid*:

> Je chante les combats, et ce Prélat terrible
> Qui par ses longs travaux, et sa force invincible,
> Dans un illustre Église exerçant son grand coeur,
> Fit placer à la fin un Lutrin dans le Choeur.*

This was the trivial basis of the affair. Without prior warning the Treasurer of the Sainte-Chapelle had positioned a large lectern just in front of the Precentor's stall, thereby outraging the Precentor himself, who took this as a calculated insult. The bitter wrangle which followed was turned by Boileau's poem into one of the most famous ecclesiastical disputes in history.

Gargantua at Notre-Dame

While Sainte-Chapelle was building, the crown of thorns was temporarily lodged in Notre-Dame. This great church, which took shape between the mid-12th and mid-13th centuries, has

---

* I sing of the fights and the fearsome prelate, who through lengthy toil and unconquerable resolution, displaying his great spirit in an illustrious church, managed to have a lectern placed in the choir.

probably elicited more tedious descriptions than any other building in Paris. Nowhere does the novelist's prose slip more readily into the bland tones of the guidebook. Encountering yet another hymn to soaring buttresses and historic stones, the reader's eyes inevitably begin to glaze. To this surfeit of decorum the indecorous writings of François Rabelais (1494?–1553?) provide a welcome antidote. One of the early tourists to visit Notre-Dame was his giant Gargantua:

> Some days after they had finished their refreshment, Gargantua went to see the sights of the town, and everyone stared at him in great wonder. For the Parisians are such simpletons, such gapers, and such feckless idiots that a buffoon, a pedlar of indulgences, a mule with bells on its collar, or a fiddler at a crossroad will draw a greater crowd than a good preacher of the Gospel.
>
> The people so pestered him, in fact, that he was compelled to take a rest on the towers of Notre-Dame; and when from there he saw so many, pressing all around him, he said in a clear voice:
>
> 'I think these clodhoppers want me to pay for my kind reception and offer them a *solatium*. They are quite justified, and I am going to give them some wine, to buy my welcome. But only in sport, *par ris*.'
>
> Then, with a smile, he undid his magnificent codpiece and, bringing out his john-thomas, pissed on them so fiercely that he drowned two hundred and sixty thousand, four hundred and eighteen persons, not counting the women and small children.
>
> A number of them, however, were quick enough on their feet to escape this piss-flood; and when they reached the top of the hill above the University, sweating, coughing, spitting, and out of breath, they began to swear and curse, some in a fury and others in sport (*par ris*): 'Carymary, Carymara!* My holy tart, we've been drenched in sport! We've been drenched *par ris*.'
>
> Hence it was that the city was ever afterwards called Paris. Formerly it had been named *Leucetia*, as Strabo tells

---

* A cabalistic spell.

us in his fourth book; which in Greek signifies *white place.*
This was on account of the white thighs of the ladies of that
city. And since at this re-christening all the spectators swore,
each by the saints of his own parish, the Parisians, who are
made up of all nations and all sorts, have proved by nature
both good swearers and good men of law, also somewhat
overbearing. For which reason Joaninus de Baranco in *libro
de copiositate reverentiarum,* considers that they derive
their name of Parrhesians from the Greek, in which language the word signifies bold of speech.

After this exploit Gargantua examined the great bells that
hung in those towers, and played a harmonious peal on
them. As he did so it struck him that they would serve very
well for cow-bells to hang on the collar of his mare, which he
had decided to send back to his father, loaded with Brie
cheese and fresh herrings. So he took them straight off to his
lodgings.[7]

Thomas Coryate on the feast of Corpus Christi

From its earliest days Notre-Dame became the focal point of
Paris's major religious festivals and state religious occasions. It
was at the season of one of these festivals, the feast of Corpus
Christi, that Thomas Coryate happened to be in Paris in 1608.
The son of a Somerset vicar, he was on the first leg of the
European journey he describes in the comprehensively entitled
*Coryat's Crudities Hastily gobled up in five Moneths travells
in France, Savoy, Italy, Rhetia commonly called the Grisons
country, Helvetia alias Switzerland, some parts of high Ger-
many and the Netherlands; Newly digested in the hungry aire
of Odcombe in the County of Somerset, and now dispersed to
the nourishment of the travelling Members of this Kingdome.*
Coryate was not a man to hide his prejudices. This account
of the Corpus Christi procession manages to be both idiosyn-
cratic and at the same time highly representative. Coryate's
narrative catches a tone which we hear with some frequency
from English observers of Paris over the next three centuries:

About nine of the clock the same day in the morning, I went
to the Cathedrall Church which is dedicated to our Lady (as

I have before written) to the end to observe the strange ceremonies of that day, which for novelty sake, but not for any harty devotion I was contented to behold, as being the first that ever I saw of that kinde, and I hartily wish they may be the last. No sooner did I enter into the Church but a great company of Clergy men came forth singing, and so continued all the time of the procession. [...] Also in the same traine there were many couples of little singing choristers, many of them not above eight or nine yeares old, and few above a dozen: which prety innocent punies were so egregiously deformed by those that had authority over them, that they could not choose but move great commiseration in any relenting spectator. For they had not a quarter so much haire left upon their heads as they brought with them into the world, out of their mothers wombs, being so clean shaved away round about their whole heads that a man could perceive no more then the very rootes. A spectacle very pittifull (me thinks) to behold, though the Papists esteeme it holy. The last man of the whole traine was the Bishop of Paris, a proper and comly man as any I saw in all the city, of some five and thirty yeares old. He walked not sub dio, that is, under the open aire, as the rest did. But he had a rich cannopy carried over him, supported with many little pillers on both sides. [...] As for the streets of Paris they were more sumptuously adorned that day then any other day of the whole yeare, every street of speciall note being on both sides thereof, from the pentices of their houses to the lower end of the wall hanged with rich cloth of arras, and the costliest tapestry that they could provide. The shewes of our Lady street being so hyperbolical in pomp that day, that it exceeded the rest by many degrees.[8]

When Coryate saw it, Notre-Dame was still a relatively youthful building. By the time Victor Hugo's *Notre-Dame de Paris* was published in 1831, it was beginning to show signs of wear. The Revolution had turned it first into a temple to Reason, then into a temple to the Supreme Being, and had finally settled on using it as a foodstore. The stonework was in disrepair; the decorations were crumbling. 'On the face of this ancient queen of our cathedrals', wrote Hugo, 'beside each wrinkle one invariably finds a scar.' It was in response to this that he set out to harness the romantic mood of the moment on its behalf. His story of the hunch-backed bell-ringer and the beautiful gypsy was a powerful catalyst to the work of restoration which took place between 1845 and 1864 under the supervision of Viollet-le-Duc. The building that we see now owes a significant debt to Hugo's novel.

The quai aux Fleurs—Héloïse and Abélard

It may be that part of Hugo's success lay in giving back to the church its mediaeval context. Rising sheer above the cluttered hovels of the island, its very presence must have seemed almost supernatural to those who lived beneath it. But the cathedral was only the last of a long line of places of worship, stretching back to the temple of Jupiter which the Romans erected on this site early in the first century. Immediately before the construction of Notre-Dame there was a Romanesque church here, also dedicated to Our Lady, and amongst its canons was one whose implacable character has ensured the survival of his name.

If you walk beside the cathedral along the rue du Cloître-Notre-Dame and then turn left up the quai aux Fleurs, you will find at no. 9 a plaque to the memory of two of Paris's most celebrated lovers. This was the site of Canon Fulbert's house, where he lived in the early 12th century with his niece Héloïse. What happened when the brilliant young Peter Abélard was engaged as her tutor is described by Abélard himself in the autobiography he wrote a few years before his death in 1142:

> Now there dwelt in that same city of Paris a certain young girl named Héloïse, the niece of a canon who was called Fulbert. Her uncle's love for her was equalled only by his desire that she should have the best education which he could possibly procure for her. Of no mean beauty, she stood out above all by reason of her abundant knowledge of letters. Now this virtue is rare among women, and for that very reason it doubly graced the maiden, and made her the most worthy of renown in the entire kingdom. It was this

young girl whom I, after carefully considering all those qualities which are wont to attract lovers, determined to unite with myself in the bonds of love, and indeed the thing seemed to me very easy to be done. So distinguished was my name, and I possessed such advantages of youth and comeliness, that no matter what woman I might favour with my love, I dreaded rejection of none. Then, too, I believed that I could win the maiden's consent all the more easily by reason of her knowledge of letters and her zeal therefor; so, even if we were parted, we might yet be together in thought with the aid of written messages. Perchance, too, we might be able to write more boldly than we could speak, and thus at all times could we live in joyous intimacy.

Thus, utterly aflame with my passion for this maiden, I sought to discover means whereby I might have daily and familiar speech with her, thereby the more easily to win her consent. For this purpose I persuaded the girl's uncle, with the aid of some of his friends, to take me into his household —for he dwelt hard by my school—in return for the payment of a small sum. My pretext for this was that the care of my own household was a serious handicap to my studies, and likewise burdened me with an expense far greater than I could afford. Now, he was a man keen in avarice, and likewise he was most desirous for his niece that her study of letters should ever go forward, so, for these two reasons, I easily won his consent to the fulfillment of my wish, for he was fairly agape for my money, and at the same time believed that his niece would vastly benefit by my teaching. More even than this, by his own earnest entreaties he fell in with my desires beyond anything I had dared to hope, opening the way for my love; for he entrusted her wholly to my guidance, begging me to give her instruction whensoever I might be free from the duties of my school, no matter whether by day or by night, and to punish her sternly if ever I should find her negligent of her tasks. In all this the man's simplicity was nothing short of astounding to me; I should not have been more smitten with wonder if he had entrusted a tender lamb to the care of a ravenous wolf. When he had thus given her into my charge, not alone to be taught but even to be disciplined, what had he done save to give free scope to my desires, and to offer me every opportunity, even if I had not sought it, to bend her to my will with threats and blows if I failed to do so with caresses? There were, however, two things which particularly served to allay any foul suspicion: his own love for his niece, and my former reputation for continence.

Why should I say more? We were united first in the dwelling that sheltered our love, and then in the hearts that burned with it. Under the pretext of study we spent our hours in the happiness of love, and learning held out to us the secret opportunities that our passion craved. Our speech was more of love than of the books which lay open before us; our kisses far outnumbered our reasoned words. Our hands sought less the book than each other's bosoms; love drew our eyes together far more than the lesson drew them to the pages of our text. In order that there might be no suspicion, there were, indeed, sometimes blows, but love gave them, not anger; they were the marks, not of wrath, but of a tenderness surpassing the most fragrant balm in sweetness. What followed? No degree in love's progress was left untried by our passion, and if love itself could imagine any wonder as yet unknown, we discovered it. And our inexperience of such delights made us all the more ardent in our pursuit of them, so that our thirst for one another was still unquenched.[9]

In due course the lovers had a son whom they quaintly called Astrolabe. For a time it seemed that a reconciliation with Fulbert might be possible. But the canon's revenge, when it came, was fearful. Abélard was castrated by Fulbert's kinsmen, Héloïse ended her life in a nunnery.

The Hôtel-Dieu

Just beyond the quai aux Fleurs, fronting the quai de Corse, are the heavy stone walls of the Hôtel-Dieu. This hospital, which now occupies the area between the pont Notre-Dame and the pont d'Arcole, is a construction of the late 19th century. It used to stand, equally forbidding, on the other side of the island, roughly where the statue of Charlemagne is today, in front of Notre-Dame.

Through all the accounts of mediaeval Paris it is one of the names which recur most frequently. In his biography of François Villon, D. B. Wyndham Lewis describes how the harsh beginnings of the 15th century gave way after the end of the English occupation to even worse:

> In 1438 it seemed as though all the long-drawn-out miseries of the Hundred Years' War had culminated in a final onslaught on the unhappy town. The winter was terrible: famine raged; a plague carried off 45,000 inhabitants. The sick lay starving in the Hostel-Dieu, or dropped in the grass-grown streets to freeze to death; and the cry *'Hélas, doux Dieu! je meurs de faim et de froit!'* arose day and night. Bands of cutthroats prowled the suburbs. The wolves, ravening in that dreadfull cold, slunk freely across the frozen Seine and in and out of the town, and more than once carried off infants alive.[10]

Inside the Hôtel-Dieu the sick survived as best they could during the Middle Ages, naked and on average three to a bed, though the number sometimes rose to eight. According to a common saying, there were on each pallet 'the sick, the dying, and the dead'. For a long time the hospital's mortality rate remained staggeringly high. From the late 17th century its dead were taken off to be buried in the cimetière de Clamart in the rue des Fossés-Saint-Marcel, just to the south of the modern Jardin des Plantes. There were no tombstones; it was the cemetery of the poor. In his *Tableau de Paris* (1781–9) Louis-Sébastien Mercier paints a grim picture of the daily cortège:

> The bodies which the Hôtel-Dieu vomits forth daily are carried to Clamart, a huge cemetery whose pit is ever open. These corpses have no bier; they are sown up in rough cloth. They are removed from their beds with dispatch, and more than one sick man who had been supposed dead has come to life under the urgent hand that was enclosing him in this

coarse shroud; others have called out that they were alive in the very cart that was taking them to the grave.

The cart is pulled by twelve men. A wretched priest in filthy vestments, a bell, a cross—such is the ceremony that awaits the poor.

This gloomy cart leaves the Hôtel-Dieu every day at 4 a.m.; it makes its journey in the silence of the night. As it goes by, the bell which precedes it awakens those who sleep. You have to be there when it passes to get a real idea of the effect it has, the sound of this cart. It casts a shadow over the soul.

At times of high mortality it has been known to go by as many as four times in twenty-four hours. It can hold up to fifty bodies, with the children between the legs of the adults. The corpses are tipped into a broad deep pit, then quick-lime is thrown onto them; and this unclosing maw tells the horrified spectator that it would have no difficulty in devouring every person who dwells in the capital.[11]

The Morgue

Next to the Hôtel-Dieu, appropriately enough, was the Morgue. 'Those who have never seen the Morgue', wrote Dickens in *The Uncommercial Traveller* (1861), 'may see it perfectly, by presenting to themselves an indifferently paved coach house accessible from the streets by a pair of folding gates ...'[12] It moved to the quai du Marché-Neuf in 1804 and stayed there for sixty years, becoming in the course of time a tourist attraction which exercised a peculiar fascination over certain writers, of whom Dickens was one. 'Whenever I am in Paris', he confessed, 'I am dragged by an invisible force into the Morgue.'[13] And Wilkie Collins, who accompanied Dickens on a number of his trips to Paris, was also sensitive to its appeal. It is in the Paris Morgue that we get our last glimpse of the villainous Count Fosco at the end of *The Woman in White* (1859–60), 'unowned, unknown, exposed to the flippant curiosity of a French mob!'

Another writer whose imagination was caught by this grim place was Emile Zola. He came here while researching the background for his novel *Thérèse Raquin*—with suitably macabre results. Laurent, having murdered Thérèse's husband, starts keeping a daily check on the Morgue to see if his body has yet been fished out of the river:

> When he entered, a stale odour, the odour of washed flesh, nauseated him, and cold chills ran over his skin; the dampness of the walls seemed to saturate his clothes, which grew heavier on his shoulders. He went directly to the glass partition that separates the visitors from the corpses; he pressed his pale face against the panes and looked about. Before him were the rows of grey slabs. Here and there on the slabs naked bodies made patches of green and yellow, of white and red. Some bodies still kept their uncorrupted flesh in the stiffness of death; others looked like heaps of bloody, rotting meat. Behind, on the wall, hung pitiful rags, rumpled skirts and trousers gawking from the bare plaster. At first, Laurent saw nothing but the general duskiness of the slabs and the walls, stained with rusty brown and black by the clothing of the corpses. There was a singing sound of running water.[...]
>
> Every morning, during all the time he was there, he heard the sound of spectators arriving and leaving behind him.
>
> The Morgue is a show within reach of every purse, a spectacle of which passers-by, poor or rich, may avail themselves for nothing. The door stands open, anyone is allowed in. There are connoisseurs who go out of their way in order not to miss a single one of these performances staged by death. When the slabs are empty, people go out disappointed, cheated, muttering. When the slabs are well filled, when there is a fine display of human flesh, spectators crowd one another, indulge in cheap emotions, are horrified, joke, applaud or catcall, as at the theatre, and leave contented, saying that the Morgue has a hit today.[14]

The Conciergerie

Across the boulevard du Palais from the site of the Morgue, the quai des Orfèvres curves round towards the tip of the island. If

the name of quai des Orfèvres can stir memories in many who
have never set foot in Paris, it is largely the achievement of one
man.

In 1929 a little-known Belgian writer called Georges Simenon left Paris by boat for a two-year tour of the European
canals. It was in the course of this trip, during a stopover in the
Netherlands, that Inspector Maigret was born. While his boat
was being recaulked, Simenon passed the time by writing
Pietr-le-Letton (1931). It opens in Maigret's office at police
headquarters, 36 quai des Orfèvres. The setting was to recur in
later novels, as was the bulky figure of Maigret himself, refill-
ing his pipe as he turns his attention to another case:

> It was November. Dusk was falling. From his office window
> he could see a stretch of the Seine, the Place Saint-Michel,
> and a floating wash-house, all shrouded in a blue haze
> through which the gas lamps twinkled like stars as they lit
> up one by one.[15]

The view, the office, the quai des Orfèvres, the Brasserie
Dauphine in the adjoining square – all were to become, over
the next forty years, part of a familiar landscape to millions of
readers.

The complex of buildings in which Maigret had his office
has gradually swallowed up the whole area between the quai
des Orfèvres and the quai de l'Horloge, and with it a handful
of streets that included the rue de Jérusalem and the rue de
Nazareth, the birthplaces respectively of Boileau and Voltaire.
It is from the quai de l'Horloge that one enters the turreted
precincts of the Conciergerie. Originally the prison of the
King's Palace, the Conciergerie was later used to accommo-
date the overflow of criminals from the Grand Châtelet. During the Revolution its role changed again: Danton, Robespierre and Charlotte Corday all passed through its gates, and
it was from here, on 16 October 1793, that Marie Antoinette
was led out to the guillotine. A modified version of the cell in
which she spent her final weeks is still on view to the public.

The poet André Chénier (1762–94) made a shorter stay. He
was brought here for a single night, before being taken out to
the eastern reaches of the city to be guillotined in the place de la

Nation. Like many others with liberal inclinations, he had hoped to see the social changes of the Revolution co-exist with an adherence to the monarchy. It was a mistake which in the 1790s could have only one issue.

The prison, even with its electric lights and clattering parties of tourists, is a cheerless place. At the time of the Revolution its inmates had little to hope for. Sir William Codrington, who had been arrested as an enemy alien in 1794, was one of the few whose imprisonment there did not lead to the guillotine:

> Two of us procured the seventeenth part of a small apartment. The beds were placed so near together that one was obliged to get in at the feet; and though we paid for them apart, it was three weeks before I could get any sheets; and when at last I had them, I could with great facility have crept through them. But the room being very small and the ceiling so very low, and so many persons stove in so narrow a compass, the air was so bad we could none of us sleep, at least not for more than an hour, often less, and sometimes not at all.
>
> As we were locked up every evening about five o'clock, and the door not opened until near ten the next morning, a tub was placed in the room ... We had with us a tolerably good physican, who advised us to burn incense every night before we went to bed, in order to purify the air, and to take a mouthful of brandy every morning as soon as we got up, as a preventive against infection. We all of us rose in the morning with a great dryness in the throat or something of a soreness. At twelve o'clock every night we used to be visited by three or four turnkeys, with as many great dogs. With large staves they used to thump against the ceiling, open the windows, and with an iron hammer beat against the bars to see that all was safe and sound. [...]
>
> Four months I passed in this pleasing abode, having seen half my room companions quit me to take their final leave; and the half of that half have since shared the same fate.[16]

After the Revolution the Conciergerie continued to be used as a prison throughout the 19th century,[17] and in 1852 it played host to another eminent man of letters. Prosper Mérimée, the author of *Carmen*, had rashly intervened in the case of a friend accused of theft. Despite the fact that he was by then an officer of the Legion of Honour and a member of the Académie Française, he was sentenced to a fortnight's imprisonment for having insulted the officers of the court. Since he was also Inspector-General of Historic Monuments, his confinement in the Conciergerie was not without a certain irony. Nonetheless, he installed himself comfortably enough, passing the hot July days in the embrasure of his cell window, which he had furnished with cushions and a Persian rug. To Mme de Circourt he wrote on the 15th of the month:

> Madame, don't you think I was well-advised to keep cool in the Palace of St. Louis during this appalling heatwave. People bring me fearful reports of it in the tower where I am installed at the moment. I have already accustomed myself to my new life-style, and I no longer hear the bell that is rung in the morning to wake the prisoners. I read, I write trivia, and I receive the honest fellows who haven't forgotten me. Monsieur Bocher has been here for about a week and we make a merry business of the bad dinners that are sent over from the tap-room of the *Messieurs*. In the evening we walk in the *cour des femmes*,* where we find four very agreeable cats. Although they're attached to the Prefecture of Police, their manners are so elegant and so well-bred that one would take them for court cats. The company here is very diverse, as you would expect. We do not make any visits and we have no contact with our neighbours on the corridor other than to lend them the newspaper. One of them is a M. Lusarda, a Portuguese, who throws nitric acid in the faces of people who find his wife attractive. The other is a poor devil who in '49 took it into his head to speak ill of the Republic.[18]

It is a lighter note than most on which to leave the Conciergerie, and with it the Ile de la Cité. There is little else to detain the visitor who has already strolled along the quais and down

---

* This sad little patch of open ground, where the women prisoners washed their clothes and where the daily farewells were made by those on their way to the guillotine, can still be seen by visitors to the Conciergerie.

to the tip of the island. Since the days of Haussmann, writers have often enough admired its outline from a distance, but for the new streets and the monumental buildings that went with them there has been little enthusiasm.

The Ile Saint-Louis

'There is an island in Paris [...] the inhabitants of which are quite separate from the rest of [the city], they dine at a different hour, their manners are different; and they talk of crossing the bridge as the ancients talking of crossing the Hellespont and they never signalized themselves by any excesses in the revolution ...'[19]

These strange aboriginals observed by the sister of the novelist Maria Edgeworth in the early 19th century were the natives of the Ile Saint-Louis. Their habits, it is true, have over the years fallen more into line with the rest of Paris, but a sense of remoteness, noticeable as soon as one crosses the pont Saint-Louis, still lingers over the island. The change is immediate. There are no métro stations here, no large banks, no supermarkets, little evidence of the hustle of business; the 20th century, held at bay by the wealth of the island's modern inhabitants, has touched it lightly. 'If you walk along the streets of the Ile Saint-Louis,' wrote Balzac, 'do not ask why you feel gripped by a sort of nervous sadness. For its cause you have only to look at the solitude of the place, at the gloomy aspect of its houses and its large empty hôtels.*'[20] Even today the streets have changed remarkably little since the 1650s. 'One of the loneliest places in Paris,' Vincent Cronin called it in his *Companion Guide*.

It is perhaps this loneliness that prompts nostalgia. In Hemingway's *The Sun Also Rises* (1926), Jake Barnes, the drifting, disillusioned narrator, crosses over to the island with a friend for dinner. Afterwards they walk together round the quais. Hemingway's description takes in all the classic elements—the *bateau mouche*, the night-time silhouettes, the black water, the lovers under the bridge—and in doing so

---

* The word hôtel/hotel can be confusing. Where it is used in the sense of a large private residence, I have retained the French accent.

captures something both of his narrator's sense of separate-
ness and of the melancholy that permeates the island:

> We walked along under the trees that grew out over the river
> on the Quai d'Orléans side of the island. Across the river
> were the broken walls of old houses that were being torn
> down.
>   'They're going to cut a street through.'
>   'They would,' Bill said.
>   We walked on and circled the island. The river was dark
> and a *bateau mouche* went by, all bright with lights, going
> fast and quiet up and out of sight under the bridge. Down
> the river was Notre Dame squatting against the night sky.
> We crossed to the left bank of the Seine by the wooden
> foot-bridge from the Quai de Béthune, and stopped on the
> bridge and looked down the river at Notre Dame. Standing
> on the bridge the island looked dark, the houses were high
> against the sky, and the trees were shadows. [...] We leaned
> on the wooden rail of the bridge and looked up the river to
> the lights of the big bridges. Below, the water was smooth
> and black. It made no sound against the piles of the bridge.
> A man and a girl passed us. They were walking with their
> arms around each other.[21]

This was a part of Paris that Hemingway knew well, since the
offices of Ford Madox Ford's *Transatlantic Review* were at 29
quai d'Anjou,[22] along with the Three Mountains Press. 'We
printed and published in a domed wine-vault, exceedingly old
and cramped, on the Ile Saint-Louis with a grey view of the
Seine below the Quais.'[23] Hemingway was both a contributor
to the magazine and a reader for the publishing house. In
summer he would read the manuscripts outside by the river,
within easy reach of the Rendez-vous des Mariniers, a hotel
and restaurant on the quai which had been discovered by John
Dos Passos during the First World War and in which he had
written his novel *Three Soldiers* (1921) with its affectionate
recollections of post-war Paris.

The same restaurant was later frequented by Cyril Connolly. It was natural that a writer so nostalgic in temperament

should have felt drawn to the island. From the drab world of wartime London, where he was editing the literary magazine *Horizon*, he looked back to Paris for images of a life from which he was now cut off: 'Tout mon mal vient de Paris. There befell the original sin and the original ecstasy; there were the holy places—the Cross Roads and the Island. Quai Bourbon, Rue de Vaugirard, Quai d'Anjou.'[24] The Island was of course the Ile Saint-Louis, where he had lived for a time before the war. His evocation of it strikes a characteristic note:

> The Ile Saint-Louis strains at her moorings, the river eddies round the stone prow where tall poplars stand like masts, and mist rises about the decaying houses which seventeenth-century nobles raised on their meadows. Yielding asphalt, sliding waters; long windows with iron bars set in damp walls; anguish and fear. Rendez-vous des Mariniers, Hôtel de Lauzun: moment of the night when the saint's blood liquefies, when the leaves shiver and presentiments of loss stir within the dark coil of our fatality.[25]

Today the hôtel de Lauzun, at 17 quai d'Anjou, is owned by the City of Paris and hired out for public lectures. Its past has sometimes been less respectable. Built in the mid-17th century by Louis Le Vau, it was later to become, under the name of hôtel Pimodan, one of the centres of the literary and artistic bohemia of the 19th century and the meeting-place of le Club des Hachichins. Théophile Gautier, the flamboyant author of *Mademoiselle de Maupin* (1835), joined the Hashish Eaters one December evening in the 1840s:

> Although it was only six o'clock, the night was dark. A fog, made thicker by the nearness of the Seine, veiled every object in a cloak which at long intervals was rent by the reddish haloes of the street lamps and the gleams of light escaping from illuminated windows.
>
> The paving stones, slick with rain, glistened under the lamps ... A keen wind, mingled with hail, lashed one's face, and its guttural whistles were like the high notes of a symphony of which the swollen waves breaking against the arches of the bridges were the bass. The evening lacked none of the harsh poetry of winter.

1 Traffic on the Pont Neuf in the eighteenth century. Strollers and sideshows take advantage of the raised pavements

2 Nineteenth-century visitors to the Morgue

It was not easy, along this deserted quai, among this mass of sombre buildings, to distinguish the house I was looking for; but my coachman, standing up in his seat, managed to read on a marble plaque the name, from which half the gilt had peeled away, of the ancient hôtel which was the meeting-place of the adepts.

I raised the carved door-knocker—for the use of copper door-bells had not yet penetrated these remote regions—and several times I heard a vain grating sound. Finally, yielding to a more forceful tug, the old rusted bolt gave way and the door with its massive panels could turn on its hinges.[26]

From one of the bowls of Japanese porcelain displayed inside Gautier is served a green morsel of hashish and then, according to his highly coloured account, he settles to an evening of visions and nightmares in the company of his fellow bohemians.

Later, Gautier himself went to live in the hôtel de Lauzun, following the example of Charles Baudelaire whom he had first met there in 1843 when the poet was renting a two-room apartment on the top floor. Baudelaire had just moved to the Ile Saint-Louis, explaining in a letter to his mother that he was drawn to it by the sense of isolation. He took care, however, that the isolation should not be unrelieved. A few minutes away, in the house which still stands at 6 rue Le Regrattier, he also furnished a small apartment for his mulatto mistress Jeanne Duval. He was twenty-two and had just met her. Known as the *Vénus noire*, she was to become the muse of such poems as 'Les bijoux', 'La chevelure', and 'Parfum exotique'.

The streets of the Ile Saint-Louis, particularly the quais, have exerted a continuing attraction over widely different kinds of writer. It was the building at 1–3 quai d'Anjou of which André Gide noted in his Journal, 'that's the house I should most like to live in'. 'Le seul endroit du monde pour un poète,' Charles-Louis Philippe had written to Francis Carco when the young poet of Montmartre first came to live on the island. But to Carco the atmosphere of the quai de Bourbon seemed oppressive: 'The place was too calm, too secluded, with its melancholy trees, the river, its old houses.'[27] And yet in the end he was drawn back. It was on the second floor of the hôtel Richelieu, at 18 quai de Béthune, that Carco died in 1958.

Gradually the island is changing. The graceless building opposite the pont Marie may perhaps turn out to be a sign of things to come. But for the moment the Ile Saint-Louis manages to remain aloof in the centre of Paris, still displaying the elegant balconies which so attracted Baudelaire, still the island of Connolly's nostalgic memories.

The Seine and its bridges

The Pont Neuf

'A dirty nasty Ditch of a River' was how William Cole described the Seine in 1765. But then Cole, a clergyman and antiquary from Cambridge, was nothing if not patriotic, and the fashion for crying up things French at the expense of their English counterparts exasperated him:

> The Bridges over the Seine at Paris are about 5 or 6, & nothing remarkable for their Beauty: tho' to hear the Descriptions of the Pont-Neuf, & the Pont-Royal, one would suppose that there were not two such Bridges to be met with anywhere. The Pont-Neuf is built over a Part of the River where a small Island divides it about the middle; so that it has an Advantage that none of our most noble, truly royal, & excellently constructed Bridges over the Thames at London & Westminster, had in their Formation: they being all founded in the Bed of the River. [...]
>
> How must a vain & fantastical Frenchman be inwardly chagrined, mortified & struck dumb, on taking a Boat on a fine day & being rowed from Westminster down the River below London Bridge! If such a Sight will not make him blush at his Vanity in supposing Paris the Centre of every Thing great & noble: if Truth will not make him acknowledge the *Petitesse*, the Littleness, the Nothingness of Paris

in Respect to the Beauty, Grandeur & Superiority of London, he must be ashamed of nothing; indeed a very Frenchman.[28]

Cole's dismissive verdict on the Pont Neuf was eccentric. From the time of its completion in the early 1600s it had been generally admired. It was the first of the Seine's bridges not to be lined with houses, so that Parisians could actually see the river as they crossed it. Another feature was the high pavements which protected pedestrians from the muddy passage of the carriages and made the bridge a pleasant spot to loiter. It became the site of Paris's first *bouquinistes*, and in spite of opposition from the traditional shops, this distinctively Parisian form of bookselling had by the end of the 17th century spread to the neighbouring quais, where the battered green boxes still open every afternoon for their trade in prints and books. Among other attractions of the Pont Neuf were the city's most famous mountebank team, Mondor and Tabarin, whose antics to promote the sale of their spurious balms provided material for Molière's *Les fourberies de Scapin* (1671). The general atmosphere of the bridge in its heyday is well described in John Russell's *Paris* (1960):

> The Pont Neuf was not just a beautiful bridge; it was fairground, department store, employment exchange, picturegallery and poor man's Harley Street. You could have a tooth out, go through the 'Situations Vacant', watch the tight-rope dancers, buy a Lancret or a Fragonard, join the army, pick up the new Marivaux or a first edition of *Manon Lescaut*, and arrange to go up in a balloon, watch a bullfight, take fencing-lessons and attend a surgical demonstration.[29]

The Pont Neuf, as Sébastien Mercier noted, had become the heart of Paris. It was a fashionable place, and in 1768 it duly found its way into that fashionable book, *A Sentimental Journey*. Laurence Sterne's phenomenal success with *Tristram Shandy* had been overshadowed by his declining health. In 1765 he took a trip through France and Italy in an effort to purchase a few more years of life. *A Sentimental Journey* sets

out as a whimsical account of these travels. Inserted towards
the end is a fragment of a story which Sterne claims to have
found on a sheet of paper being used to wrap a pat of butter. It
concerns a notary who has quarrelled with his wife. Not
wishing to share the only bed with her, he takes his hat and
cane and short cloak and walks out through the windy night
towards the Pont Neuf:

Of all the bridges which ever were built, the whole world
who have passed over the *Pont Neuf* must own, that it is the
noblest—the   finest—the   grandest—the   lightest—the
longest—the broadest that ever conjoined land and land
together upon the face of the terraqueous globe—
   *By this, it seems, as if the author of the fragment had not
been a Frenchman.*
   The worst fault which divines and doctors of the Sorbonne can allege against it, is, that if there is but a cap-full of
wind in or about Paris, 'tis more blasphemously *sacre
Dieu*'d there than in any other aperture of the whole city—
and with reason, good and cogent Messieurs; for it comes
against you without crying *garde d'eau*, and with such
unpremeditable puffs, that of the few who cross it with their
hats on, not one in fifty but hazards two livres and a half,
which is its full worth.
   The poor notary, just as he was passing by the sentry,
instinctively clapped his cane to the side of it, but in raising it
up, the point of his cane catching hold of the loop of the
sentinel's hat, hoisted it over the spikes of the balustrade
clear into the Seine—
   —'*Tis an ill wind*, said a boatsman, who catched it, *which
blows nobody any good.*
   The sentry, being a Gascon, incontinently twirled up his
whiskers, and levelled his harquebuss.
   Harquebusses in those days went off with matches; and
an old woman's paper lanthorn at the end of the bridge
happening to be blown out, she had borrowed the sentry's
match to light it—it gave a moment's time for the Gascon's
blood to cool, and turn the accident better to his
advantage—'*Tis an ill wind*, said he, catching off the not-

ary's castor, and legitimating the capture with the boatman's adage.[30]

The deprived notary walks off along the rue Dauphine to further adventures, but Sterne declines to tell us how they end. The other stray sheets of paper are not to be found.

Seine water

If opinions were more or less united about the Pont Neuf, they were less so about the water which ran beneath it. Sanitation was as much of a problem for the Parisians as for the inhabitants of any other large city, and until well into the 19th century it was the Seine which suffered the worse consequences of this. As early as 1713, Robert Chasles recorded in *Les illustres françoises* a story which illustrates graphically the hazards of entrusting oneself too blithely to the river. Monsieur Dupuis, the hero of the story, prompted by an urge to go swimming in the Seine, gets together a party:

> These gentlemen stayed by the boat, while Gallouin and I, who enjoyed swimming and diving, went straight under the Pont Neuf where we climbed onto the bathing machine and leapt from the top of the second storey. There was a crowd of people watching us swim over and under each other, amongst them a knave of a soldier who was on the edge of the bridge where the rabble deposit their excrement, and with his foot he pushed some down on us. I looked up to tell him to stop and some of it fell right on my face.
> You laugh, and who wouldn't? The spectators laughed as well. Personally, I didn't laugh; I dived down to get myself clean, then, taking the shortest way between the boats, I got ashore by the steps. I went up them naked and at the mercy of the carters' whips, which did not spare me. As it happened, I got onto the Pont Neuf right beside my scoundrel of a soldier who imagined he had heard the last of the business. Seizing him by the hair, I gave him three or four punches on the nose, flung him from the top of the bridge into the river and jumped in after him. The surprise of my action and the distance of the fall had stunned him. His clothes dragged

him to the bottom of the water. If no one had come to his aid, he would have been a drowned soldier. I made quite sure it wasn't our boat that helped him. The boatman did not dare to defy a man as furious as I was.

My friends rejoined me; I was in a terrible fury, bleeding all over from the cuts of the whips. I saw no one laugh; I would not have stood for it, no matter who it was. We got dressed again and I made the boatman drop me at the quai de Conti where they had taken the scoundrel. We all looked such as to make the rabble tremble, and our footmen indicated our rank.[31]

In spite of such cautionary tales, the practice of bathing in the Seine won increasing popularity. In the early 19th century Nikolai Karamzin, a devotee of Sterne and the driving force of the Sentimental movement in Russian literature, described his own experience of the bathing facilities without any sign of misgiving:

While walking along the rue Dauphine, I noticed two Chinese pavilions on the river, which I recognized to be public baths. I went down, paid twenty-four sous, and bathed with cold water in a splendid little cabinet. The cleanliness was surprising. A special pipe conveys water from the river into each cabinet. People can also learn to swim here for thirty sous a lesson. Three men were swimming remarkably well while I was there.[32]

The bathing cabinets were a welcome innovation, but many Parisians continued to plunge cheerfully into a river clotted with ordure. Predictably, the English were less enthusiastic. A century earlier Cole had already complained bitterly about the river's impurities:

The Water of the River Seine is as thick and muddy as the Channel of the Severne which comes up to Bristol: so that to drink such Water is not practicable; besides they say it is very unwholsome, creates Gravel, & is very purgative, especially to Strangers: so that they carry clear Water about in Pails & Vessels, & sell it by the Quart or Gallon, at a very extravagant Price. I have seen People on the Pont Neuf with a large Copper Vessel on their Backs, with a Cock to it, selling drinking Water to the Passengers. [...]

Notwithstanding the Beastliness & Filth of the River Water, both sides of the Seine in the City of Paris, are covered with large covered Boats, or rather Water-Houses, in which live all the Washer-Women of Paris; who hang continually over the Sides of the Boat & so beat the Linen with flat Peices of Wood to get them clean; from whence they are sent out to the neighbouring fields to be dried: & this is all the cleaning they have: & their Ironing is full as bad as their Washing; so that it is no wonder that your Linen comes back torn to Peices, dirtier than when it first went there, & just of the nasty dirty yellowish Colour of that beastly River. It is Pity they should have much good Linen to spoil: as to their own, it is no great matter what becomes of it: for it is generally both very coarse & of a bad Colour.[33]

Suicide in the Seine

But though the water was bad to drink and dirty to swim in, it did offer a fairly reliable means of committing suicide; and this became an increasingly important consideration from the Romantic period onwards. The literature of the 19th and 20th centuries is rich in examples. Time and again the novelist's hero looks down at the dark water from one of the bridges of the Seine. For Frédéric Moreau in Flaubert's *L'education sentimentale* it is the pont de la Concorde, for Claude Lantier in Zola's *L'oeuvre* it is the pont du Carrousel, for Mathieu Delarue in Sartre's *L'âge de raison* it is the Pont Neuf. Between them the disappointed lover, the frustrated artist and the disillusioned philosopher probably cover most of the ground.

'Hé, little one. Is it for tonight the suicide?' calls a passing youth, as Marya Zelli, the heroine of Jean Rhys's *Quartet*, stands on the quai des Orfèvres looking down at the trembling necklaces of light in the water.[34]

More often than not the night-time act is contemplated rather than committed; but behind all the desperate figures who lean out over the parapets of the Seine there is the ghost of one of the great literary suicides of the 19th century. Javert, the ruthless police inspector who has pursued Jean Valjean throughout the long span of Hugo's *Les misérables*, finds at last that his rigid devotion to justice will no longer suffice. Hugo selects the spot with precision:

> Between the Pont Notre-Dame and the Pont-au-Change [...] the Seine forms a sort of pool traversed by a swift current. It is a place feared by boatmen. Nothing is more dangerous than that current, aggravated in those days by the piles of the bridges, which have since been done away with. The current speeds up formidably, swelling in waves which seem to be trying to sweep the bridges away. A man falling into the river at this point, even a strong swimmer, does not emerge.[35]

Javert contemplates the rushing water, then walks back across the silent square to the police station in the place du Châtelet. Having made his final arrangements, he returns:

> It was the sepulchral moment that succeeds midnight, with the stars hidden by cloud and not a light to be seen in the houses of the Cité, not a passer-by, only the faint, distant gleam of a street-lamp and the shadowy outlines of Notre-Dame, and the Palais de Justice.
>
> The place where Javert stood, we may recall, was where the river flows in a dangerous rapid. He looked down. There was a sound of running water, but the river itself was not to be seen. What lay below him was a void, so that he might have been standing at the edge of infinity. He stayed motionless for some minutes, staring into nothingness. Abruptly he took off his hat and laid it on the parapet. A moment later a tall, dark figure, which a passer-by might have taken for a ghost, stood upright on the parapet. It leaned forward and dropped into the darkness.
>
> There was a splash, and that was all.[36]

In his novel *Les beaux quartiers* (1936) the poet and one-time surrealist Louis Aragon offered a glimpse of the less romantic figures to be found along the banks of the river—and sometimes in its waters:

Old men, garbage of a world; young men, tragic in their unfulfilment; equivocal shadows of the lowest kind of prostitution; the sudden apparition of a little old woman, neat with the neatness of the provinces, her black hat and folding chair ... Each of these figures represents the conclusion of a long story of common life which takes on the note of grandeur at just the moment when it reaches the last act. Like iron hands, the arches of the bridges join their dark fingers over the tempting water.[37]

The temptation remains. 'I was there when it happened,' writes Jacques Prévert in 'Encore une fois sur le fleuve', one of the poems from *Histoires* (1963):

> ... J'étais là quand la chose s'est passée
> à côté du Pont-Neuf
> non loin du monument qu'on appelle
> la Monnaie
> J'étais là quand elle s'est penchée
> et c'est moi qui l'ai poussée
> Il n'y avait rien d'autre à faire
> Je suis la Misère
> j'ai fait mon métier
> et la Seine a fait de même
> quand elle a refermé sur elle
> son bras fraternel ...*

Lovers by the Seine

By day, the banks of the Seine are traditionally the preserve of lovers. In the early years of the century Guillaume Apollinaire gave poignant voice to these associations in 'Le Pont Mirabeau', which celebrates his love affair with the painter Marie Laurencin. The bridge, out to the south-west of Paris, was a familiar landmark in the progress of their relationship,

---

* I was there when it happened, by the Pont-Neuf, not far from the building called the Mint. I was there when she leaned over and it is I who pushed her. There was nothing else to be done. I am Misery. I did my job and the Seine did likewise when it closed its brotherly arm around her.

for Marie Laurencin had been living at the time with her mother in Auteuil, while Apollinaire himself was in the nearby rue Gros.

LE PONT MIRABEAU

Sous le pont Mirabeau coule la Seine
Et nos amours
Faut-il qu'il m'en souvienne
La joie venait toujours après la peine.

Vienne la nuit sonne l'heure
Les jours s'en vont je demeure

Les mains dans les mains restons face à face
Tandis que sous
Le pont de nos bras passe
Des éternels regards l'onde si lasse

Vienne la nuit sonne l'heure
Les jours s'en vont je demeure

L'amour s'en va comme cette eau courante
L'amour s'en va
Comme la vie est lente
Et comme l'Espérance est violente

Vienne la nuit sonne l'heure
Les jours s'en vont je demeure

Passent les jours et passent les semaines
Ni temps passé
Ni les amours reviennent
Sous le pont Mirabeau coule la Seine

Vienne la nuit sonne l'heure
Les jours s'en vont je demeure*

* Under the pont Mirabeau flows the Seine / And our loves / Must I remember / Joy always came after pain. / Let night come let the hour sound / The days go by I remain. / Hand in hand let us stay face to face / While under / The bridge of our arms passes / The tired wave of eternal

Emile Zola's long series of novels about the Rougon-Macquart family often seem to be as much concerned with Paris itself as with the characters who live there. In *L'oeuvre* (1886) it is the Seine and its two islands to which Zola keeps returning. They are used as a measure of the developing relationship between the artist Claude Lantier (based partly on Cézanne, partly on Zola himself) and Christine, the girl he finds sheltering outside his house on the Ile Saint-Louis at the start of the novel. In the early days of their relationship they often walk along the embankment from the Hôtel de Ville to the pont Royal, entranced by the different sights and sounds: the flower market, the booksellers, the passers-by, the roof-tops caught in sunlight. Later, when their love has begun to fade, they take the same walk. It is one of the last fine days of summer, and in this lingering view of the Seine, its islands and bridges, the note of melancholy seems an inescapable accompaniment:

> They followed the embankment, under the plane-trees, seeing the past rise up at every step as the landscape opened out before them: the bridges, their arches cutting across the satin sheen of the river; the Cité covered with shadow, dominated by the yellowing towers of Notre-Dame; the great sweeping curve of the right bank, bathed in sunshine, leading to the dim silhouette of the Pavillon de Flore; the broad avenues, the buildings on either bank, and between them, the Seine, with all the lively activity of its laundry-boats, its baths, its barges. As in the past, the setting sun seemed to follow them along the riverside, rolling over the roofs of the distant houses, partially eclipsed for a moment by the dome of the Institut. It was a dazzling sunset, finer than they had ever seen, a slow descent through tiny clouds which gradually turned into a trellis of purple with molten

---

glances. / Let night come let the hour sound / The days go by I remain. / Love goes by like this running water / Love goes by / How slow life is / And how violent Hope is. / Let night come let the hour sound / The days go by I remain. / The days pass by and the weeks pass by / Neither time past / Nor loves come back / Under the pont Mirabeau flows the Seine. / Let night come let the hour sound / The days go by I remain.

gold pouring through every mesh. But out of the past they were calling to mind nothing reached them but an unconquerable melancholy, a feeling that it would always be just beyond their reach, that it would be impossible to live it again. The time-worn stones were cold and the ever-flowing stream beneath the bridges seemed to have carried away something of their selves, the charm of awakening desire, the thrill of hope and expectation. Now they were all in all to each other, they had forgone the simple happiness of feeling the warm pressure of their arms as they strolled quietly along, wrapped, as it were, in the all-enveloping life of the great city.[38]

CHAPTER 2

Central Paris

The place du Carrousel

By day, cities offer themselves to the spectator in fragments. It is only in the calmer light of dusk or dawn that they take on a fleeting coherence. There is a moment in Romain Rolland's ten-volume novel *Jean-Christophe* (1903–12) when the hero pauses beside the Seine to contemplate the city around him. With his back to the Invalides Jean-Christophe looks out over the river and sees the shape of Paris outlined against the evening sky like a dead giant lying prone upon the plain. 'He stopped to gaze at the gigantic fossils of a fabulous race, which had long ago become extinct, [...] the race whose helmet was the dome of the Invalides and whose girdle was the Louvre.'[1]

There is no mistaking the centre of this vision of Paris. The Palace of the Louvre has been acquiring its present aspect bit by bit since the early 16th century, and the process still goes on. First opened to the public in 1793, the Grande Galerie is now at the heart of one of the richest collections in the world. Looking back to his childhood in mid-19th century Paris, Henry James wrote of 'going and coming along that interminable and incomparable Seine-side front of the Palace against which young sensibility felt itself almost rub, for endearment and consecration, as a cat invokes the friction of a protective piece of furniture.'[2] Inside the Palace 'the pictures, the frames themselves, the figures within them, the particular parts and features of each, the look of the rich light, the smell of the massively enclosed air' all imparted 'a sense of freedom of contact and appreciation' which was the opening of a new world.[3]

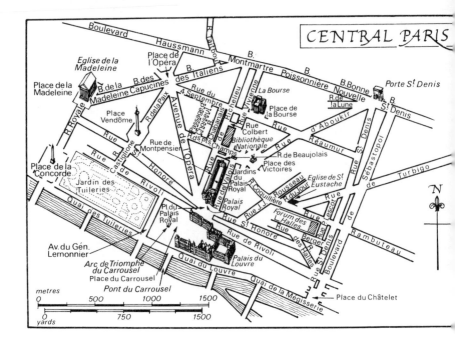

But it is not a literary world, nor perhaps one that literature can do much to enhance. For today's visitor, as for James, it is the paintings and sculptures that are the imaginative life of the place and to them that it should be left.

About the palace itself writers have tended to be less interesting than about the dissolute buildings which once stood in its shadow. From the 17th century the north-eastern part of what is now the place du Carrousel consisted of a tangle of narrow streets which grew shabbier and shadier as the decades passed. Amongst them was a wretched little cul-de-sac called the impasse du Doyenné. It was here that the formidable heroine of Balzac's *Cousine Bette* (1838) had her home:

> Beyond the archway leading from the pont du Carrousel to the rue du Musée, anyone visiting Paris, even for a few days, is bound to notice a number of houses with decayed façades, whose discouraged owners do no maintenance work upon them. These are all that remains of an old quarter, in process of demolition since the day when Napoleon decided to complete the Louvre. The rue du Doyenné and the blind

alley of the same name are the only passages that penetrate this sombre and deserted block, inhabited presumably by ghosts, for one never catches sight of anyone here. [...]

These houses, submerged and darkened by the raising of the Square, also lie wrapped in the perpetual shadow cast by the high galleries of the Louvre, blackened on this side by the north wind. The gloom, the silence, the glacial air, the hollow sunken ground level, combine to make these houses seem so many crypts, or living tombs. If, passing in a cab through this dead area, one happens to glance down the impasse du Doyenné, a chill strikes one's heart, one wonders who can possibly live here and what may happen here at night, at the hour when the alley becomes a place of cutthroats, when the vices of Paris, shrouded in night's mantle, move as they will.[4]

It was not in reality quite such an abandoned area as Balzac makes out. At about the time that he was writing *Cousine Bette* the impasse du Doyenné was even acquiring in its decrepitude a certain vivacity, for it had become the home of a number of young Bohemian writers, including Théophile Gautier and Gérard de Nerval. Their disreputable life-style excited its full measure of bourgeois disapproval, but it was fondly remembered by those who had shared in it. In his *Confessions* (1885) Arsène Houssaye sketches the scene in the impasse du Doyenné when pleasure was taking second place to poetry:

In the large drawing-room there was space for everybody. One of us would be writing by the fireside, another inditing verses in a hammock. Théo, stretched out on his stomach, penned admirable chapters while stroking the cats. Gérard, elusive as always, walked to and fro with the faint uneasiness of those who seek for something in vain.[5]

By the time Houssaye wrote these lines the impasse du Doyenné had disappeared, demolished in the early 1850s to make way for the place du Carrousel. Along with it went such other relics of the 17th century as had survived, amongst them all that was left of the hôtel de Rambouillet. It was here, in her

famous 'chambre bleue'—so called because it was hung with
blue rather than the usual red—that the marquise de Rambouillet established the salon which was to have a decisive
effect on the manners and literature of her society. La Rochefoucauld, Voiture, Mlle de Scudéry and Mme de Sévigné all
frequented it, and for the first half of the 17th century, the era
of the *précieuses*, it was one of the centres of French culture.

The Tuileries

At the western end of the place du Carrousel stands the triumphal arch. For six years this was the site of the four bronze
horses plundered from Venice by Napoleon. From 1809 until
they were returned to St Mark's in 1815 they looked out from
the top of the arch, which was then the main entrance-way to
the Palace of the Tuileries. Built for Catherine de Médicis in
the 16th century, the palace was situated along the line of the
modern avenue du Général-Lemonnier, so that it more or less
enclosed the area between the wings of the Louvre which
contained the impasse du Doyenné and the triumphal arch. In
1871, during the period of the Commune, the whole palace
was burnt to the ground by arsonists, leaving the prospect
open, with the arch isolated and somewhat diminished at the
edge of the long expanse of the Tuileries Gardens.

Once a rendezvous of duellists and a meeting-place for
courtiers and pleasure seekers, the Gardens now look rather
naked for much of the year. In the days of Louis XIV their
aspect was more luxuriant. Martin Lister, an eminent zoologist who came to Paris in 1698, was particularly impressed:

> This [Garden] of the *Tuilleries* is vastly great, has shaded
> Tarrasses on two sides, one along the River *Seine*, planted
> with Trees, very diverting, with great Parterrs in the middle,
> and large Fountains of Water, which constantly *Play*; one
> end is the Front of that Magnificent Palace the *Louvre*; the
> other is low, and for Prospects, open to the Fields. The rest is
> disposed into Alleys, and Grass-Plots, and Copses of Wood;
> with a *great number of Seats* upon Down in all parts, for the
> Accommodation of the Weary. [...]

3 A summer evening on the boulevard Montmartre in 1860

4 Les Halles in the nineteenth century: the scene at daybreak on the rue Rambuteau

5 The arcades of the Palais-Royal in 1815: The scene outside the gambling-house at No. 113

Nothing can be more pleasant, than this Garden, where in the Groves of Wood the latter end of *March, Black-Birds* and *Throstles*, and *Nightingales* sing most sweetly all the morning, and that as it were within the City; for no Birding is suffered here near this City, and the Fields round the Town, are all, everywhere, full of Partridges, and Hares, and other Game.[6]

Other visitors were less appreciative. Earlier in the same year the poet and diplomatist Matthew Prior (1664–1721) had noted sourly in a letter to a friend in England: 'The women here are all practiced jades, *unam cogneras omnes noras*; they are all painted and instructed so that they look like one another. They have nothing of nature nor passion. The men neglect them and make love to each other to a degree that is incredible, for you can pick your boy at the Tuileries or at the play.'[7]

In spite of the attendant catamites—or perhaps because of them—the Tuileries were the gardens generally favoured by Paris's upper classes. Forbidden to soldiers and servants except on *jours de fête*, they offered a promenading place for the well-to-do and for members of the court—even, on occasions, for royalty. From October 1789 Louis XVI was a virtual prisoner in the Palace of the Tuileries. One of the last glimpses of him enjoying the relative liberty of a walk in the Gardens was recorded by an English visitor, Arthur Young. A farmer turned agricultural theorist, Young had come to France primarily to collect information on farming methods. In the event, his *Travels in France* (1792) acquired a historical interest of a quite different kind:

JAN. 4th [1790]. After breakfast, walk in the gardens of the Tuileries, where there is the most extraordinary sight that either French or English eyes could ever behold at Paris. The King, walking with six grenadiers of the *milice bourgeoise*, with an officer or two of his household, and a page. The doors of the gardens are kept shut in respect to him, in order to exclude everybody but deputies, or those who have admission-tickets. When he entered the palace, the doors of the gardens were thrown open for all without distinction, though the Queen was still walking with a lady of her court. She also was attended so closely by the *gardes bourgeoises*, that she could not speak, but in a low voice, without being heard by them. A mob followed her, talking very loud, and paying no other apparent respect than that of taking off their hats wherever she passed, which was indeed more than I expected. Her Majesty does not appear to be in health; she seems to be much affected, and shows it in her face; but the King is as plump as ease can render him. By his orders, there is a little garden railed off for the Dauphin to amuse himself in, and a small room is built in it to retire to in case of rain; here he was at work with his little hoe and rake, but not without a guard of two grenadiers.[8]

In August 1792, within three years of Young's visit, the palace was sacked and the gardens left strewn with the bodies of the king's Swiss guard. After the Revolution, however, the Tuileries more than recovered their former beauty – to judge, at least, from Hazlitt's response to them in 1824:

This is an enclosure of all sweet sights and smells, a concentration of elegance. The rest of the world is barbarous to this 'paradise of dainty devices', where the imagination is spellbound. It is a perfectly-finished miniature set in brilliants. It is a toilette for nature to dress itself; where every flower seems a narcissus! The smooth gravel-walks, the basin of water, the swans (they might be of wax), the golden fishes, the beds of flowers, the chineasters, larkspur, geraniums, bright marigolds, mignonette ('the Frenchman's darling') scenting the air with a faint luscious perfume, the rows of orange-trees in boxes, blooming verdure and vegetable gold, the gleaming statues, the raised terraces, the stately avenues of trees, and the gray cumbrous towers of the Tuileries overlooking the whole, give an effect of enchantment to the scene.[9]

Tourist hotels in the rue de Rivoli, rue de Castiglione and place Vendôme

As the city's central pleasure gardens, the Tuileries were largely responsible for making this the most popular area for the great tourist hotels of the 19th century. Of these the one especially dear to English visitors was the Hotel Meurice, later one of the headquarters of the German occupying forces during the Second World War and still in business at 228 rue de Rivoli. It was here that Charles Dickens stayed in July 1844, when he passed through Paris on his first trip to France. Like many others who visited the city in the 1840s, he would have been well aware of Thackeray's advice in the passage from *The Paris Sketch Book* (1840) which describes the author's arrival. The coach has carried Thackeray through the outskirts of Paris and down to the Porte Saint-Denis (the rue de Bourbon Villeneuve is now the rue d'Aboukir):

Passing, then, *round* the gate, and not under it (after the general custom, in respect of triumphal arches), you cross the Boulevard [Saint-Denis], which gives a glimpse of trees and sunshine, and gleaming white buildings; then, dashing down the Rue de Bourbon Villeneuve, a dirty street, which seems interminable, and the Rue St. Eustache, the conductor gives a last blast on his horn, and the great vehicle clatters into the court-yard, where its journey is destined to conclude.

If there was a noise before of screaming postilions and cracked horns, it was nothing to the Babel-like clatter which greets us now. [...] Half-a-dozen other coaches arrive at the same minute—no light affairs, like your English vehicles, but ponderous machines, containing fifteen passengers inside, more in the cabriolet, and vast towers of luggage on the roof: others are loading: the yard is filled with passengers coming or departing;—bustling porters and screaming *commissionaires*. These latter seize you as you descend from your place,—twenty cards are thrust into your hand, and as many voices, jabbering with inconceivable swiftness, shriek into your ear, 'Dis way, sare; are you for ze 'Otel of Rhin? '*Hôtel de l'Amirauté!*'—'Hôtel Bristol,' sare!—*Monsieur, 'l'Hôtel de Lille?' Sacr-rrré nom de Dieu, laissez passer ce petit, Monsieur!* 'Ow mosh loggish 'ave you, sare?'

And now, if you are a stranger in Paris, listen to the words of Titmarsh.—If you cannot speak a syllable of French, and love English comfort, clean rooms, breakfasts, and waiters: if you would have plentiful dinners, and are not particular (as how should you be?) concerning wine; if, in this foreign country, you *will* have your English companions, your porter, your friend, and your brandy-and-water—do not listen to any of these commissioner fellows, but with your best English accent, shout out boldly, 'MEURICE!' and straightway a man will step forward to conduct you to the Rue de Rivoli.

Here you will find apartments at any price: a very neat room, for instance, for three francs daily; and English breakfast of eternal boiled eggs, or grilled ham; a nondescript dinner, profuse but cold; and a society which will rejoice your heart. Here are young gentlemen from the universities; young merchants on a lark; large families of nine daughters, with fat father and mother; officers of dragoons, and lawyers' clerks. [...]

It is, as you will perceive, an admirable way to see Paris, especially if you spend your days reading the English papers at Galignani's [at 224 rue de Rivoli], as many of our foreign tourists do.[10]

By the time Oscar Wilde and his wife arrived for their honeymoon in the summer of 1884, the choice of respectable hotels was considerably wider.[11] They stayed a few doors away from the Meurice at the Hotel Wagram, 208 rue de Rivoli. 'We have an *appartement* here of three rooms,' wrote Constance Wilde to her brother on 3 June, '20 francs a day: not dear for a Paris hotel: we are *au quatrième* and have a lovely view over the gardens of the Tuileries ...'

As a rule, our impression of such hotels comes from their patrons rather than from their staff; but in the autumn of 1919 one of the hotels just off the rue de Rivoli made the mistake of taking on a down-at-heel Englishman who had applied for a job there. George Orwell had been in Paris for something over a year when he went to work as a *plongeur* in the Hotel Lotti at 7 rue de Castiglione. In *Down and Out in Paris and London* (1933) he gives a characteristically unappetising account of backstage life in the luxury hotels of that time:

It was amusing to look round the filthy little scullery and

think that only a double door was between us and the dining-room. There sat the customers in all their splendour—spotless table-cloths, bowls of flowers, mirrors and gilt cornices and painted cherubim; and here, just a few feet away, we in our disgusting filth. For it really was disgusting filth. There was no time to sweep the floor till evening, and we slithered about in a compound of soapy water, lettuce-leaves, torn paper and trampled food. A dozen waiters with their coats off, showing their sweaty armpits, sat at the table mixing salads and sticking their thumbs into the cream pots. The room had a dirty, mixed smell of food and sweat. Everywhere in the cupboards, behind the piles of crockery, were squalid stores of food that the waiters had stolen. There were only two sinks, and no washing basin, and it was nothing unusual for a waiter to wash his face in the water in which clean crockery was rinsing. But the customers saw nothing of this. There were a coco-nut mat and a mirror outside the dining-room door, and the waiters used to preen themselves up and go in looking the picture of cleanliness.[12]

Beyond the rue Saint-Honoré, the rue de Castiglione opens almost immediately into the place Vendôme. The elegant harmonies of the square's early 18th-century buildings provide an appropriate setting for some of the most exclusive shops in Paris, as well as for one of its most celebrated hotels. The discreet awnings of no. 15, beside the Ministry of Justice, mark the entrance to the Ritz. This was the hotel favoured in the years between the wars by English writers such as Somerset Maugham who could afford to keep company with the well-to-do. It also had a following among the younger Americans, including Hemingway and Scott Fitzgerald. When Hemingway entered Paris in 1944 with the advancing American troops, one of his first projects, he claimed, was 'to liberate the cellar of the Ritz', and it was here, in Room 31, that he spent the first days after the end of the German Occupation. In recognition of his fondness for the place, the hotel now has a Bar Hemingway. On the eve of the war the French poet Léon-Paul Fargue paid fitting homage to the Ritz in *Le piéton de Paris* (1939):

Not many people know that the founder of the Ritz Hotel was a man like you or me, someone who was actually called plain Mr Ritz, just as Flaubert was called Flaubert and M. Thiers M. Thiers. People who live far from Paris, in exactly those places where the Ritz recruits its most glittering clients, tend to believe that Ritz is a word more like Obelisk, Eiffel Tower, Vatican or Westminster, even Jerusalem or the Himalayas. And there is something to be said for this point of view. I mentioned one evening to Marcel Proust, who as it happened had just ordered, at midnight, chilled melon for us in the Ritz, that I had a fantasy of putting together a catechism for the use of beautiful women travellers equipped with even more beautiful luggage. The idea for it had been furnished by a drawing-room conversation I had had with the finest pair of eyes in Chile:
— What do rich girls dream about?
— The hotel life.
— Which hotels do they like best?
— They all like the same one best: the Ritz.
— What is the Ritz?
— It's Paris.
— And what is Paris?
— The Ritz.

'It couldn't be put better,' murmured Proust, who always had an affection tinged with curiosity for this establishment. What he liked, he who was so communicative, was that they observed with great seriousness at the Ritz the first and noblest rule of hotels: discretion. Absolute discretion, bound with hoops of steel, of the sort that said 'nothing doing'. He had also one evening shown himself deeply interested in the hotelier's trade; he found it one of the most humane of all jobs and the best in which to gather, breathing, sincere and detailed, the secrets of the human heart.[13]

The Grands Boulevards

It was not merely the proximity of the Tuileries and the Seine that led to a concentration of expensive hotels in this area of central Paris. For the 19th-century Englishman on release from Victorian England there were equally pressing attractions in the other direction. Just to the north of the place Vendôme were the lights of the Grands Boulevards.

This was the heart of fashionable life in the city. The boulevard de la Madeleine, the boulevard des Capucines, the boulevard des Italiens—stroll along them today and you find a predominantly middle-class shopping area, sprinkled with cinemas and airline offices. But their wide sweep leaves us room to imagine what they must have been like in the middle years of the last century.

The period of the Second Empire was transforming Paris into a city of pleasure. Its focus, of course, was sexual. Diaries, letters, novels, poems all transmit an atmosphere of sensual excitement along the boulevards which is almost tangible. In a letter to an old school-friend, written in 1842, Gustave Flaubert (1821–80) describes his emotions as a young provincial encountering Paris at the age of twenty-one:

> What strikes me as most splendid about Paris is the boulevard. Each time I walk along it, when I get there in the morning, I feel a shock from the asphalt pavement on which every evening so many whores drag their feet and trail their rustling skirts. At the hour when the gas lamps shine in the windows and the knives ring on the marble tables, I wander out there, tranquil, enveloped in the smoke of my cigar, casting glances at the women who go by. This is where prostitution displays itself to the world, this is where eyes shine![14]

What Flaubert describes is the evening world in which Georges Duroy, the hero of Maupassant's *Bel-Ami* (1885), finds himself at the start of the novel:

> He liked the places where tarts congregate in swarms—their dancing-halls, their cafés, their streets; he liked to rub shoulders with them, to talk familiarly with them, to snuff their crude perfumes, to feel himself close to them. They were women, after all, women whose business was love. He had none of the family man's innate contempt for them.
>
> He turned towards the Madeleine and followed the crowds streaming along in the oppressive heat. The big

cafés, full of people, were overflowing onto the pavement, displaying their clientèle in the harsh blaze of their illuminated frontages. On the little square or round tables in front of the customers the glasses contained liquids of every shade of red, yellow, green, brown, and in the carafes you could see the glint of the large transparent cylinders of ice that were chilling the fine clear water.[15]

As both Flaubert and Maupassant indicate, the centres of excitement on the Grands Boulevards were the cafés, and along the short stretch of the boulevard des Italiens were gathered the most famous ones in Paris. Approaching them from the direction of the Madeleine: at no. 24 was the café de Paris, at no. 22 Tortoni's, at no. 20 the Maison Dorée, at no. 16 the café Riche, at no. 13 the café Anglais. Then, just beyond, on the corner of the rue Richelieu and the boulevard Montmartre, was Frascati's, the café where Lucien de Rubempré goes to gamble in Balzac's *Les illusions perdues*. For readers of Balzac, Flaubert and Zola each of these establishments has its own associations. It is with one of Tortoni's celebrated ices that Peyrade is poisoned in Balzac's *Splendeurs et misères des courtisanes*, to the café Anglais that Frédéric and Rosanette go for their interrupted supper in Flaubert's *L'éducation sentimentale*, across the road in the café Riche that Maxime seduces his step-mother in Zola's *La curée*. Of another of these cafés, Francis Carco writes:

> ... The Café de Paris occupied the building which forms the angle of the Boulevard and the rue Taitbout. 'You reached the *grands salons* of the ground floor', recalls one of those who frequented it, 'by a flight of several steps, similar to the one at Tortoni's.' Musset, Balzac and Alexandre Dumas used to go there to enjoy casseroled veal, which, they claimed, could not really be appreciated anywhere else. [...]
> It was while he was passing this establishment at about 4 in the morning that Méry bumped into Balzac and asked him what brought him to these parts on his own. Balzac was wearing dress trousers and a frock-coat with velvet lapels. Immediately pulling out of his pocket an almanac which noted that sunrise was at 4.45, he replied: 'I'm being pur-

sued by bailiffs and forced to hide during the day ... but at this hour they can't arrest me: so I walk.'[16]

These cafés were the haunts, in some cases practically the homes, of many of the great figures of 19th-century French literature, amongst whom were the brothers Edmond (1822–96) and Jules (1830–70) de Goncourt, authors of such novels as *Soeur Philomène* (1861) and *Germinie Lacerteux* (1864). Day by day they noted down with an unforgiving pen the details of their social and literary life in a journal which, as they hoped, has ensured their immortality. This entry describes a fairly typical evening in October 1857:

> The Café Riche seems to be on the way to becoming the head-quarters of those men of letters who wear gloves. It is strange how places make the people who frequent them. Beneath that white and gold, on that red plush, none of the guttersnipes of literature would dare to venture. Murger, with whom we had dinner, made his profession of faith to us. He is rejecting Bohemia and passing over bag and baggage to the side of the gentlemen of letters: a new Mirabeau. [...]
>
> At the entrance, in the room separated from ours by two pillars, you can see here and there a few ears pricked up and drinking in the talk of our circle. They belong either to dandies frittering away the last of their little fortunes, or to young men from the Stock Exchange, Rothschild's clerks, who have brought along some high-grade tarts from the Cirque or Mabille to offer their little appetites the satisfaction of some fruit or a cup of tea and to point out from a distance the leading players in our company.
>
> Baudelaire had supper at the table next to ours. He was without a cravat, his shirt open at the neck and his head shaved, just as if he were going to be guillotined. A single affectation: his little hands washed and cared for, the nails kept scrupulously clean. The face of a maniac, a voice that cuts like a knife, and a precise elocution that tries to copy Saint-Just and succeeds. He denies, with some obstinacy and a certain harsh anger, that he has offended morality with his verse.[17]

The site of the café Riche is now occupied by a less than decorative bank, but in the seduction scene of *La curée* Zola recalls with some precision this classic setting for transient passages of love in 19th-century Paris. Maxime's young step-mother, Renée, wants to see something of a racier world, but the party to which they go does not turn out well. Deciding to have supper together at the café Riche, they go up to the entresol and are shown into a private room. Renée looks around:

> It was a square room in white and gold with pretty boudoir furniture. Apart from the table and chairs, there was a sort of low console from which the food was served and a large divan, effectively a bed, which stood between the fireplace and the window. The white marble mantelpiece was deco-rated with a clock and two Louis XVI candlesticks. But the special feature of the private room was the mirror, a fine square-cut mirror which women's diamonds had scored all over with names, dates, lame verses, prodigious sentiments, striking avowals. Renée thought she had caught sight of an obscenity among them but had not the courage to satisfy her curiosity. She looked at the divan, felt a new flush of embar-rassment, and in order to keep herself in countenance began to look at the ceiling and the gilt copper chandelier with five burners. But the uneasiness she felt was delicious. While she looked up with a serious face, lorgnette in hand, as though to study the cornice, she was taking a profound pleasure in the ambiguous furnishings which she was aware of around her—in this mirror, serene and cynical, whose purity, scarcely ruffled by the ribald scrawlings, had been of service in adjusting so many false coils of hair; in this divan which shocked her by its size; in the table, in the very carpet, in which she noticed the same smell as on the staircase—a faint smell of dust, pervasive, almost religious. [...]
>
> It was not yet midnight. Below, on the boulevard, she could hear the roar of Paris as it prolonged the hectic day before deciding to make for bed. The rows of trees marked off with an indistinct line the light of the pavements from the uncertain darkness of the road, along which passed the

rumbling wheels and swift lanterns of the carriages. [...]
Maxime pointed out to Renée the bright windows of the
Café Anglais opposite them. The high branches of the trees
made it slightly difficult for them to see the houses and the
pavement on the other side of the road. They bent down and
looked across. There was a continual coming and going;
people out for a walk went by in groups; tarts, in couples,
trailed their skirts, which they raised from time to time with
a languid movement as they looked around with weary and
smiling glances. Just under the window, the tables of the
Café Riche were set out in the incandescent light of its
chandeliers, whose glare reached right to the middle of the
road; and it was above all at the heart of this fierce blaze of
light that Maxime and Renée could see the pale countenances and empty laughter of the passers-by. At the little
round tables women and men, mingled together, were
drinking.[18]

The Banque Nationale de Paris has spread itself extensively
along this section of the boulevard. Another building now
taken over by it is the old Maison Dorée which, with its heavily
gilded balconies, stands a couple of doors away at no. 20. This
café restaurant, the setting for Villiers de l'Isle Adam's sinister
tale 'Le convive des dernières fêtes', occupied the ground floor
and entresol. It is again the Goncourts who give us the most
vivid image of the less engaging aspects of this social world:

The other day, or rather the other night—it was four o'clock
in the morning—we were in Room No. 7 at the Maison
d'Or, a room with the wall-panels edged with strips of
gilded wood, and decorated with big flowers in bright red
and white and broad leaves in relief imitating Coromandel
lacquer. On the red velvet sofa a red-haired woman was
sprawled on her belly, a street-walker called Sabine with
something of the she-wolf, the lioness, and the cow about
her, wearing neither a corset nor a dress, her breasts bare
and her chemise hitched up above her knees. There was a
basket of fruit standing untouched on the mantelpiece.
    Now and then she uttered the cries of a drunken woman,

her eyes red, her lips feverish. Then she would swear, grind
her teeth, and try to bite; I raised her head whenever she let it
fall. She vomited, swearing all the while.

In the meantime Charles was weeping on Edmond's
shoulder, saying: 'Louise! I love her! I love her!' He was
talking about La Rouvroy. There was some sort of coolness
between them at this time. She was giving him the cold
shoulder to get some more money out of him. The tart kept
sitting up to watch him crying and in between hiccoughs she
said to him: 'Cry, that's right, cry, Monsieur le Comte, I like
to see a good cry! She doesn't love you! She'll never love
you! Go on, Charles, you can cry better than that. And then,
with a thousand-franc note ... Or take her two thousand-
franc notes!' As for myself, I kept pouring the names of all
her lovers over his head, like so much cold water.

'Come now,' said Edmond, 'dammit all, forget about that
bitch and let's go to the brothel. La Rouvroy doesn't love
you, it's time somebody told you that to your face. She's
making a fool of you. Why, the other day I felt positively
indignant: you send her your carriage to cart her family to
the theatre, you go to see her in the box you have taken for
her, and she fobs you off with a few words.... You are a
laughing-stock at her theatre. They know she can do what
she likes with you.'

'I've bought her twelve hundred francs' worth of jewels,'
said Charles, and great tears trickled down one by one on to
his big black beard.

'Oh, get along with you! You're young, you've got a
review, a carriage and a theatre, and one day you'll have an
income of eighty thousand francs a year. Why, with all that,
I'd walk on a woman as if she were a pavement!'

The tart started vomiting again. Edmond, sitting opposite
with his chin in his hands, seemed to be looking into Villedeuil's future. Villedeuil, his long hair falling into his red
eyes, was sobbing and kissing a miniature of La Rouvroy. I
threw some iced water over the tart's head.

And the crossing-sweepers on the boulevard below, raising their eyes, envied all the pleasure which seemed to shine
in the fading light of the candles in Room No. 7.[19]

The limits of this region of fashionable pleasure were clearly defined. At the western end was the place de la Madeleine where at no.2, on the corner of the rue Royale, stood the restaurant Durand in which Zola wrote 'J'accuse', his bitter indictment of the French establishment's handling of the Dreyfus affair. The square is dominated by the neo-classical église de la Madeleine. When Mrs Trollope strolled down from Tortoni's in 1835 to view it by moonlight, it had only been built a few years and was regarded with more admiration than most of today's visitors are likely to muster. 'Did Greece', she asks, 'ever show any combination of stones and mortar more graceful, more majestic than this?'[20] Soon it was to become the Society church *par excellence*, and it is here that in *Bel-Ami* Georges Duroy puts the seal on his conquest of the Parisian haute-bourgeoisie by marrying his boss's daughter, Mlle Walter.

To the east, few of the denizens of the Grands Boulevards would have considered venturing much beyond Frascati's, except perhaps to visit the Théâtre des Variétés, which still stands at 7 boulevard Montmartre. It was under the direction of Nestor Roqueplan in the 1840s that the foundations of the theatre's prosperity were laid. Later, the actress Hortense Schneider won huge success in the works of Offenbach, notably *La Belle Hélène*. It is at the Variétés that the career of the heroine of *Nana* (1880) begins, and Zola's novel opens with the first night of a play, *La Blonde Vénus*, which is clearly intended to evoke the productions of Offenbach.

The rue Vivienne and the Bourse

Close to the Théâtre des Variétés is the northern end of the rue Vivienne, where in 1870 Isidore Ducasse was living at no.15. He was twenty-four and this was the last year of his life. Born in Montevideo, he had been sent over to France for his education, and there, under the name of the comte de Lautréamont, he wrote the savage *Chants de Maldoror* (1868), later hailed by surrealists as a work which brilliantly foreshadowed their own. Lautréamont already knew the rue Vivienne and had perhaps lived there before. In the sixth of the *Chants* he describes it in passing: 'The shops of the rue Vivienne display their riches to wondering eyes. Lit by numerous gas-lamps, the mahogany caskets and the gold watches flash dazzling gleams of light through the windows. The clock on the Bourse has tolled eight.'

The place de la Bourse, about half-way down the rue Vivienne on the left-hand side, is the centre of the city's commercial life, the Paris equivalent of London's Stock Exchange. Its fascination for men of letters in the 20th century has not been great, but in the 19th it was rightly recognised as a transforming influence on the nature of Parisian society. The pleasures of the Grands Boulevards had to be paid for one way or another, and the fortunes which were made and lost at dizzying speed on the stock market had much to do with the conspicuous consumption of the Second Empire. The successful speculator who could provide a lavish apartment for his mistress and expensive entertainment for her friends was an important feature of these years. In a letter to his biographer John Forster, Dickens notes that amongst the other guests at an exquisite dinner party he had attended:

… a little man dined who was blacking shoes 8 years ago, and is now enormously rich—the richest man in Paris—having ascended with rapidity up the usual ladder of the Bourse. By merely observing that perhaps he might come down again, I clouded so many faces as to render it very clear to me that *everybody present* was at the same game for some stake or other! [...] If you were to see the steps of the Bourse at about 4 in the afternoon, and the crowd of blouses and patches among the speculators there assembled, all howling and haggard with speculation, you would stand aghast at the consideration of what must be going on. Concierges and people like that perpetually blow their brains out, or fly into the Seine, 'à cause des pertes sur la Bourse.' I hardly ever take up a French paper without lighting on such a paragraph. On the other hand, thoroughbred horses without end, and red velvet carriages with white kid harness on jet black horses, go by here all day long; and the pedestrians who turn to look at them, laugh, and say, 'C'est la Bourse!'[21]

Cyril Connolly in the rue Colbert

Those who preferred to spend their money more discreetly were well catered for in neighbouring streets such as the rue Colbert. Business was still brisk in this region of Paris when Cyril Connolly found his way there, as a schoolboy of seventeen, shortly after the First World War. An incident which took place then provides the material for an entertaining passage in his *Enemies of Promise* (1938):

One event in Paris upset me. On a sultry evening as I was walking back to my hotel after dinner, I was accosted outside the Café de la Paix [on the corner of the boulevard des Capucines and the place de l'Opéra] by a pimp with a straw hat and an umbrella. He offered to take me to a music-hall. I was too nervous to refuse and he then informed me it would be 'rather a rough kind of place, you understand'. I was now too frightened and excited to turn back and he took me to a brothel in the Rue Colbert. I was overcome with guilt and apprehension as I sat with the pimp in the little gilded *salon* while he spoke to the Madame. The mechanical piano played, at last the girls filed in and I was asked to choose two of them. Voiceless I pointed with a trembling finger. They stayed behind and a bottle of champagne appeared. We all had a glass and then another bottle. Drink made no impression, I was paralysed with fear, partly of being hit on the head and waking up in Buenos Aires, partly of saying the wrong thing. Then it was suggested that I should go upstairs with the two ladies. It was then a new panic arose. How much was all this? In a shrunken voice I asked for the bill. '*Quoi. Déjà?*' '*Oui, oui, oui. Toute suite.*' I explained to Madame that I did not know if I would have enough money to pay. She was astounded. 'But I thought Monsieur was a gentleman!' When the bill arrived it was for almost ten pounds, mostly for champagne and with a bonus of course for the pimp. I explained that I could not pay at once, that the ladies must leave immediately, that I would give her all the money I had (about four pounds), and find the rest within the week. I gave her my card, on which I had written the address of my hotel. My father was waiting up for me and I told him I had lost my way.

The rest of my time in Paris was spent in anguish. At any moment I expected to see Madame and the pimp arrive to ask for me. Meals in the hotel were a torture which I could not bear for I would be sure to see the pimp with his umbrella or Madame with my visiting card directed to our table by the concierge. No time of day was safe. I wrote to my grandmother who, I knew, was giving me five pounds for my birthday and asked her to send it to Paris in advance as the shops were better there than they would be in Belgium and I wanted to buy some presents for my friends. It seemed as if her letter would never arrive; my worst moment was in the Musée de Cluny, beside the iron crown of Receswinth. I went out and sat in a cold sweat on a bench in the garden.

Next day the money arrived and I rushed round to the brothel. It was eleven o'clock in the morning; no one remembered me, another Madame was on duty and listened in bewilderment while I explained, stuffing money into her hand, and wondering if it would seem impertinent to ask for my card back. At last I was safe. I bought Charles Milligan, Denis, and Freddie a few cheap presents and shortly afterwards attained my eighteenth birthday, still without having kissed anyone.[22]

It was not until 1946 that the brothels of Paris were officially closed. For the better part of a hundred years they had been one of the city's major tourist industries and since the middle of the previous century the facilities on offer, especially in these streets of central Paris, had grown increasingly elaborate. The 1880s and 1890s saw the publication of numerous 'bachelor's guides' which tabulated their various attractions. Typical of these helpful reference books was *The Pretty Women of Paris, Being a complete Directory or Guide to Pleasure for Visitors to the Gay City*. Its entries make curious reading. A stone's throw from the rue Colbert, for example, the house which stands at 12 rue Chabanais enjoyed a particularly high reputation. It was known to its patrons, who included the Prince of Wales, simply as the Chabanais:

> The finest bagnio in the world. Each room is decorated in a different style, regardless of expense. The bathing chamber is sumptuously arranged and may be used in company of a chosen nymph, for the charge of 100 francs. The management issue an illustrated book giving a view of the principal saloons. A negress is kept on the establishment. This is a favourite resort of the upper ten, and many ladies, both in society and out of it, come here alone, or with their lovers, for Lesbian diversions.

Chamfort in the rue des Petits-Champs

By a quirk of historical irony 'the finest bagnio in the world' was situated next door to the house, still there today at 10 rue Chabanais, in which the great moralist Chamfort had died in 1794. Chamfort belonged to the other class of people who haunt these streets—the users of the Bibliothèque Nationale at 58 rue de Richelieu. It is perhaps the spirit of the great library which has drawn to the rue de Richelieu its succession of literary inhabitants, among them such varied figures as Molière, Tallemant, Diderot, Stendhal, Balzac, and Thomas Paine.[23] But Chamfort had a more direct association with the Bibliothèque Nationale, since in 1792 he was appointed its keeper. In the collection of maxims and anecdotes which are his lasting monument he analysed with disillusioned clarity the folly and corruption of French society in the days before the Revolution. 'A man must swallow a toad every morning', he remarked, 'if he wishes to be sure of finding nothing still more disgusting before the day is over.'[24] His opinion of Paris was low: 'One could apply to the city of Paris just the terms which St. Theresa used to define hell: the place where it stinks and where there is no love.'[25]

Chamfort welcomed the Revolution, but he was too uncompromising a man to make the sort of accommodations necessary for survival in that turbulent period. Arrested once and then released, he went back to live in the rue des Petits-Champs at the southern end of the rue Chabanais and the Bibliothèque Nationale. Before long, he heard that he was to be re-arrested. His determination never to return to prison was absolute. The rest is told in a breathless narrative set down by one of his contemporaries:

> Chamfort retires to his study at the end of the gallery which contained his library. He shuts himself in, loads a pistol, tries to fire it at his forehead, smashes the upper part of his nose and staves in his right eye. Astonished to be still alive and determined to die, he seizes a razor, tries to slit his throat, then makes several further attempts, cutting his flesh to ribbons. The weakness of his hand does nothing to change the resolution of his spirit; he strikes several blows at his heart, and, as he begins to lose consciousness, tries by a last effort to hamstring himself and to open all his veins. Finally overcome by pain, he lets out a cry and throws himself onto a chair, where he remains almost lifeless. The blood streams out under the door. The housekeeper hears the cry, sees the blood; she calls for help, people come; she bangs on the door with redoubled force; they break it down; the sight which greets them puts a stop to any questioning. Everyone hastens to staunch the flow of blood with handkerchiefs, scraps of linen, bandages. The dying man is carried to his bed. Doctors and civil officers are called. While the former are preparing the instruments needed for the treatment of so many wounds, Chamfort dictates in a firm voice to the police commissioner of the Lepelletier section the following declaration:
>
> 'I, Sébastien-Roch-Nicolas Chamfort, declare that I wish to die a free man rather than to be taken back like a slave into a place of imprisonment. I declare that if I am nonetheless to be dragged thither by violence in my present state, I have enough strength left to finish what I have started. I am a free man; while I live, I shall never again be forced to enter a prison.'[26]

Chamfort accepted his failed suicide with equanimity: 'I've got the bullet in my head, which is the main thing. A little sooner, a little later, that's all it amounts to.' As things turned out, it was not much later. Looked after by friends, Chamfort seemed for a while to be recovering, but some seven months later he suffered a relapse and died in the house to which he had moved at 10 rue Chabanais.

The Palais-Royal

In Chamfort's time the resorts of pleasure in central Paris were not dispersed among different streets, they were focused, with wonderful convenience, on the Palais-Royal. Built in the 1630s for Cardinal Richelieu, this palace eventually passed into the possession of the duc d'Orléans. A glimpse of it in the mid-18th century is provided by Diderot at the start of *Le neveu de Rameau* (the allée d'Argenson was the avenue of trees on the east side of the garden near the rue de Valois, and the allée de Foy that on the west near the rue de Richelieu):

> Come rain or shine, my custom is to go for a stroll in the Palais-Royal every afternoon at about five. I am always to be seen there alone, sitting on a seat in the Allée d'Argenson, meditating. I hold discussions with myself on politics, love, taste or philosophy, and let my thoughts wander in complete abandon, leaving them free to follow the first wise or foolish idea that comes along, like those young rakes we see in the Allée de Foy who run after a giddy-looking little piece with a laughing face, sparkling eye and tip-tilted nose, only to leave her for another, accosting them all, but sticking to none. In my case my thoughts are my wenches. If it is too cold or wet I take shelter in the Café de la Régence and amuse myself watching people playing chess. Paris is the place in the world, and the Café de la Régence the place in Paris where this game is played best ...'[27]

There are only hints in this passage of the Palais-Royal of the future. Shortly afterwards it passed into the hands of the licentious Louis-Philippe-Joseph, who was to become fifth duc d'Orléans and later took the name Philippe Egalité. Heavily in debt, Philippe decided in the 1780s to turn the Palais-Royal to profit and accordingly opened up the three arcaded galleries that we see around the gardens now. It was a move that was looked on with some disdain at court. 'So, cousin, you've turned shop-keeper,' remarked Louis XVI. 'No doubt we shall only see you on Sundays in future.' Undeterred, Philippe d'Orléans went ahead with the project and the Palais-Royal was transformed. The cafés, shops and gambling-houses which occupied the arcades quickly made the place notorious as a centre of debauchery. This was the state of things when William Wordsworth (1770–1850) visited 'the Palace huge/ Of Orleans' in December 1791 and, as he guardedly puts it, 'coasted round and round the line/Of Tavern, Brothel, Gaming-house, and Shop ...'[28]

The Palais-Royal seems to have been one of the few places on which the Revolution had little effect. In 1801 J. G. Lemaistre, who had travelled to Paris on legal business, found the scene of Wordsworth's coasting largely unchanged:

What an extraordinary place is the Palais-Royal! There is nothing like it in any town in Europe. I remember hearing an English epicure once observe, 'that as soon as the peace took place, he would give himself the happiness of passing six weeks in the Palais-Royal without once going out of its gates.' Certainly, if a man be contented with sensual pleasures, there is not one which he may not gratify within the walls of this building. *Restaurateurs*, or taverns, where dinners are served from two sols to two louis a head. Coffee houses, where the man of pleasure, at the risk of all that is dearest to him in life, purchases the anxious feelings which fear and hope excite, and where the *chevalier d'industrie* finds the disgraceful means of a dishonourable existence. Tailors, haberdashers, silversmiths, and watchmakers, offer every variety of clothing, of ornament, and of machinery. Book-sellers' shops are in every corner, where the *homme de lettres* finds his favourite authors, the romantic lady her novels, and the politician his pamphlets. Opticians, where the frequenter of *spectacles* purchases his opera glass, and the philosopher his telescope. Crowds of unfortunate, and sometimes lovely females challenge with every variety of dress the attention of passengers, and while they offer a too easy banquet to libertines and dotards, fill every reflecting mind with pity and sorrow. [. . .] Puppet shows, dwarfs, giants, quack doctors, vociferating newsmen, and quiet vendors of libels, who in a whisper offer you indecent and forbidden publications, complete the catalogue of many-coloured curiosities which this place presents.[29]

Among the most famous of the new establishments in the redesigned palace was the Restaurant des Trois Frères Provençaux at 88 Galerie de Beaujolais at the northern end of the gardens. This survived for almost a century and was later popular with the bohemians of the impasse du Doyenné when they were in funds. It was also patronised by some of the more discerning foreigners, including Dickens and Bulwer-Lytton. In his novel *Pelham* (1828) Lytton portrays the typical figure of the young dandy in the early years of the 19th century, for whom a connoisseur's knowledge of Paris was of course essential: 'I dined the next day at the Frères Provençaux, an excellent restaurateur's, by the by, where one gets irreproachable *gibier*, and meets no English. After dinner, I strolled into the various gambling houses, with which the Palais-Royal abounds.'[30]

Since the duc d'Orléans had always forbidden the police to enter his property, the Palais-Royal enjoyed a degree of licence that was unknown in the rest of Paris. The gambling-houses were one consequence of this. Sir Walter Scott, who was in Paris the year after Waterloo, viewed them with abhorrence; but his detailed account perhaps also suggests a certain fascination. The proprietors would clearly have had little to learn from their modern counterparts:

The Palais-Royal, in whose saloons and porticos Vice has established a public and open school for gambling and licentiousness, far from affording, as at present, an impure and scandalous source of revenue to the state, should be levelled to the ground, with all its accursed brothels and gambling houses,—rendezvouses, the more seductive to youth, as being free from some of those dangers which would alarm timidity in places of avowedly scandalous resort. Gaming is indeed reduced to all the gravity of a science, and, at the same time, is conducted upon the scale of the most extensive manufacture. In the *Sallon des Étrangers*, which I had the curiosity to visit, the scene was decent and silent to a degree of solemnity. An immense hall was filled with gamesters and spectators; those who kept the bank and managed the affairs of the establishment were distinguished by the green shades which they wore to preserve their eyes, by their silent and grave demeanour, and by the paleness of their countenances, exhausted by constant vigils. There was no distinction of persons, nor any passport required for entrance, save that of a decent exterior; and on the long tables, which were covered with gold, an artizan was at liberty to hazard his week's wages, or a noble his whole estate.

The profits of the establishment must indeed be very large to support its expenses. Besides a variety of attendants who distribute refreshments to the players gratis, there is an elegant entertainment, with expensive wines, regularly prepared about three o'clock in the morning, for those who choose to partake of it. With such temptations around him, and where the hazarding an insignificant sum seems at first venial or innocent, it is no wonder if thousands feel themselves gradually involved in the whirlpool whose verge is so little distinguishable, until they are swallowed up with their time, talent, and fortune, and often also both body and soul. This is Vice with her fairest vizard; but the same unhallowed precincts contain many a secret cell for the most hideous and unheard of debaucheries, many an open rendezvous of infamy, and many a den of usury and treason; the whole mixed with a Vanity-fair of shops for jewels, trinkets, and baubles, that bashfulness may not lack a decent pretext for adventuring into the haunts of infamy. It was here where the preachers of the Revolution first found, amidst gamblers, desperadoes, and prostitutes, ready auditors for their doctrines, and active hands to labour in their vineyard. In more recent times, it was here that the plots of the Buonapartists were adjusted, and the number of their partisans recruited and instructed concerning the progress of the conspiracy; and from hence the seduced soldiers, inflamed with many a bumper to the Exile of Elba, under the mystic names of *Jean de l'Epée*, and *Caporal Violet*, were dismissed to spread the news of his approaching return, and prepare their comrades to desert their lawful sovereign. In short, from this central pit of Acheron,—in which are openly assembled and mingled those characters and occupations which, in all other capitals, are driven to shroud themselves in separate and retired recesses—from this focus of vice and treason have flowed forth those waters of bitterness of which France has drunk so deeply.[31]

It is in one of these gambling-houses that the young Raphael loses his last gold coin at the start of Balzac's *La peau de chagrin* (1831) and in another of them, at no. 9, that the hero of *Le père Goriot* (1834) hazards the hundred francs of Delphine de Nucingen, while she waits in a carriage outside. Rastignac goes to the roulette table and throws them down on 21, the number of his age, then doubles his winnings by placing them on red. Delphine is temporarily saved.

Today there is little to remind the visitor of the Palais-Royal's gaudy past. Around the gardens, the shops, deeply arcaded, could hardly be more discreet. Couples walk sedately along the aisles between the young trees or sit around the central fountain with faces held to the sun. Single men feed the birds. This is the scene on which both Colette and Cocteau looked out during the closing years of their lives, Colette from 9 rue de Beaujolais, Cocteau from 36 rue de Montpensier. At night it is a shadowy place with little movement. Of the various literary figures who were associated with it in earlier days, perhaps the one who would be least dismayed by the modern tranquillity of the Palais-Royal would be the poet Gérard de Nerval. His fondness for it owed nothing to rowdy pleasures. In the early 1850s it was his custom to walk in the gardens with a lobster to which he had attached a blue ribbon. 'I like lobsters,' he explained, 'because they are calm, serious, and know the secrets of the sea ...'[32]

The rue Jean-Jacques-Rousseau

From the place du Palais-Royal it is only a few yards east along the rue Saint-Honoré to the rue Jean-Jacques-Rousseau. In the 18th century, when it was called the rue Plâtrière, this was a street of substantial hôtels, one of which, on the site of the present nos. 52–4, had been divided into apartments. Rousseau himself occupied the top floor of this building from 1770 to 1778. Two years after he moved in he was visited there by Bernardin de Saint-Pierre, an admirer who later enjoyed wide success with his Rousseauist novel *Paul et Virginie* (1787):

> In the month of June 1772 a friend who had suggested taking me to see Jean-Jacques Rousseau led me to a house in the rue Plâtrière, just about opposite the hôtel de la Poste. We went up to the fourth floor. We knocked and Mme Rousseau came to open the door to us. She said: 'Come in, gentlemen, you'll find my husband.' We walked into a very small ante-room where household utensils were neatly arranged. From there we went into a room in which Rousseau was seated, in frock coat and blue cap, busy copying some music. He got up with a cheerful countenance, set chairs in place for us and then went back to work, conversing with us at the same time. [...]
>
> Near him was a spinet on which he tried out tunes from time to time. The furniture consisted of two small beds with cotton covers, blue and white striped, like the hangings in the room, a chest of drawers, a table and a few chairs. Pinned to the walls were a map of the forest and park of Montmorency where he used to live and an engraving of the king of England, who had been his benefactor. His wife was sitting down, sewing linen; a canary was singing in its cage suspended from the ceiling; sparrows came to eat bread at the open windows above the street, and on the window-sill you could see window-boxes and flower-pots filled with the sort of plants which grow naturally in these conditions. Altogether, the little household had a pleasing air of neatness, peace and simplicity.[33]

Saint-Eustache—Molière's funeral

Intersecting the rue Jean-Jacques-Rousseau just beside the site of Rousseau's house is the rue de la Coquillière. At the eastern end of this street, on the edge of the rue du Jour, stands the église de Saint-Eustache. Towering beside the former site of les Halles, this great 16th-century church presents a stark and impressive contrast to the chrome and glass of the new Forum. It was here that the French poet Voiture was buried in 1684 and that the funeral of La Fontaine was held in 1695. But the church also had dealings with a less respectable side of the literary world in the person of Molière.

On the night of 17 February 1673 the playwright was taken ill while playing *Le malade imaginaire* at a theatre whose site is now marked by a plaque at the south-east corner of the place du Palais-Royal. He managed to get back to his home in the rue de Richelieu, but despite the efforts of his wife Armande to tend him, he died within a matter of hours. It was then that for those around him the problems began. Saint-Eustache was Molière's parish and it was here that he had been baptised; but actors in general were disliked by the clergy, and the author of *Tartuffe* more so than most. The vicar of Saint-Eustache piously refused to bury a man of his profession in consecrated ground. The Archbishop was petitioned; he referred the matter to one of his officers. The King was petitioned; he pondered the risks of offending the clergy. Meanwhile, the days passed and Molière remained unburied. Finally, under tactful pressure from the King, the Archbishop accepted a compromise: 'We authorize the vicar of Saint-Eustache to give ecclesiastical burial to the body of the deceased Molière in the cemetery of the parish on condition that there shall be no ceremony, with two priests only, after nightfall, and that there shall be no solemn service for him either in the parish of Saint-Eustache or elsewhere, in any church of the regular clergy.'[34]

The meagre concession came too late. When Molière was eventually buried on 21 February 1673, the Archbishop's instructions were quite disregarded. Four priests carried the body, three churchmen officiated, six children in blue carried wax candles in silver candlesticks, lackeys bore torches of white wax, hundreds of Molière's friends followed his body to the grave with lighted tapers. In consequence of the huge crowd, the occasion later degenerated into a near-riot. Even this was not the end; in after years the rumour persisted that

Molière had in fact been cheated of his place in consecrated ground and buried in a remote corner of the cemetery among the suicides and the stillborn.

The Cemetery of the Holy Innocents

Churlish priests were not the only impediment to a decent burial in Paris. Over a century earlier Rabelais' giant, Pantagruel, had remarked that 'it was a good town to live in, but not to die in, for that the grave-digging rogues of St. Innocent used to warm their backsides with dead men's bones'. The church Rabelais refers to stood directly across the Forum des Halles from Saint-Eustache, at the corner of the rue Berger and the rue Saint-Denis—and its cemetery was notorious. Two centuries after Rabelais it was sought out by William Cole. His visit was one of the less happy experiences of his stay, but it gives a remarkable picture of what remained, until a few years before the Revolution, the central burying-ground of Paris.

'From St. James de la Boucherie I went to the Church and *Cimetière* of the Holy Innocents in St. Denis's Street: one of the most filthy and nasty places I ever was in.' The church itself Cole finds 'small and antient and very gloomy', but it is the cemetery which really upsets him:

From the Church I stepped into the Church Yard, which is, of all the Places I ever saw in my Life, without the least Exaggeration, the most shocking to mortal Pride and Vanity, the most stinking, loathsome & indecent. [...]

As I came out from the Church, under a Covering & close to the Wall, my smelling Faculty was so powerfully offended that I could stay there no longer, & thought of leaving a Place so necessarily unwholesome: but observing my two Servants very busily employed, at a good Distance from me, towards the South West Corner, or rather more to the Middle of it, inclining to the West End, in peeping into a Cave or great Hole, I went up to them, & saw such a Scene as might do much Good to the Soul but smelt such a Stink as was enough to poison one, & to frustrate all the good Effects arising from sober Reflections upon the Equality that Death makes of us all, & the necessary unavoidable Consequence of Putrefaction, rottenness & Corruption, after a fleeting & short Life of Delicacy, Luxury & Dissipation. In this Cave, about 30 Feet Square, cheifly covered over by Boards & Planks, were a great Variety of Coffins of different Sizes & most of them ordinary ones, ill jointed & sadly made, according to French Joinery; so that it was unavoidable but that the Smell should find its way out of such ill jointed Boxes: indeed it is inconceivable what a Stench issued from such an Aggregation of mortifying & putrefying Carcasses: enough to give the Plague to the whole City: the Smell, literally speaking, did not get out of my Head or Fancy for many Days after. In this Manner do the polite French bury their Dead, leaving them above Ground to poison the Living! for when one Stage is full, they cover it over with a Layer of Sand, as I conceive, & then lay another Pavement of Coffins upon that, which is also covered with Sand when the Floor will hold no more; & so on 'till the Cave is quite full to the Top.[35]

Today the southern part of the rue Saint-Denis is given over to glossy tourist restaurants interspersed with the neon lights and rustling curtains of the sex shops and peep-shows. Altogether, the scene offers a contrast with Cole's description which might be relished by even the most jaded moralist.

Les Halles

For centuries the church of Saint-Eustache and the church of the Holy Innocents straddled the central market-place of Paris. That time is now past. When the 19th-century pavilions of les Halles were demolished in the early 1970s, a rich strand of Paris's history went with them, and for this the buildings which have risen in their place can hardly be a substitute.

Since the Middle Ages this area had been a focus of popular life in the centre of the city. For this reason the narrow streets around les Halles were for a long time a favourite resort of those who wanted a taste of the low life without venturing into the dangerous outskirts of Paris. 'I went', notes Restif de la Bretonne in the 18th century, 'to visit the cabarets of les

Halles, about which I had heard a great deal. I expected to find some fascinating sights there, but I saw nothing but debauchery: people smoking, or sleeping; lewd women with billiard or card sharks, brawling and swearing at one another; a few sad rakes who had come there looking for amusement and who were bored instead.'[36]

A century and a half later, in *Good Morning Midnight* (1939), Jean Rhys mentions an excursion to the same area:

> One day, he said: 'I'll take you to see something rather interesting.' And, wandering along the streets at the back of the Halles, we came to a café where the clients paid for the right, not to have a drink, but to sleep. They sat close-pressed against each other with their arms on the tables, their heads in their arms. Every place in the room was filled; others lay along the floor. We squinted in at them through the windows. 'Would you like to go in and have a look at them?' he said, as if he were exhibiting a lot of monkeys. 'It's all right, we can go in—the chap here knows me. There's one fellow who is usually here. If you stand him a few drinks and get him really going he tries to eat his glass. It's very curious. You ought to see that.'
>
> When I said: 'Not for anything on earth,' he thought I had gone shy or sentimental. 'Well,' I said, 'all right. I'll watch you eating a glass with pleasure.' He didn't like that at all.[37]

More often it was in the early morning that the curious and those in search of entertainment found their way to the Halles. Back in the 1860s the Goncourts make reference to the four-sous bowl of soup that was to be had in a filthy tavern in the rue Basse—soup rather than anything else, because its onion soup was one of the market's particular attractions. When the night-clubs of Montmartre finally closed, revellers could come here to mark the end of one day at the spot where Paris was just beginning to wake to another. And so it is that early in 1929 we find Evelyn Waugh and his party drinking 'fine, pungent onion soup' (see p. 213) in the café Au Père Tranquille which still stands on the corner of the rue Pierre-Lescot and the rue Rambuteau.

It was not merely the socialites who ended up at les Halles.

Other habitués of Montmartre also tended to make for it in the early morning, amongst them the group of poets and painters celebrated by Francis Carco:

> It's the 'violet hour' which we never dared to admit that we had seen dawning through the windows of the bar in Montmartre where we had spent the night, for that meant a round for everyone at the expense of the sleep-lover who allowed himself to give the signal for us to break up.
>
> The city is coming to life ... A gilt paper-doll, lost by a party-goer, flaps in the edge of a gutter: a tramp picks it up. We were all twenty, even the 'old men', who were thirty. Jean Pellerin recited his poetry to us. Les Halles overflowed with strawberries, cabbages, porters, *fortes femmes* in sweaters, pleated skirts and clogs, sides of beef, down and outs, neighing horses, carts. The Grand Comptoir never emptied. Its night-time customers were followed by its dawn customers to be followed in turn by its real day-time customers. Standing at a zinc bar, we drained the 'last of the last', only to have another a bit further along. In this way we went from calvados to red wine, then to spiked black coffee, and finally to the *café crème* into which we plunged our croissants.[38]

But at this hour neither artists nor socialites were more than a frivolous addition to the real business of les Halles, which was being carried on by the porters and the *fortes femmes*. Dawn was always the most exciting time here, and it is the scene in the first stirrings of daylight that most people who had the fortune to know this part of Paris before the days of Pompidou will best remember. Zola's *Le ventre de Paris* (1873) marks the literary apotheosis of les Halles. The novel opens with the carts converging on the market-place. Dawn is breaking and the hero Florent, who has just arrived in Paris, is faint from hunger. He stands at the edge of the market, near the western end of the rue Rambuteau:

> At present the luminous dial of Saint-Eustache was paling as a night-light does when surprised by the dawn. The gas-jets in the wine-shops in the neighbouring streets went out one

by one, like stars extinguished by the brightness. And Florent gazed at the vast markets now gradually emerging from the gloom, from the dreamland in which he had beheld them, stretching out their ranges of open palaces. Greenish-grey in hue, they looked more solid now, and even more colossal with their prodigious masting of columns upholding an endless expanse of roofs.

[...] And by degrees, as the fires of dawn rose higher and higher at the far end of the Rue Rambuteau, the mass of vegetation grew brighter and brighter, emerging more and more distinctly from the bluey gloom that clung to the ground. Salad herbs, cabbage-lettuce, endive, and succory, with rich soil still clinging to their roots, exposed their swelling hearts; bundles of spinach, bundles of sorrel, clusters of artichokes, piles of peas and beans, mounds of cos-lettuce, tied round with straws, sounded every note in the whole gamut of greenery, from the sheeny lacquer-like green of the pods to the deep-toned green of the foliage; a continuous gamut with ascending and descending scales which died away in the variegated tones of the heads of celery and bundles of leeks. But the highest and most sonorous notes still came from the patches of bright carrots and snowy turnips, strewn in prodigious quantities all along the markets and lighting them up with the medley of their two colours.

At the crossway in the Rue des Halles cabbages were piled up in mountains; there were white ones, hard and compact as metal balls, curly savoys, whose great leaves made them look like basins of green bronze, and red cabbages, which the dawn seemed to transform into superb masses of bloom with the hue of wine-lees, splotched with dark purple and carmine. At the other side of the markets, at the crossway near Saint-Eustache, the end of the Rue Rambuteau was blocked by a barricade of orange-hued pumpkins, sprawling with swelling bellies in two rows one on top of the other. And here and there gleamed the glistening ruddy brown of a hamper of onions, the blood-red crimson of a heap of tomatoes, the quiet yellow of a display of marrows, and the sombre violet of the aubergine; while numerous fat black radishes still left patches of gloom amidst the quivering brilliance of the general awakening.[39]

As the sun rises and the carts continue to unload their produce, Florent stands lost in the midst of it all:

On his left some waggons were discharging fresh loads of cabbages. He turned his eyes, and away in the distance saw carts yet streaming out of the rue Turbigo. The tide was still and ever rising. Florent had felt it about his ankles, then on a level with his stomach, and now it was threatening to drown him altogether. Blinded and submerged, his ears buzzing, his stomach overpowered by all that he had seen, he asked for mercy; and wild grief took possession of him at the thought of dying there of starvation in the very heart of glutted Paris, amidst the effulgent awakening of her markets. Big hot tears started from his eyes.[40]

CHAPTER 3

The Marais and the East

The place du Châtelet

The place du Châtelet was a less agreeable spot for a mid-day drink in the 17th century than it is today. There was the same fine view across the Seine to the towers of the Conciergerie, but one's enjoyment of it would at best have been fitful:

> The noise of the mills on the pont Marchand, the shrieks of the fowl and lambs being slaughtered along the quai de la Mégisserie, of the cows and calves having their throats slit on the rue de la Tuerie, the cries of the fishwives and hawkers in the place du Châtelet, the screams of the tortured, the stench of the morgue, ... the stale smell from the blood-soaked cobbles—all this made the district truly one of the most fearful in Paris.[1]

The sounds of torture which mingle with the other noises of street life in Jacques Hillairet's sketch are not just the product of a historian's imagination. There were two places of execution within this area (in front of les Halles and on the place de Grève), and at its centre was the city's main prison. For nine hundred years or more the bridge leading to the rue Saint-Denis was guarded by a fortress which in the 16th and 17th centuries took its final form in the gloomy structure of the Grand Châtelet. Walk across the square from the pont au Change and you will find a plaque to its sinister memory on either side of the Chambre des Notaires.[2] With its formidable round towers and conical roofs, it stood a few yards to the west of the centre of the modern square.

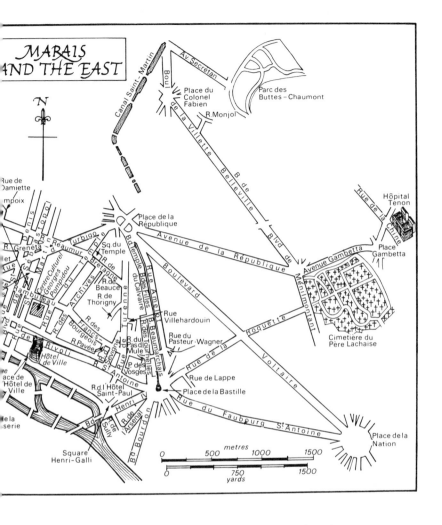

MARAIS AND THE EAST

In an age when prisons were anyway vile, the Châtelet seems to have been a place of peculiar horror. In 1526 the poet Clément Marot, an important forerunner of Ronsard and the Pléiade, was convicted of eating meat in Lent and shut up there. After a short time his friends managed to get him transferred to a prison in Chartres, but the experience of the Châtelet had left him scarred. While in the prison 'claire et nette' of Chartres, he wrote a bitter and moving attack on his earlier prison in a poem called 'L'Enfer' ('Hell'). The smell of the Châtelet is worse than sulphur:

> Si ne croy pas qu'il y ait chose au monde
> Qui mieulx ressemble ung Enfer tresimmonde:
> Je dy Enfer et Enfer puys bien dire;*

One of the most striking passages of the poem is his account of how the criminal investigator goes to work to wheedle a confession from the prisoner, assuring him that if he will say who was really responsible for the crime he will be able to leave this place of torment,

> Pour t'en aller aux beaulx champs-Elysées,
> Où liberté faict vivre les esprits
> Qui de compter vérité ont appris.†

But if the prisoner refuses, he is taken down to the depths of this Hell, 'where his veins and sinews are stretched', to try what torture can do where mildness has failed.

With the honourable exception of Montaigne, Marot was practically alone in protesting against this habitual use of torture in the interrogation of people suspected of crimes. His plea for compassion went unheeded. Torture not only continued to be practised but became on occasions something of a tourist attraction. Over a century later, in the spring of 1651, the English diarist John Evelyn visited the Châtelet to see one of its prisoners put to the question. Evelyn was a civilised man, whose main literary topics, apart from the doings recorded in his celebrated diary, were the cultivation of trees and the dangers of air pollution. The scene with which he was confronted in this dark fortress was perhaps less diverting than he had hoped:

> This morning I went to the *Chastlett* or prison, where a Malefactor was to have the *Question* or Torture given to him, which was thus: They first bound his wrists with a strong rope or smalle Cable, & one end of it to an iron ring made fast to the wall about 4 foote from the floore, & then his feete, with another cable, fastned about 6 foote farther than his uttmost length, to another ring on the floore of the

---

* And I do not believe that there is anything in the world which more closely resembles a hideous Hell. I say Hell and I may well say it.
† To go off to the beautiful Champs-Elysées, where freedom gives life to souls who have learnt to tell the truth.

roome, thus suspended, & yet lying but a slant; they slid an
horse of wood under the rope which bound his feete, which
so exceedingly stiffned it, as severd the fellows joynts in
miserable sort, drawing him out at length in an extraordinary manner, he having only a paire of linnen drawers on his
naked body: Then they question'd him of a robery, (the
Lieutennant Criminal being present, & a clearke that wrot)
which not confessing, they put a higher horse under the
rope, to increase the torture & extension: In this Agonie,
confessing nothing, the Executioner with a horne (such as
they drench horses with) struck the end of it into his mouth,
and pour'd the quantity of 2 boaketts of Water downe his
throat, which so prodigiously swell'd him, face, Eyes ready
to start, brest & all his limbs, as would have pittied &
almost affrited one to see it; for all this he denied all was
charged to him: Then they let him downe, & carried him
before a warme fire to bring him to himselfe, being now to
all appearance dead with paine. What became of him I know
not, but the Gent: whom he robbd, constantly averrd him to
be the man; & the fellows suspicious, pale lookes, before he
knew he shold be rack'd, betraid some guilt: The *Lieutennant* was also of that opinion, & told us at first sight (for he
was a leane dry black young man) he would conquer the
Torture & so it seemes they could not hang him; but did use
in such cases, where the evidence is very presumptuous, to
send them to the *Gallies*, which is as bad as death. There was
another fat Malefactor to succeede, who he said, he was
confident would never endure the Question; This his often
being at these Trials, had it seemes given him experience of,
but the spectacle was so uncomfortable, that I was not able
to stay the sight of another: It represented yet to me, the
intollerable suffering which our B.S. must needes undergo,
when his blessed body was hanging with all its weight upon
the nailes on the Crosse.[3]

The place de l'Hôtel-de-Ville

For many of those who confessed to real or fictitious crimes it
was only a short journey to the place of execution. A hundred

yards away, in front of the Hôtel de Ville, the place de Grève (now the place de l'Hôtel-de-Ville) had been one of the main sites of these public entertainments since early in the 14th century. The *Journal d'un bourgeois de Paris sous François I*^{er} records with impassive regularity such entries as, 'Le jeudy XXVIe octobre [1525], fust pendue et estranglée unne femme Picarde devant l'ostel de la ville, pour avoir desrobé quelque argent à sa maitresse.' (Thursday 26 October, a woman from Picardy was hanged in front of the Hôtel de Ville for stealing some money from her mistress.) In the summer of 1665 it was the turn of Claude Le Petit. The unlucky poet had left a window open one day in the room where he had been working. A gust of wind plucked from the desk one of his papers, which fluttered to the ground at the feet of a passing priest. The priest read it and recoiled. Le Petit's blasphemy was at once relayed to the authorities. He was a man of dissipated life, whose uncompromising satires had frequently given cause for offence.[4] It was decided to act with firmness. On 1 September 1665 his hand was cut off in front of the Hôtel de Ville and he was then burned at the stake. He was thirty years old, and the place de Grève had already cast a pale shadow across his verse. Ten years earlier, in his *Chronique scandaleuse ou Paris ridicule*, he had offered this sardonic comment on the advantages of having a place of execution by the edge of the river:

> Malheureux espace de terre,
> Au gibet public consacré;
> Terrain où l'on a massacré
> Cent fois plus d'hommes qu'à la guerre;
> Certes, Grève, après maint delict,
> Vous estes, pour mourir, un lit
> Bien commode pour les infasmes,
> Puisqu'ils n'ont qu'à prendre un bateau,
> Et, d'un coup d'aviron, leur âmes
> S'en vont au Paradis par eau. *

---

* Wretched patch of earth devoted to the public gallows. Site where a hundred times more men have been slaughtered than in war. Truly, Grève, you are a very convenient bed on which to die for villains who have committed many an offence, since they only have to take a boat, and, with a stroke of the oar, their souls go off to Paradise by water.

On execution days the square was a sea of onlookers, surrounding windows were rented out at extravagant prices, the roofs were turned into grandstands. In the 18th century, the writer Restif de la Bretonne attended one of these spectacles with his friend Du Hameauneuf. His account of it in *Les nuits de Paris* pays, as usual, full tribute to his own sensitivity:

The crier had announced a death sentence during the day ... We were proceeding towards the place de Grève. It was late, and we thought the execution over. But the gaping mob proclaimed the contrary.

'Let us go on,' said Du Hameauneuf, 'since the opportunity offers itself.'

As he spoke, I caught sight of some movement on the steps of the Hôtel de Ville. It was the first of the three convicts going to meet his end! ... When the penalty is too great for the crime it is an atrocity and the effect is lost; it inspires not dread, but outrage.

The man was broken on the wheel, as were his two companions. I could not endure the sight of that execution; I moved away; but Du Hameauneuf watched it all stoically. I turned to look at something else. While the victims suffered, I studied the spectators. They chattered and laughed as if they were watching a farce. But what revolted me most was a very pretty girl I saw with her sweetheart. She uttered peals of laughter, she jested about the victims' expressions and screams. I could not believe it! I looked at her five or six times. Finally, without thinking of the consequences, I said to her, 'Mademoiselle, you must have the heart of a monster, and to judge by what I see of you today, I believe you capable of any crime. If I had the misfortune to be your sweetheart, I would shun you forever.'

As she was no fishwife, she stood mute! I expected some unpleasant retort from her lover—he said not a word.... Then, a few steps away I saw another young girl, drenched in tears. She came to me, leaned upon my arm, hiding her face, and she said, 'This is a good man, who feels pity for those in anguish!'

Who was that compassionate girl? ... A poor thing who

had abandoned herself to the procurers on the Quai de la Ferraille! I looked at her; she was tall and attractive. I led her to the Marquise's shelter without waiting for Du Hameauneuf.[5]

The rue Bourg-l'Abbé

The area to the north of the Châtelet and the place de Grève was a warren of narrow and dangerous streets. It is now much changed, but vestiges of the earlier streets still remain—as, for example, at the western end of the rue Greneta, not far from the site of the cour des Miracles described in Hugo's *Notre-Dame de Paris*. The miracles that took place in this criminal enclave—roughly where the rue de Damiette is today—were those performed by the apparently crippled and mutilated beggars who each evening threw off their pretended afflictions when they got back here. It was an underworld kingdom with its own language and its own elected monarch, where the forces of law rarely penetrated.

Until the mid-19th century the rue Greneta and the rue aux Ours were linked by a disreputable alley called the rue Bourg-l'Abbé* which found its way into the memoirs of François-René de Chateaubriand (1768–1848). Later Chateaubriand was to become famous as the author of *Le génie du Christianisme* and the precursor of French Romanticism, but at the time of this episode he was only twenty years old and the Revolution was a year away. What led him to seek out the rue Bourg-l'Abbé was the account given by Marshal Bassompière of an adventure he had undertaken in 1606. Bassompière was a cynical and accomplished diplomat in the reign of Louis XIII who made the mistake of giving offence to Cardinal Richelieu. Consigned for twelve years to the Bastille, he took the opportunity to write his often scandalous memoirs. The reminiscence which caught Chateaubriand's imagination two hundred years later is an eerie, inconclusive tale, which nonetheless gives something of the atmosphere of the Paris of its time, a city of narrow, lampless streets 'where robbers and murderers

---

* The present rue Bourg-l'Abbé, to the east of the boulevard Sébastopol, is a different street, which used to be called the rue Neuve-du-Bourg-l'Abbé.

lay in wait and where meetings took place either by torchlight or in total darkness'. Chateaubriand tells the story in Bassompière's own words:

'Five or six months ago,' writes the Marshal in his Memoirs, 'every time I crossed the Petit-Pont'—for at that time the Pont Neuf was not yet built—'a pretty woman, a sempstress at the sign of the two Angels,* made deep curtseys to me and followed me with her eyes as far as she could; and as I had noticed this, I looked at her too and greeted her with greater attention. It happened that one day when I was coming into Paris from Fontainebleau, as soon as she saw me crossing the Petit-Pont she stood at the door of her shop and said as I passed: 'Monsieur, I am your servant.' I returned her greeting, and looking round from time to time, I saw that she followed me with her eyes as far as she could.'

Bassompière obtained an assignation.

'I found,' he says, 'a very beautiful woman, twenty years old, wearing a nightcap and dressed in nothing but a very fine shift and a little petticoat of green wool, with slippers on her feet and a wrapper around her. She pleased me greatly. I asked her if I could not see her again. 'If you wish to see me again,' she replied, 'it will be at the house of an aunt of mine, who lives in the Rue Bourg-l'Abbé, near the Market, next to the Rue aux Ours, the third door going towards the Rue Saint-Martin; I will wait for you there from ten o'clock till midnight, and later if need be; I will leave the door open. Inside there is a little passage through which you must go quickly, for the door of my aunt's room opens on to it, and you will find a staircase leading to the second floor.' I arrived at ten o'clock and found the door she had indicated, and a bright light, not only on the second floor but on the third and first too; but the door was closed. I knocked to show that I had come, but I heard a man's voice ask who I was. I returned to the Rue aux Ours, and coming back a second time and finding the door open, I went up to the second floor, where I found that the light came from the

---

* Buildings were identified by signs rather than numbers until the late 18th century.

straw of the bed which was being burnt, and saw two naked bodies lying on the table in the room. I withdrew in great perplexity, and on my way out I met some funeral mutes who asked me what I was looking for; and I, to make them stand aside, drew my sword and went out, returning to my quarters, somewhat disturbed by this unexpected sight.[6]

Chateaubriand cannot resist the temptation to retrace the Marshal's steps, but he finds at the address only an innocent house, its upper window hung with a garland of flowers.

From the boulevard de Sébastopol to the square du Temple

Thirty years later, in the first decade of the 19th century, the Grand Châtelet was demolished; but the maze of surrounding streets remained intact—and politically dangerous. How well they lent themselves to the activities of insurrectionists can be gathered from Victor Hugo's account in *Les Misérables* (1862) of the uprising of June 1832, which was centred on these streets. Easily barricaded by a handful of men, they offered little room for manoeuvre to the opposing government forces. It is no accident that most of the streets Hugo mentions had already disappeared by the time he was writing. This was precisely what Napoleon III's minister, Haussmann, had in mind. The wide new boulevard de Sébastopol, opened by the emperor himself in 1858, was specifically designed to cut a swathe through this densely populated area and thereby act as a strategic firebreak.

With the demolition of the Châtelet and the construction of the boulevard Sébastopol and the two theatres in the place du Châtelet, the area began to take on its modern shape. But while it ceased to be the desperate region of former times, it never quite acquired the elegance the planners had intended, hovering always, in spite of its dignified façades, on the edge of something rather less respectable. From the start it was a poor relation of the Grands Boulevards, the haunt of cheaper prostitutes and a less discriminating clientèle. For the novelist Charles-Louis Philippe (1874–1909) it was as good a place as any to observe the daily process by which modest dreams succumb to a sordid reality. His novel *Bubu de Montparnasse* (1901) opens there at half past nine on the evening of 15 July. The big stores along the boulevard have put up their shutters:

It was the hour when passers-by no longer pause before shop windows. Night, with other aims in view, had come to life. There were lanterns on the carriages: the cabs with bright lights shining like two pleasure-hungry eyes, and the trams with red or green beacons roaring like an impatient crowd. They followed one another, crossed, stamped the ground and rolled on. On the horizon, in the direction of the Grands Boulevards, the light was far brighter and rose into the sky as though drawn by some luminous power. At this hour, the Boulevard Sébastopol, with its closed shops was no longer the goal. Cabs rushed by. Those bound for the Grands Boulevards went towards the light, hastening there like people attracted by a show.

The whole of the Boulevard Sébastopol lives on the pavement. On this broad area, in the blue air of a summer night, the day after the 14th July, Paris sifts and trails the residue of the holiday. The arc-lights, the trees' foliage, the moving vehicles, the diverse excitement of the passers-by, create something dense and sharp, an atmosphere both alcoholic and tired. A nightly spectacle, and yet many a façade and street corner retains a reminder of the day before. Certain noises, certain cries, recall the songs of last night's revellers. A few flags and lanterns hang at windows and seem to clamour for a renewal of festivities. One can guess what is taking place in people's minds. Those who enjoyed themselves yesterday are on the alert for some new delight. This is because men who have once known pleasure seek it eternally. While the others, those who are poor, those who are ugly, and those who are shy, make their way through the remains of the holiday and nose in the corners for some debris of pleasure that has been overlooked. This is because men who have never known pleasure are in torment and seek for it day after day until they grow weary of never having had anything at all.

The air seemed to vibrate about them. Spruce young men

passed by in groups of two and three and went their way. They wore stiff new collars, elegant and sober ties pierced with gaudy tie pins, and they hastened off, with money in their pockets, towards the light. Shop clerks chatted together: 'We danced until midnight. She was willing enough. I took her to a hotel in the rue Quincampoix. She was just dying for it!' Two men followed in the footsteps of two little misses. Accosted, the girls looked at each other and broke into laughter. Young men with burning eyes ogled the woman when a couple passed ...[7]

It was in these pages about the boulevard Sébastopol that T. S. Eliot encountered the image of the mixing of memory and desire which he borrowed for the opening of *The Waste Land*. As a man walks along, says Philippe, he carries in his head all the aspects of his life ... 'Notre chair a gardé tous nos souvenirs, nous les mêlons à nos désirs.'

Running parallel to the boulevard Sébastopol is the ancient rue Saint-Martin, along which Bassompière walked to his assignation. Beyond it lies the general district known as the Marais. That we can still see so many of the original buildings in this quarter is largely thanks to the writer André Malraux, who, as de Gaulle's Minister of Culture in the 1960s, ensured its survival and restoration. Literally a marshland, the term Marais is now used to indicate most of the area covered by the 3rd and 4th arrondissements. It is approximately the triangle of ground bounded by the rue Saint-Martin, the river, and the curve of the inner boulevards. In the earliest times, when the rue Saint-Martin was the main route northwards, it cut a path between these marshlands to the east and the forest of Rouvray (of which the Bois de Boulogne is a remnant) to the west. Later it became a Roman road. Ironically, it was on the edge of this street that in the early 1970s the outline began to take shape of the most defiantly modern building in Paris, the Centre Culturel Georges Pompidou.

The Centre's main cultural activities are artistic and musical, but it also houses the Bibliothéque d'Information Publique. On the top floor the charmless café offers a spendid view south and west across the city over a skyline that for years to come will probably be dominated by the giant orange and yellow cranes which nod like grazing dinosaurs above the roofs of Paris.

The rue Rambuteau, running across the northern end of the open square in front of the Cultural Centre, was another 19th-century development that swallowed a number of the old streets. It takes its name from the comte de Rambuteau who, as Prefect of the Seine, was responsible in 1844 for one small but enduring change in the appearance of the city. From Casablanca to Martinique one can spot the vestigial presence of France in the familiar street plaques of blue enamel, dear to Francophiles, which Rambuteau originally decreed for the capital.

As it moves eastward, the rue Rambuteau crosses the rue du Temple, where at no. 122 Balzac spent his adolescence. The street gets its name from the enclosure of the Knights Templar, the entrance to which was at no. 158. This powerful and secretive body of men, whose most famous literary representative was Brian de Bois-Guilbert, the villain of Scott's *Ivanhoe*, has cast a faintly sinister shadow in the popular imagination. As the heroine's father remarks of Bois-Guilbert: 'They say he is valiant as the bravest of his order; but stained with their usual vices, pride, arrogance, cruelty and voluptuousness.'[8]

Founded at Jerusalem after the First Crusade, the order of Templars reached its zenith in France in the 13th century. Its ostensible purpose was to protect pilgrims to the Holy Land, but over the years it had managed to amass fantastic wealth. Secure behind the twenty-five-foot walls of its enclosure, it effectively constituted an independent state. When, in 1306, Philippe le Bel was fleeing from popular reaction to another of his periodic currency devaluations, he took refuge with the Templars. It is perhaps unwise to entertain kings too lavishly. As soon as he got out, he accused them, in concert with Pope Clement V, of a range of delinquencies from sacrilege to sodomy. Within a few years the order was suppressed and fifty-four of the Templars were tortured and burned at the stake. Finally, on 12 March 1314, the Grand Master of the Order was burnt alive in the presence of the King on the south side of what is now the place Dauphine. Though the assets of

the Templars were confiscated—most of them being appropri-
ated by the King—the enclosure itself survived for almost five
centuries, until it was demolished by Napoleon.

Mlle de Scudéry in the rue de Beauce

It was a few yards from the square du Temple, on the corner of
the rue de Beauce and the rue des Oiseaux, that Mlle de
Scudéry lived during the last half of the 17th century. With the
dispersal of the salon of the marquise de Rambouillet in 1665,
the rue de Beauce became the focal point of the blue stockings.
Celebrated for such lengthy novels as *Le Grand Cyrus* (1649–
53) and *Clélie* (1654–60), Madeleine de Scudéry ended up as a
sort of literary shrine, to which a stream of notable visitors,
including Queen Christina of Sweden, came to pay homage.
The zoologist Martin Lister, who was one of the more entertaining of 17th- and 18th-century English travellers, did not
reach Paris until 1698. This was late in the day for Mlle de
Scudéry, but Lister did not intend to be cheated of his visit. In
the event, his account seems to owe more to the zoologist than
to the literary pilgrim:

> Amongst the Persons of Distinction and Fame, I was de-
> sirous to see *Madamoiselle de Scuderie*, now 91 years of
> Age. Her Mind is yet vigorous, tho' her Body is in Ruins. I
> confess, this Visit was a perfect Mortification, to see the sad
> Decays of Nature in a Woman once so famous. To hear her
> Talk, with her Lips hanging about a Toothless Mouth, and
> not to be able to Command her Words from flying abroad at
> Random, puts me in mind of the *Sibyl's* uttering Oracles.
> Old Women were employed on this Errand, and the Infant-
> World thought nothing so Wise, as Decayed Nature, or
> Nature quite out of Order; and preferred Dreams before
> reasonable and waking Thoughts.
>
> She shewed me the Skeletons of two *Chameleons*, which
> she had kept near four years alive. In Winter she lodged
> them in Cotton; and in the fiercest Weather she put them
> under a Ball of Copper, full of hot Water.

In her Closet she shewed me an Original of Madame Maintenon, her old Friend and Acquaintance, which she affirmed was very like her: and, indeed, she was then very beautiful.[9]

Mme de Sévigné in the rue de Thorigny

Mlle de Scudéry and her circle were a literary phenomenon, but it is significant that their base should have been out on the fringes of the Marais. To reach the centre of this district, and of 17th-century Paris, we must turn to a woman whose character and interests were altogether different.

At the time when Mlle de Scudéry moved into the rue de Beauce, Mme de Sévigné (1626–96) was living a few streets away at 8 rue de Thorigny. As well as anyone, Mme de Sévigné sums up through her letters the world of the Marais in the *grand siècle*. She was born only a short distance away at 1 bis place Royale (now the place des Vosges) and lived most of her life within half a mile of this hub of 17th-century French society, writing endless letters about its day-to-day concerns to the daughter on whom she doted. This address in the rue de Thorigny was her home from 1669 to 1671, and it was from here that she sent one of her most vivid letters, written on 20 February 1671 (the comte de Guitaut's house was in the same street at what is now no. 4):

> You must know, then, that the night before last after I had returned from Mme. de Coulanges' house, where we had been making up our packets for post day, it occurred to me to go to bed. That is nothing out of the common, but what follows is very much so. At three o'clock in the morning I heard a cry of 'thieves! fire!' It sounded so loud that I had no doubt it was in the house; and I thought I heard people speaking about my grand-daughter—I feared she must be burned. In this fear I got out of bed without a light, and I was trembling so much I could hardly stand. I ran to her room (which is yours) and found everything quiet there; but I saw that the Guitauts' house was all on fire, and the flames were

spreading to the house of Mme de Vauvineux. Both M. de Guitaut's courtyard and our own were illuminated with terrifying clearness; all was shouting and confusion; beams and joists were falling with a frightful noise. I had my door opened, and all my people went to help. M. de Guitaut sent me a packet of valuables, which I put in my cabinet; and then I went into the street to gape like the rest. There I found M. and Mme. de Guitaut (who were almost naked), Mme. de Vauvineux and the Venetian Ambassador with all his people. They were carrying to the Ambassador's house the little Vauvineux (who was fast asleep) and also a lot of furniture and silver plate. Mme. de Vauvineux had already removed all her goods. [...]

The good Capuchins worked with so much skill that they prevented the fire from spreading further. They kept pouring water on the places where it was still burning, and at last the battle ceased for want of combatants—that is to say, after all those parts of the first and second storeys which are on the right-hand side of the salon had been entirely consumed. We thought it a piece of good fortune that so much of the house was saved; but poor Guitaut will lose at least 10,000 crowns. They count on restoring the apartment which was painted and gilded. The loss includes several fine pictures belonging to M. le Blanc, who owns the house; also pieces of furniture, mirrors, miniatures and tapestries. They are greatly concerned about some letters—I take them to be letters from *M. le Prince*.[10]

It was another fire which, long after she had left, destroyed Mme de Sévigné's own house at no. 8. The building which now carries her imprint more strikingly than any other is the hôtel Carnavalet, close by at 23 rue de Sévigné. Mme de Sévigné moved into it in 1677 and spent the last nineteen years of her life there, enjoying, she said, 'fine air, a fine courtyard, a fine garden, a fine district'. One of her rooms on the first floor, in which hangs a portrait of her by Robert Nanteuil, can still be seen in the musée Carnavalet. This excellent historical museum, which now occupies the hôtel, does much to recapture something of the climate of her times.

The place des Vosges

The centre of the social world in which Mme de Sévigné moved was the place Royale, which had itself only come into being at the start of the 17th century. At the time of Bassompière's assignation (see page 79) Paris was still for the most part a city of narrow streets and huddled buildings; it lacked any open space suitable for official festivities. In 1605 Henri IV decided to take over the horse market which had previously occupied the site and to set about building a new square. The place des Vosges as we see it today has changed remarkably little from the square in which Mme de Sévigné was born. Throughout the 17th century it was to remain the focus of French literary and social life. Jacques Wilhelm gives us a modern historian's impression of the surrounding streets during this period:

At the beginning of the century you could come across magistrates making their way to the Palace on mules. Many noblemen went around on horseback, escorted by their retinue, whose size was in proportion to the rank of their master. A Guise would never have left his hôtel in the rue du Chaume [rue des Archives] without an escort of dozens of nobles, pages and valets. A Rohan contented himself with slightly fewer. The idleness of practically all the nobility allowed each of its members generally to be surrounded by a handful of friends. And prudence often made this necessary; there was always the fear of encountering a rival and his partisans, or even a band of vagabonds, who, in the time of Louis XIII, were quite ready to attack in broad daylight. [...]

But as the century progressed, the number of carriages quickly multiplied, particularly in this district where the population was so rich. These heavy vehicles with vermilion wheels, drawn by two or four large horses, were cumbersome in the narrow streets. For a long time they had no glass in the windows and the passengers were protected from the cold by leather curtains. When some noblewoman left her hôtel, the opening of the *porte-cochère* and the departure of the equipage put the whole street in an uproar. The coachman on his seat, the lackeys clinging to the vehicle's frame, and sometimes two or three noblemen on horseback beside its doors—all this made for a spectacle the crowd appreciated.[11]

Wilhelm goes on to talk of the large number of military and ecclesiastical figures who were normally to be seen in the streets of Paris at the time—monks, priests, officers, members of the King's bodyguard and so forth. Among them he pictures the musketeers in their red mantles with large white cross passing through the Marais on their way to the Arsenal to guard Nicolas Fouquet, Louis XIV's ex-Minister of Finance, who had fallen from grace in 1661, undermined by his own extravagance and the machinations of Colbert. Fouquet had been a close friend of Mme de Sévigné, and when he was charged with corruption, she took a detailed interest in his fate. On one occasion she had the opportunity to watch him from a window as he walked back to his prison in the Arsenal. Her subsequent letter offers at the same time a glimpse of the figure who, as a result of the work of Alexandre Dumas, was to become two centuries later the most famous of all the musketeers:

> Thursday 27th November, 1664.
> I must tell you what I did. Some ladies of our acquaintance (you can guess which) proposed that we should go to a house facing the Arsenal, which would give us a good view of our poor friend on his way back from the trial. I wore a mask but I could see him a good way off. M. d'Artignan walked beside him, while fifty musketeers followed about thirty or forty paces behind. He looked as if his thoughts were far away. When I saw him my legs trembled, and my heart beat so quickly I could hardly bear it. As he came near, M. d'Artignan touched him on the shoulder and pointed in our direction. When he turned to salute us we saw once more that engaging smile you know so well. I don't think he recognized me, but I confess I was deeply affected when I saw him re-enter that little door. If you knew what a misfortune it is to have a heart like mine, I am sure you would pity

me; but from what I know of you I doubt if you would have got off more cheaply.[12]

Its social prominence made the place Royale a convenient place for noblemen to conduct their duels, sometimes by night, sometimes by day. One winter's night in 1614 the two parties and their seconds fought together, each with a flaming torch in one hand and a sword in the other. Thirty years later, the subject of another of the square's famous duels, Mme de Longueville, sat with friends watching the fatal outcome from the window of no. 18.

Less reputable entertainment was on one occasion provided by the duc de Candalle and his friend Ruvigny, marquis de Benneval:

> Monsieur de Candalle had brought back with him from Venice two or three Albanian soldiers in the service of the Venetian Republic. He and Ruvigny once came upon one of them lying with a drab in the place Royale. Ruvigny said to him: 'There's a gold crown for you if you'll fuck her tomorrow, at mid-day, in the square.' The man agreed and, while he was performing his promise, M. de Candalle, Ruvigny and a few others deliberately created a din. All the women put their heads out of the window and saw this fine spectacle.[13]

The writer who passes this story down to us was Ruvigny's brother-in-law, Tallemant des Réaux, a 17th-century chronicler with an incorrigible taste for scandal. It was he who relayed much of the gossip about contemporary life around the place Royale. There is a cheerful lack of propriety about the way he exposes the details of life behind the elegant façades of the square. At no. 19, for example, on the corner of the rue des Francs-Bourgeois, lived Robert Aubry. The fact that he was président à la Chambre des Comptes left his small and resolute wife unimpressed. Such was her contempt for him, Tallemant informs us, 'qu'elle a pissé plus d'une fois dans les bouillons qu'elle lui faisait prendre'.[14] Today more traditional dishes are served at this address in the Brasserie Ma Bourgogne, one of Maigret's favourite haunts.

Tallemant shows an equal relish for the misfortune which befell the duchesse de Rohan in the rue Saint-Antoine:

> One evening as she was returning from a ball,* she ran into some robbers. At once she put her hand to her pearls. To force her to let go of them, one of these gallants made to catch hold of her in that spot which women are normally most concerned to protect. But he was dealing with a shrewd woman: 'The fact is,' she told him, 'you won't take that away with you, but you would take my pearls.' In the course of this exchange, some other people came up and she escaped being robbed.[15]

No one catered more readily for Tallemant's taste for scabrous gossip than the mistress of one of the most popular literary salons of the day. Ninon de Lenclos lived just off the northeast corner of the place Royale. If you leave the square by the rue du Pas-de-la-Mule and walk a few yards up the rue des Tournelles, you will find at no. 36 the original 17th-century building which was her home. It was the resort of Molière and La Fontaine, of Boileau, La Rochefoucauld and Mme de Lafayette. Even Mme de Sévigné was occasionally to be seen there, despite the fact that Ninon had at different times been the mistress of both her husband and her son. Molière read *Tartuffe* here, and when the young Voltaire was presented to Ninon shortly before her death at eighty-five, she was sufficiently impressed by his qualities to bequeath him a thousand francs with which to buy books.

Saint-Simon sang her praises, Saint-Evremond wrote poems about her. For someone whose immoral life had caused her to be confined to the prison of the Madelonnettes on the order of the Queen, she had made a striking comeback. This is one of Paris's great courtesan success stories. Long after her physical charms had ceased to attract, her wit and understanding enabled her, in a ruthless society, to preserve the friendships and associations of her youth—'chose étrange', as Saint-Simon affirms with a hint of perlexity.

She died in this house on 17 October 1705. Already the

---

* She would have been making for the hôtel de Rohan-Guéménée at 6 place des Vosges. See p. 93.

centre of French social life had begun to shift westwards towards the faubourg Saint-Germain on the left bank and the area round the Palais du Louvre on the right. The *grand siècle* was over, and with it the zenith of the Marais.

Those literary figures to be found here in the 18th century were unlikely to be part of the mainstream of Paris's social and literary life. The heyday of the elder Crébillon (1674–1762) was in the first decades of the century, when his classical tragedies were the most admired productions on the French stage. By the time Sébastien Mercier visited him in 1760, his day was long past. The house he lived in still stands at 17 rue Villehardouin[16] (then called rue des Douze-Portes), a couple of minutes' walk from that of Ninon in the rue des Tournelles. It was here that Mercier sought him out, two years before his death:

He lived at that time in the Marais, Rue des Douze-Portes, where, one day, I sounded his knocker; there followed an outburst of barking from fifteen or twenty dogs inside, who surrounded me as I entered, and escorted me in none too friendly fashion to the poet's own room. The staircase was foul with the excrements of these brutes; they announced, and ushered me in to their master.

His room was bare. A pallet bed, two stools, seven or eight tattered armchairs—this was all the furniture. I saw for an instant as I came through the door a woman's figure, four feet high and three wide, disappearing into the next room. The chairs were all occupied by dogs, all growling. The old man, with bare legs and breast and head uncovered, was smoking a pipe. His eyes were very large, very bright blue, his white hair scanty above a most expressive face. He quieted the dogs with some difficulty, and, whip in hand, obliged one of them to quit his armchair and make room for me. He took his pipe from his mouth a moment, civilly, to greet me; then replaced it, and without a word continued to smoke with a satisfaction which his mobile features most vividly expressed.

He remained in silent meditation some time, his blue eyes fixed on the floor; then spoke a word or two. The dogs growled, and bared their teeth at me. At last he put down his pipe, and I asked him: 'Monsieur, when shall we see your *Cromwell*?' 'It is not yet begun,' said he. I asked if I might be privileged to hear a verse or two. 'After one more pipe,' said he. At this the woman I had seen before came in, a bandy-legged dwarfish creature, with the longest nose, and the brightest most wicked eyes I ever saw in my life—the poet's mistress. The dogs evidently respected her; she was conceded a chair, and sat down facing me. When the second pipe was finished, Crébillon recited a few incomprehensible verses from some romantic tragedy or other not yet written; I could not make out a word of the plot, nor yet its development, but the lines were in the nature of fierce reproaches to the gods, and denunciation of kings, for whom he had no love. He seemed a good old fellow, wrapped up in his thoughts, and no talker; his mistress's expression bore out the malicious promise of her eyes. His lines spoken, the poet filled another pipe, while I talked with the woman. My eye kept wandering, intrigued by the extreme shortness of her legs; his shins on the contrary were bare as an athlete's, resting after his turn in the arena. I rose at last to go, to the relief of the dogs, who rose too in a body, barking, and escorted me to the street door as before. The old poet scolded them gently; love showed through the harshness of the words. No other man could have borne to live in an atmosphere so polluted with dogs' filth.

I remembered enough of my classics to remind him that Euripides too was a dog-lover, and that he was in a fair way to outlive that other ancient playwright, Sophocles; he was at this time eighty-six years old. I had the luck to please him, and he gave me a tiny piece of pasteboard on which, in very fine characters, was inscribed his name; this card was a kind of passport to one of his plays; but since Voltaire saw to it that these were not often performed, I had nine months to wait before I could put it to any use. The old man had warned me that it might be so, and told me the reason, as he conceived it; he spoke of his rival as 'a very wicked fellow,' in tones of entire benevolence.[17]

As Mercier implies, Crébillon was by this time little more than a name. Literary honours had passed to his son, whose delicately erotic novels did not prevent his taking over his father's post as official literary censor. A man of singular urbanity, he distinguished himself in this office by issuing the famous imprimatur: 'By order of Mgr. the Chancellor I have read the work entitled *The Koran* by Mr. Mahomet and have found in it nothing contrary either to religion or to morality; signed: Crébillon fils.'

Until the Revolution, the world of literature and the social world moved more or less in unison, but by the 19th century their ways had parted. Although the Marais never recovered its social position, it did briefly become once again the resort of some of France's major writers in the middle and late years of the century. Gautier and Daudet both lived for a time in the place des Vosges—as did Victor Hugo, who is now commemorated by the museum at no. 6.

The musée Victor Hugo is the former hôtel of the Rohan-Guéménée, in which Hugo and his family lived until 1848, when a band of revolutionaries almost set fire to it. Among the works he composed here were the verse drama *Ruy Blas* (1838) and the volumes of lyric poetry *Les chants du crépuscule* (1835), *Les voix intérieures* (1837) and *Les rayons et les ombres* (1840). It was at this address that in January 1847 he was visited by Charles Dickens, who afterwards passed on his impressions to Lady Blessington:

We were at his house last Sunday week. A most extraordinary place, looking like an old curiosity shop, or the Property Room of some gloomy vast old Theatre. I was much struck by Hugo himself, who looks a Genius, as he certainly is, and is very interesting from head to foot. His wife is a handsome woman with flashing black eyes, who looks as if she might poison his breakfast any morning when the humour seized her. There is also a ditto daughter of fifteen or sixteen, with ditto eyes, and hardly any drapery above the waist, whom I should suspect of carrying a sharp poignard in her stays, but for her not appearing to wear any. Sitting among old armour, and old tapestry, and old coffers, and grim old chairs and tables, and old Canopies of state from old palaces, and old golden lions going to play at skittles with ponderous old golden balls, they made a most romantic show, and looked like a chapter out of one of his own books.[18]

Daudet in the hôtel Lamoignon

Shortly before moving into the place des Vosges, Alphonse Daudet had been living nearby in part of one of the oldest hôtels in Paris, which still stands on the corner of the rue Pavée and the rue des Francs-Bourgeois and now houses the Bibliothèque historique de la Ville de Paris. It was while Daudet was here that he wrote his novel set in the Marais, *Fromont jeune et Risler aîné* (1874). Years later his son Léon recalled the period in *Paris vécu* (1928):

We lived in the hôtel Lamoignon at 24 rue Pavée in the Marais. It was a magnificent-looking 17th-century residence, converted into several apartments which were full of character, as the saying goes, but not very comfortable. We had one of these apartments.

Almost every Wednesday evening Flaubert, Zola, Turgenev and Edmond de Goncourt used to meet in our modest dining-room. I called them 'the giants', because Flaubert and de Goncourt were so tall: 'Mummy, is it the day the giants come?' Flaubert and my father brought everything to life with their jokes, their laughter, their stories. Regularly, as soon as he arrived, Flaubert would say to my father: 'Good day, Alphonse, how do I look? ... Young as ever, I trust?' This 'young as ever' sent the giants off into roars of laughter, which I joined in with a will. My mother had made me learn by heart the opening of *Salammbô*, 'C'était à Mégara, faubourg de Carthage, dans les jardins d'Hamilcar.' I used to recite this beautiful line to its author, who would catch hold of me and lift me in his strong arms, and I would see in close-up his Vercingetorix moustache and his large shiny cheeks.[19]

The hôtel Sully

Another ancient residence which survives not far from the hôtel Lamoignon is the hôtel Sully at 62 rue Saint-Antoine. It was built in the 1620s for a banker and sold about ten years later to the duc de Sully, who was by that time in his seventies. Tallemant paints a colourful portrait of the duc, who, after a lucrative career as the King's Treasurer, took to dancing pavanes in his old age with doubtful young women brought to him by two of his former secretaries. At other times he would dress himself up in the fashions of Henri IV, by now long dead, and, decked with ornamental chains and diamond stars, parade around under the arcades of the place Royale. 'In his speech,' writes Tallemant, 'he was the foulest man in the world. One day some gentleman or other, very handsome in appearance, came to dine with him. Mme de Sully, his second wife, who is still alive, could not take her eyes off the visitor. "Confess, madame," said he out loud, "confess that you'd be prettily caught if our friend turned out to have no—." ' [20] But on the whole, he took his young wife's infidelities philosophically, paying out her liberal allowance in three parts: 'so much for the house, so much for you, so much for your lovers'. Reluctant to have them cluttering the stairs, he installed a separate staircase leading to his wife's apartments. Today certain parts of the hôtel, which is now the information centre on historic monuments, can be seen by guided tour.

It was while he was dining here with one of the later ducs de Sully in December 1725 that Voltaire received a message that someone was waiting at the gate of the hôtel with information about a plot against him. Voltaire was then thirty-one and already a successful and lionised author. He went down the staircase, across the courtyard, and straight into the trap laid for him by the duc de Rohan, three of whose lackeys set about Voltaire with sticks. The duc, meanwhile, doubled up with laughter, shouted occasional directions from the opening of the rue de l'Hôtel-Saint-Paul just opposite.

This was Rohan's less than heroic retaliation for a trivial incident at the theatre a few days earlier. Voltaire was now set on challenging him to a duel and to this end started taking fencing lessons. But it was not an era in which to try conclusions with the aristocracy. Before anything dramatic could occur, Rohan prudently arranged to have his would-be adversary shut up in the Bastille. As it happened, this was not Voltaire's first visit to the fortress. Nine years earlier he had been imprisoned there as the suspected author of some verses intimating that the Prince Regent was guilty of incest with his daughters. The verses had suggested that, like Lot in the Bible, the Prince might be fathering a new race of Moabites and Ammonites. Voltaire defended himself in a neat little rhyme which concluded by pointing out that the only Old Testament race likely to be known to a poet educated by Jesuits was the Sodomites.

Neither of his stays in the Bastille was long, and on this second occasion he was given leave after a few weeks to decamp to England.

The Bastille

The Bastille itself lives in our imagination more as a product of literature and myth than of historical reality. Though the fortress had been built in the last part of the 14th century, it was not until Richelieu's day, two and a half centuries later, that it became commonly used as a prison, and then only for a small number of people. Imprisonment in the Bastille carried no stigma. Until the years of its decline it housed a consistently distinguished clientèle. Most of them were consigned thither by the notorious system of *lettres de cachet* which simply requested the Governor of the Bastille to receive the individual in question and detain him until further orders.

The regime was not unduly harsh. 'I only took with me two valets and a cook,' remarks the maréchal de Biron of his stay in 1631. And people there were still eating well in the 18th century. The marquis de Sade was shuffled off to the lunatic asylum at Charenton only a few days before the Bastille fell, and his menus, some of which are preserved in the Bastille archives, included such items as turkeys, truffled chickens, pigeons, oysters, patés and large quantities of wine and brandy.[21] This was by no means exceptional. It contrasts oddly with the traditional image of life in the Bastille, epitomised by the figure of Dickens's Dr Manette, buried for almost eighteen years in Number One Hundred and Five, North Tower: 'These words are formed by the rusty iron point with which I write with difficulty in scrapings of soot and charcoal from the chimney, mixed with blood, in the last month of the tenth year of my captivity. Hope has quite departed from my breast ...'[22]

No doubt there were horrifying cases—it would be hard to imagine an 18th-century prison without them—but the sort of Gothic details that Dickens incorporates into *A Tale of Two Cities* belong to a mythology which derives mainly from a charlatan called Latude, who spent a large part of his thirty-five years of imprisonment there, initially because he had tried to secure a reward for himself by pretending to have discovered a plot against the life of Mme de Pompadour. After the Fall of the Bastille, Latude, whose real name was Danry, used to conduct tours round the place, recounting in pathetic terms the details of damp straw, wall chains, inadequate nourishment etc. The archives tell a different story: 'Danry is in a vile temper,' notes the harassed commandant. 'He sends for us at 8 o'clock in the evening to tell us to send his turn-key to the market to buy fish, saying that he cannot eat eggs, artichokes or spinach. Danry is just as exacting on meat days. He swore like a trooper and said to me "Commander, when I'm given fowl, it should at least be well basted." '[23]

A library of light fiction together with some scientific and philosophical works was kept for the diversion of the prisoners. Crossing off the list one of the books to be sent for binding—a lengthy poem on the grandeur of God—the 18th-century police lieutenant Berryer explains in a covering letter that this is a subject 'trop mélancolique pour des prisonniers'. His consideration shows a delicacy that seems peculiarly Gallic.

There is one inmate of the Bastille who has caught the literary imagination more forcefully than any other. His arrival was as mysterious as the rest of his story. This is part of the diary entry made by the King's lieutenant at the Bastille for Thursday 18 September 1698:

At 3 o'clock in the afternoon M. de Saint-Mars, the [new] governor of the Château of the Bastille, arrived to make his first entrance, having come from the islands of Sainte-Marguerite-Honorat and brought with him in his litter a prisoner who is kept permanently masked and whose name is never spoken. When the prisoner got out of the litter, he was put in the first room of the Bazinnière tower until nightfall, when I and M. Rosargues, one of the sergeants in the governor's suite, took him at 9 o'clock in the evening and placed him, alone, in the third room of the Bataudière tower, which I had furnished some days before his arrival in accordance with the instructions of M. de Saint-Mars.

Some five years later the same lieutenant, Etienne Du Junca, entered in his diary:

On [...] 19th November, 1703, the unknown prisoner, still in a mask of black velvet, [...] having been slightly unwell yesterday as he left mass, died at 10 o'clock in the evening. [...] Caught unawares by his death, he had not received the sacraments, and our chaplain spoke words of exhortation to him a moment before his death. This unknown prisoner, held here for so long, was buried on Tuesday, 20th November at 4 o'clock in the afternoon in the cemetery of Saint-Paul, our parish. In the register of deaths his name was entered as unknown. M. de Rosargues, major, and Arreil, surgeon, signed the register.[24]

These sparse words are the tantalising reality from which Voltaire, Dumas and others wove their speculative fantasies. A brother of Louis XIV? An illegitimate son of Charles II of England? One 19th-century scholar even reached the conclusion that the man in the 'iron' mask must have been Molière. In fact, he was probably a Mantuan diplomat, called Mattioli, who had tried for his own profit to play a double game with both Louis XIV and the Duke of Mantua.[25] Whatever the truth, his anonymous life behind a mask, even of velvet, cannot have been enviable.

By the late years of the 18th century this imposing stronghold (its walls were some seventy-five feet high) had become hopelessly uneconomic to maintain. It was already under sentence of death when the rabble who had made their way from the Invalides in order to appropriate its stock of gunpowder arrived before the main entrance on 14 July 1789. The governor of the fortress, the marquis de Launay, was courteous no doubt, but indecisive. The stories of his brutal treachery which were blazed across Paris on the day itself have long been discredited. After some half-hearted exchanges of fire the citadel was rendered on the promise of safe-conduct for its defenders. The crowd promptly killed as many of them as possible, including de Launay. The revolutionary enthusiasm for displaying people's heads was already in the air and a public-spirited youth called Desnot, an apprentice chef, undertook to tackle de Launay—cutting up meat ('travailler les viandes'), he explained, was something he knew about. With the aid of a penknife he managed it bit by bit, swigging brandy and gunpowder the while to keep himself up to the mark. Later that day de Launay's head was paraded in triumph down the rue Saint-Honoré. An inglorious episode, it was not improved by the undistinguished bag of prisoners released, seven in all—a couple of madmen, four forgers, and a young nobleman who had been committed by his family to hush up a case of incest.

Within the week, work had begun on the demolition of the Bastille. Nothing of it now remains in place. At the south-east corner of the square a line of dark brown paving stones marks the old outline of the fortress, and a plaque beside 5 rue Saint-Antoine indicates the site of what used to be the main entrance. A few of its stones can be seen in the square Henri-Galli, where the foundations of one of the towers have been placed. More recently an exhibition piece has been built into the platform (Direction Bobigny) of the Bastille métro station.

The uninspiring column in the middle of the place de la Bastille has nothing to do with the events of 1789. It was set up to celebrate another bout of revolutionary activity in 1830, which this time put an end to the Bourbon dynasty. Its base was originally intended for a quite different sort of monument. Back in 1808 Napoleon had hit on the idea of a colossal statue of an elephant. It was to be cast in bronze out of cannons captured from the Spaniards and water was to spout from its trunk. 'I imagine the elephant will be very fine . . . ,' he wrote to his minister from Madrid.

But the idea was never realised—sadly, for it would have much improved this windy and unattractive site. A model of the gigantic creature was, however, constructed out of wood and plaster and set in place at the south-eastern corner of the square. The elephant was forty feet high, with a tower the size of a house on its back and a spiral staircase inside one of its legs, leading up to an observation post. 'Outlined against the stars at night, in that open space, with its huge body and trunk, its crenellated tower, its four legs like temple columns, it was an astonishing and impressive spectacle,' wrote Victor Hugo.[26] The model stayed in place until 1845, and as the structure decayed, its belly, alive with rats, became a sort of camping ground for local vagrants. It was here that Hugo lodged his young street urchin, Gavroche, in *Les misérables*.

Dominated by such an object, the place de la Bastille must have seemed an outlandish corner of Paris through the first half of the century. Hugo appears to have had a special fondness for this unrealised monument. He kept a fine model of it, which can still be seen in his apartment in the place des Vosges (musée Victor Hugo).

Henry Miller on the boulevard Beaumarchais

The boulevard Beaumarchais, running north from the place de la Bastille, is another street which dates from the 17th century, but its aspect today—the glass-fronted cafés, the speeding cars, the modern shops—brings one unmistakably back to the 20th century. It is not easy to imagine Henry Miller devoting much time to the aristocratic hôtels of the place des Vosges, but on the boulevard Beaumarchais he is quite at home. Having given up his job with the Western Union Telegraph Company in 1924 to become a full-time writer, he moved six years later, at the age of thirty-nine, from New York to Paris. His obsessive love affair with the city is chronicled in *Tropic of Cancer* (1934), *Black Spring* (1936), *Tropic of Capricorn* (1939) and the later *Quiet Days in Clichy* (1956). This extract is taken from the first and most evocative of them, *Tropic of Cancer*:

It was a Sunday afternoon, much like this, when I first met Germaine. I was strolling along the Boulevard Beaumarchais, rich by a hundred francs or so which my wife had frantically cabled from America. There was a touch of spring in the air, a poisonous, malefic spring that seemed to burst from the manholes. Night after night I had been coming back to this quarter, attracted by certain leprous streets which only revealed their sinister splendor when the light of day had oozed away and the whores commenced to take up their posts. The Rue du Pasteur-Wagner is one I recall in particular, corner of the Rue Amelot which hides behind the boulevard like a slumbering lizard. Here, at the neck of the bottle, so to speak, there was always a cluster of vultures who croaked and flapped their dirty wings, who reached out with sharp talons and plucked you into a doorway. Jolly, rapacious devils who didn't even give you time to button your pants when it was over. Led you into a little room off the street, a room without a window usually, and, sitting on the edge of the bed with skirts tucked up gave you a quick inspection, spat on your cock, and placed it for you. While you washed yourself another one stood at the door and, holding her victim by the hand, watched nonchalantly as you gave the finishing touches to your toilet.

Germaine was different. There was nothing to tell me so from her appearance. Nothing to distinguish her from the other trollops who met each afternoon and evening at the Café de l'Eléphant. As I say, it was a spring day and the few francs my wife had scraped up to cable me were jingling in my pocket. I had a sort of vague premonition that I would not reach the Bastille without being taken in tow by one of these buzzards. Sauntering along the boulevard I had noticed her verging towards me with that curious trot-about air of a whore and the run-down heels and cheap jewelry and the pasty look of their kind which the rouge only accentuates. It was not difficult to come to terms with her. We sat in the back of the little *tabac* called L'Eléphant and talked it over quickly. In a few minutes we were in a five franc room on the Rue Amelot, the curtains drawn and the covers thrown back. [...]

As I say, she was different, Germaine. Later, when she discovered my true circumstances, she treated me nobly—blew me to drinks, gave me credit, pawned my things, introduced me to her friends, and so on. She even apologized for not lending me money, which I understood quite well after her *maquereau* had been pointed out to me. Night after night I walked down the Boulevard Beaumarchais to the little *tabac* where they all congregated and I waited for her to stroll in and give me a few minutes of her precious time.[27]

Somerset Maugham in the rue de Lappe, Simenon in the rue de la Roquette

Though Miller was writing of the Paris of the early thirties, his descriptions seem relatively undated; they have little of a period feel to them. By contrast, when Somerset Maugham comes to visit the same area a few years later, his description is heavy with the atmosphere of a pre-war world. Maugham himself, who spent much of his life travelling and in later years settled at the Villa Mauresque in Cap Ferrat, had a long-standing acquaintance with Paris, since it was at the British Embassy in the rue du Faubourg-Saint-Honoré that he had been born (see p. 158). In this scene from *The Razor's Edge* (1944) the narrator, who has agreed to show an American woman-friend the seamier side of Paris, takes her to the rue de Lappe, a couple of minutes' walk from the spot where Miller encountered Germaine. It is still a street of leprous walls and crumbling plaster, dotted now with rather tamer bars and cabarets:

It is a dingy, narrow street and even as you enter it you get the impression of sordid lust. We went into a café. There was the usual young man, pale and dissipated, playing the piano, while another man, old and tired, scraped away on a fiddle, and a third made discordant noises on a saxophone. The place was packed and it looked as though there wasn't a vacant table, but the *patron*, seeing that we were customers with money to spend, unceremoniously turned a couple out, making them take seats at a table already occupied, and settled us down. The two persons who were hustled away did not take it well, and they made remarks about us that were far from complimentary. A lot of people were dancing, sailors with the red pompon on their hats, men mostly with their caps on and handkerchiefs round their necks, women of mature age and young girls, painted to the eyes, bareheaded, in short skirts and coloured blouses. Men danced with podgy boys with made-up eyes; gaunt, hard-featured women danced with fat women with dyed hair; men danced with women. There was a frowst of smoke and liquor and of sweating bodies. The music went on interminably and that unsavoury mob proceeded round the room, the sweat shining on their faces, with a solemn intensity in which there was something horrible. There were a few big men of brutal aspect, but for the most part they were puny and ill-nourished. I watched the three who were playing. They might have been robots, so mechanical was their performance, and I asked myself if it was possible that at one time, when they were setting out, they had thought they might be musicians whom people would come from far to hear and to applaud. Even to play the violin badly you must take lessons and practise: did that fiddler go to all that trouble just to play fox trots till the small hours of the morning in that stinking squalor? The music stopped and the pianist wiped his face with a dirty handkerchief. The dancers slouched or sidled or squirmed back to their tables.[28]

This is clearly an area that recommends itself to writers who specialise in the less glamorous side of city life. At about the time that Miller and Maugham were investigating these streets in search of pleasure, Inspector Maigret passed through them on an investigation of a different sort, making his way in *Le pendu de Saint-Pholien* (1931) to a cheap hotel at 18 rue de la Roquette:

This part of the street is less than fifty yards from the place de la Bastille. The rue de Lappe, with its little dance-halls and its slums, leads into it.

Every ground floor is a bistro, and every house a hotel used by vagrants, permanent casual labourers, displaced persons, prostitutes.

Yet a few workshops are squeezed into this disturbing refuge of penury where, doors wide open, they hammer and handle oxy-acetylene blow-lamps, and there is a constant flow of heavy lorries.

There is a sharp contrast between these active lives, these regular workers and busy employees with consignment notes, and the sordid, leering figures that hang about the area.[29]

The East—Montfaucon

The curious law of urban life by which the rich gravitate towards the west and the poor towards the east is as much a feature of Paris as of London or Tokyo. Until comparatively recently neither writers nor travellers had found much to detain them in the 19th and 20th arrondissements. (Partly for this reason, no doubt, they contain some of the least spoiled areas of modern Paris.) There are just two green spaces on the map—to the east the cemetery of Père Lachaise, to the north the park of the Buttes-Chaumont.

It is the Buttes-Chaumont which Louis Aragon calls 'that great oasis in a working-class district [...] born out of the conflict between Jean-Jacques Rousseau and the economic conditions of Paris life'. The word oasis is carefully chosen. Outside the park, the streets are unlikely to encourage flights of lyricism. Back in the 18th and early 19th centuries, before it was absorbed into the city, the whole district had been little more than a vast sewer and charnel house, a dumping place for human excreta, where the carcasses of thousands of animals from the nearby butchers' yards were left daily to rot on the ground. Carried by the wind, the stench of this region could infect the whole of Paris. Earlier still, when this was open countryside, its associations were even more sinister. As a young man Francis Carco used to wander through these streets by night:

5 The Cemetery of the Innocents in the sixteenth century

7 A view of the Grand Châtelet in the late seventeenth century

8 The Bastille and Porte Saint-Antoine in the seventeenth century

9 Bodies hanging from the gibbet of Montfaucon

Certain areas harbour such presences that they put a spell on you. For example, I have for a long time wondered why, when I was strolling at night in the neighbourhood of the place du Combat [now the place du Colonel-Fabien], the avenue Secrétan and the rue Monjol, I would suddenly get the impression that I was entering forbidden ground where, in spite of the proximity of the outer boulevards, the lights, the métro, the houses, the hotels, it seemed to me that something terrible still hovered in the air. A most peculiar split would take place in me. Without going so far as to fear that it could really be a spell that I was under, I felt an equivocal delight in exposing myself to the sensation.[30]

The atmosphere brings to his mind 'La ballade des pendus' of François Villon. Later, when he looks at a map of Paris in the time of Villon, he discovers that it was amongst these streets that the gibbet of Montfaucon once stood. Its actual site was a little to the west of the rue Monjol, on the other side of the place du Colonel-Fabien. In his book on Villon, D. B. Wyndham Lewis sets the scene. Executions, he explains, were frequent and gibbets plentiful:

The most superb and ancient of all, the great gibbet of Montfaucon, is worth a passing glimpse, since its shadow looms so heavy and permanent over Villon's life and verse. Its base was a flat oblong mound fifteen feet high, thirty feet wide, and forty feet long. In a colonnade around three sides, on a raised platform, rose sixteen evenly-spaced square pillars of unhewn stone, each thirty-two feet high, linked together at the top by heavy beams, with ropes and chains festooned at short intervals. In the centre of the platform gaped an immense pit covered by a grating, for the ultimate disposal of the hanged. [...] The condemned, setting forth from prison roped and tied in their carts, accompanied by the Provost and his bodyguard of twelve mounted Sergeants and attended by Master Henry Cousin, Executioner of Paris from 1460 onwards, and his assistants, made a brief station at the convent of the Filles-Dieu by the Porte St. Denis. Here the good sisters comforted them for their last journey with a manchet of bread and a cup of wine. The slow procession then continued its way, through the St. Denis gate and into the country, preceded and followed by the spectators. The Sergeants spurred a lane through the mob; the Provost, magnificent in fur and scarlet, reined in and took up his position near the gibbet, with the birds swooping and crying around. The creaking carts reached the platform and halted, while Master Henry and his men busied themselves with the ropes, and the friar in attendance recited in a loud voice the last prayers for the dying. An official of the Prévôté unrolled a parchment and read the sentences, the nooses were fixed, the carts moved on, the condemned swung briskly into space, and the ceremony was over. They would hang there, twisting and rotting, pecked by the crows and spun like tops by the winds, until most of the flesh was off their bones.[31]

At a time when the remnants of bodies hanging from the gallows were a common enough sight (in Paris alone there were half a dozen other important gibbets, besides Montfaucon), François Villon must have had more cause to shudder than most. Born in 1431, he grew up to become a wayward student at the Sorbonne. In 1455 he killed a priest in a fight (see p. 110) and later, after taking part in a robbery at the Collège de Navarre, he was forced to flee the city and wander through France. His outlaw life, which is the main subject of his poetry, led him into further trouble after his return to Paris. In 1463 he was condemned to be 'pendu et estranglé', and it was while under sentence of death that he wrote his epitaph in the form of a ballad. Later, this sentence was commuted to ten years' banishment from the capital and Villon disappeared onto the dangerous roads that led away from Paris, leaving no further trace of his life.

Across a distance of five hundred years his poetry retains a startling intimacy of tone. Fifteenth-century Paris was still in many ways a wild place, more so by far than the London of its time; the area round the gibbet of Montfaucon must have been desolate indeed. But in most people the familiar landmark of hanging bodies can have stirred little more than foreboding. It was a strange sympathy that made these bodies speak:

Frères humains, qui après nous vivez,
N'ayez les cueurs contre nous endurcis ...

Richard Aldington's translation of the poem is less well known than Swinburne's, but it catches something of the spirit of these two verses:

Brothers among men who after us shall live,
Let not your hearts' disdain against us rise,
For if some pity for our woe ye have,
The sooner God your pardon shall devise.
Behold, here five or six of us we peise.
As to our flesh, which we fed wantonly,
Rotten, devoured, it hangeth mournfully;
And we, the bones, to dust and ash are riven,
Let none make scorn of our infirmity,
But pray to God that all we be forgiven.

. . . . . .

The rain doth weaken all our strength and lave
Us, the sun blackens us again and dries;
Our eyes the ravens hollow like a grave.
Our beards and eyebrows are plucked off by pies.
Never rest comes to us in any wise;
Now here, now there, as the wind sways, sway we,
Swung at the wind's high pleasure ceaselessly,
More pecked by birds than hazel-nuts that ripen.
Be ye not then of our fraternity,
But pray to God that all we be forgiven.

Père Lachaise

The neighbourhood of the cemetery of Père Lachaise has never been wealthy, but only a hundred years ago it could still offer the attractions of a rural retreat. The rue de la Chine, which intersects the avenue Gambetta just beside the hôpital Tenon, was a particular favourite of Joris-Karl Huysmans (1848–1907), author of *À rebours*. It represented, he claimed in his *Croquis parisiens* (1880), a denial of that 'tedious symmetry' which marked the city's great new thoroughfares. 'Under a wide sky it is a country lane where most of the people who go by seem to have had something to eat and drink; it is the refuge sought by the artist in quest of solitude; it is the haven longed for by aching souls who desire only a healing rest far from the crowd.'[32]

That was a century ago. To find any sort of tranquillity here today, you will have to turn from the streets to the cemetery. Père Lachaise is the largest and best-known of the city's cemeteries, and as such it acquired the remains of a number of literary figures who had originally been buried elsewhere. Amongst these were Abélard and Héloïse, Molière, La Fontaine and Beaumarchais. Later writers buried in the cemetery include: Louis-Sébastien Mercier (1814), Benjamin Constant (1830), Honoré de Balzac (1850), Gérard de Nerval (1855), Auguste Comte (1857), Alfred de Musset (1857), Jules Michelet (1874), Jules Vallès (1885), Villiers de L'Isle-Adam (1889), Alphonse Daudet (1897), Oscar Wilde (1900), Guillaume Apollinaire (1918), Marcel Proust (1922), Henri de Régnier (1936), Gertrude Stein (1946), Paul Eluard (1952), Colette (1954).[33]

The cemetery, which takes its name from the confessor of Louis XIV, was opened in the early years of the 19th century and made an immediate appeal to the sensibilities of the emergent Romantic Movement. It was, as the novelist Etienne Pivert de Senancour (1770–1846) pointed out, a city of the dead at the gates of the capital ... 'One day these hills with their urns and epitaphs will be all that remains of our present generations and their subtle contrivances; they will compose, as Rome was said to do, a city of memories.'[34]

For Balzac it was a city of dreams and speculations rather than of memories. 'I rarely go out,' he wrote to his sister in 1819, 'but when I do wander, I go to cheer myself up in Père Lachaise.'[35] His walks were not fruitless. The cemetery figures more than once in his work and in *Le père Goriot* (1834) it becomes the setting for the climax of the novel. The young Rastignac, whose struggle to make his mark in Paris society has led him into an affair with Goriot's ungrateful daughter Delphine de Nucingen, has developed a sort of filial intimacy with the old man. At the end of the novel he has followed Goriot's coffin to its grave and the two or three others in attendance have gone away. The closing lines of the book present an image which has over the years acquired the resonance of an archetype:

Thus left alone, Rastignac walked a few steps to the highest part of the cemetery, and saw Paris spread out below on both banks of the winding Seine. Lights were beginning to twinkle here and there. His gaze fixed almost avidly upon the space that lay between the column of the Place Vendôme and the dome of the Invalides; there lay the splendid world that he had wished to gain. He eyed that humming hive with a look that foretold its despoliation, as if he already felt on his lips the sweetness of its honey, and said with superb defiance,

'It's war between us now!'

And by way of throwing down the gauntlet to Society, Rastignac went to dine with Madame de Nucingen.[36]

CHAPTER 4

The Left Bank

François Villon in the rue Saint-Jacques

'Just say in the most natural tone: when I was in Paris, *boul'*
Mich', I used to.' In the early pages of *Ulysses* Joyce's Stephen
Dedalus rehearses the passwords of youthful sophistication.
The Latin Quarter is the heart of student Paris and the boulevard Saint-Michel is the heart of the Latin Quarter. Or so it has
seemed for the past hundred years. But in its present form the
boulevard is of fairly recent date, constructed only in the
1850s. The real backbone of the *quartier latin*—so called
because Latin was the language of the university—was for
centuries the rue Saint-Jacques. One of the oldest streets in the
city, it was originally the Roman road to Orléans and later the
road by which the mediaeval pilgrims left Paris for the shrine
of Santiago di Compostella in Spain.

A short way up it, just beyond the intersection with the
boulevard Saint-Germain, the north-eastern corner of the Sorbonne covers the site of the old church and cloister of Saint-
Bénoît. It was in this cloister in the mid-15th century that
France's greatest mediaeval poet was living with his adoptive
uncle, the priest Guillaume Villon.

On 5 June 1455, the evening of the Feast of Corpus Christi,
François Villon's life was jolted violently from its expected
course. In the company of a priest and a woman named
Ysabeau he was sitting on a stone bench beneath the tower of
Saint-Bénoît in the rue Saint-Jacques. It was about nine
o'clock. While they talked, another priest, Philip Chermoye,
came up to Villon. For whatever reason, Chermoye was out to

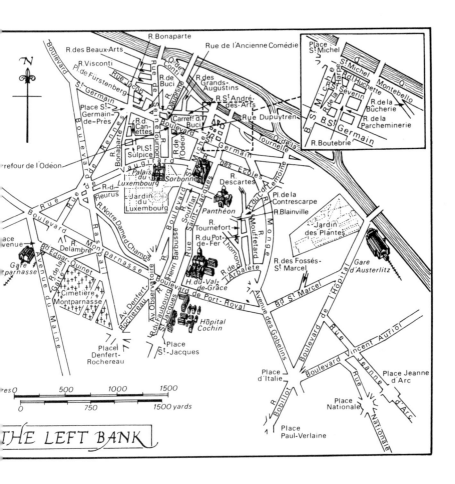

THE LEFT BANK

pick a quarrel. The story is taken up in a letter of Remission accorded to Villon by Charles VII in January 1456, of which D. B. Wyndham Lewis gives the details. The poet's companions, observing the turn events were likely to take, had slipped away:

> The said Chermoye a moment after, determining to accomplish and put into execution his wicked and damnable will, drew a large dagger from beneath his gown and struck the said petitioner in the face with it, on the upper lip, causing thereby a great flow of blood, as it appeared and appears now. Seeing this the said petitioner, who on account of the evening air was wearing a cloak, having beneath it a dagger

hanging at his belt, in order to avoid the fury and wicked will of the said Chermoye, and fearing that he would be more bitterly pressed and attacked in his person, drew the said dagger, as it seems, and struck him in the groin or thereabout, not thinking at that time that he had so struck him. [...]

Whereupon, the said Chermoye persisting in his attempt to do mischief to the said petitioner, pursuing him and hurling several threats and menaces, the said petitioner finding at his feet a stone took it and flung it in the face of the said Chermoye, and at once the said petitioner left him and departed and retired to the shop of a barber named Fouquet to have his wound dressed.[1]

After being tended in one of the houses in the cloister of Saint-Bénoît, Chermoye was on the following day removed to the hospital of the Hôtel-Dieu, where he died a few days later.

Villon did on this occasion secure a pardon, but not before he had spent long enough as an outlaw to forge the links which would determine his future.

Corneille in the rue de la Parcheminerie, Restif in the rue de la Harpe, Elliot Paul in the rue de la Huchette

The construction of the boulevard Saint-Michel, the boulevard Saint-Germain and the rue des Ecoles in the 19th century did much to change the physiognomy of this ancient region of the city, but relics of the old Paris remain, particularly in the clutch of narrow streets which separate the northern end of the boulevard Saint-Michel from the rue Saint-Jacques. In the Middle Ages the rue de la Parcheminerie was the street of public scribes and manuscript copyists. Only the name—parchment-trade—reminds us of this past, but if you walk along to the western end of the street, beyond the rue Boutebrie, you can still find houses of the kind that the dramatist Pierre Corneille must have entered when at the age of seventy-three he came here one day with a friend from Rouen. The year was 1679 and the swings of literary fashion had reduced Corneille, once the revered author of such plays as Le Cid,

Horace and *Polyeucte*, to near penury. 'Yesterday, I saw our friend and relation,' writes the man from Rouen. 'He's not doing badly for his age. We went out together after dinner and as we passed along the rue de la Parcheminerie, he went into a shop to have his shoe repaired; it had come unstitched. He sat down on a bench with me beside him and paid out the three coins that were left in his pocket. When we got home, I offered him my purse, but he would not accept it, nor any part of it. I cried to see so great a genius in this extremity of wretchedness.'[2]

Running across the end of the rue de la Parcheminerie is the rue de la Harpe. Both this and the adjoining rue de la Huchette were much truncated by the building projects of the 19th century, but they too retain something of the atmosphere of the past, an inkling even, late at night, of the streets that Restif de la Bretonne knew in the 18th century. Restif was one of Paris's great *noctambules*. His night ramblings in the last years before the Revolution led him into every corner of the city, producing the curious range of experiences and observations recorded in *Les nuits de Paris* (1788–90). This passage describes an incident that occurred one night when he was making for his lodgings on the left bank:

Returning home, I took rue Saint-Martin, rue de Gèvres, the Pont au Change and the Pont Saint-Michel. At the corner of rue de la Huchette I saw some young men hurrying up rue de la Harpe. I went to see what they had been doing, and I found—the limbs of a dismembered child. I shuddered ... But there was nothing for me to do there; I left.

The following morning I visited the apothecary there, to tell him what I had found under his windows. He laughed: 'That's what's left from a class in anatomy; medical students are not allowed to use corpses and they are obliged to steal them or buy them; they don't know how to dispose of them when they are through with the dissecting. Four students take up the segmented body; two walk ahead, and two follow to be on the alert; they know of the secret spring latches at a few entryways along their route, and are careful to keep them open—they take refuge there in case of danger.

They finally reach this spot to discard the remains, and they run off. [...]

In the evening, on my way to visit the Marquise, I intended to walk through the Saint-Séverin graveyard; it was closed. I took the little ruelle des Prêtres and I listened at the gate. I heard some sounds. I sat down to wait in the doorway of the presbytery. After an hour the cemetery gate opened and four youths went out, carrying a corpse in its shroud. They went off along ruelle des Prêtres, rue Boutebrie, and rue du Foin, and darted into a dark little house on rue de la Harpe, three or four doors from the corner.[3]

Returning from his visit to the Marquise, Restif decides to go back to the rue de la Harpe to see what the apprentice surgeons are doing with their stolen body:

I reached the downstairs door to their amphitheatre and I pushed it; it yielded, and I climbed to the third floor where I had seen a light. I stepped quietly to the doorway, and I saw ... on a large table, the body ... of a girl of eighteen, buried the day before. They had already opened the chest ... I knew the girl's parents; I withdrew in deep sorrow, but I kept silent. Would that criminals were given to the students![4]

A trace of something slightly down at heel about the rue de la Harpe and its neighbours persisted into the 20th century. In one of the more attractive books of Paris reminiscences, *A Narrow Street* (1942), the American journalist Elliot Paul gives a semi-fictionalised account of the years he spent living in the rue de la Huchette after the First World War. The result is an entertaining survey of the life of the street and the characters who inhabited it. It was, when he arrived in the 1920s, a place remote from the hustle of the neighbouring boulevard:

Most of the traffic moved through the little street in an easterly direction, entering from the place St. Michel. This consisted mainly of delivery wagons, makeshift vehicles propelled by pedalling boys, pushcarts of itinerant vendors, knife-grinders, umbrella menders, a herd of milch goats and the neighbourhood pedestrians. The residents could sit in doorways or on kerbstones, stroll up and down the middle of the way, and use the street as a communal front yard, in daylight hours or in the evening, without risk of life or limb from careening taxis. In fact, at dawn and dusk a pair of bats, never more or less than two, zigzagged back and forth at the level of the second-storey windowsills and, when confronted by noise and lights in the *place*, or the rue des Deux Ponts, faltered, wheeled and started back again.[5]

This is no longer a quarter for timid bats. During the evening the bright windows of the Tunisian patisseries, the scores of cheap restaurants, the colourful buskers, and the scent of roasted chestnuts drifting over from the boulevard Saint-Michel combine to lend a certain air of carnival, even in the depths of winter, to these seething streets.

Expatriates

In the years before the First World War, the cafés of the boulevard Saint-Michel—d'Harcourt, la Source, le Panthéon, and pre-eminently la Vachette, where Verlaine used to pass his days—had already welcomed a younger clientèle, as the artistic community of Montmartre began to switch its allegiance to the left bank.[6] Then, with the end of the war, a new element was introduced on the scene, and one which was to have a crucial effect on the literary tone of the area for the next twenty years. Others, besides Elliot Paul, were moving into its narrow streets.

There had been Americans in Paris before, of course. James Fenimore Cooper had lived there as a diplomat in the 1830s, Henry James had worked there as a journalist in the 1870s, Gertrude Stein had been living at 27 rue Fleurus since 1903, Ezra Pound had been doing research in the Bibliothèque Nationale in 1911; but it was the war which introduced a whole generation of young writers to Paris. Hemingway, Dos Passos and Cummings were among the many who had their first taste of the city during this period. When the war ended, a variety of factors drew them back: infatuation with the place itself, dislocation from their roots in America, a favourable exchange rate and, from 1920, the horrors of Prohibition.

Early in *The Sun Also Rises* (1926) Hemingway gives us what is almost a street map of the expatriate territory. Jake Barnes, the narrator, and Bill Gorton have dined on the Ile Saint-Louis. After walking round the island, they turn to the left bank:

> We crossed the bridge and walked up the Rue du Cardinal Lemoine. It was steep walking, and we went all the way up to the Place Contrescarpe. The arc-light shone through the leaves of the trees in the square, and underneath the trees was an S bus ready to start. Music came out of the door of the Negre Joyeux. Through the window of the Café Aux Amateurs I saw the long zinc bar. Outside on the terrace working people were drinking. In the open kitchen of the Amateurs a girl was cooking potato-chips in oil. There was an iron pot of stew. The girl ladled some on to a plate for an old man who stood holding a bottle of red wine in one hand.
>
> 'Want to have a drink?'
>
> 'No,' said Bill. 'I don't need it.'
>
> We turned to the right off the Place Contrescarpe, walking along smooth narrow streets with high old houses on both sides. Some of the houses jutted out towards the street. Others were cut back. We came on to the Rue du Pot de Fer and followed it along until it brought us to the rigid north and south of the Rue Saint Jacques and then walked south, past Val de Grace, set back behind the courtyard and the iron fence, to the Boulevard du Port Royal.
>
> 'What do you want to do?' I asked. 'Go up to the café and see Brett and Mike?'
>
> 'Why not?'
>
> We walked along Port Royal until it became Montparnasse, and then on past the Lilas, Lavigne's, and all the little cafés, Damoy's, crossed the street to the Rotonde, past its lights and tables to the Select.[7]

The rue du Cardinal-Lemoine

The long walk up the rue du Cardinal-Lemoine does not attract many tourists, but it takes Hemingway's characters past a number of literary landmarks. No. 2, for example, on the corner of the quai de la Tournelle, is where Verlaine was living at the time of the Commune. Further up on the other side of the road, between nos. 55 and 63, is the site of the convent at which George Sand was educated from 1817 to 1820. (By coincidence, both her mother and grandmother had been imprisoned there when it was turned into a jail during the days of the Revolution.) For the English visitor the site has another curious association. One of the prioresses of this convent of English Augustinians was a Mrs Fermor, niece to the Arabella Fermor who was the heroine of Pope's *Rape of the Lock*. In 1775 Dr Johnson and Mrs Thrale visited her during their stay in Paris, and when Mrs Thrale returned to the city in 1784, she took the opportunity to visit the convent again:

Mean time I have stolen a day to visit my old acquaintance the English Austin Nuns at the Fossée, and found the whole community alive and cheerful; they are many of them agreeable women, and having seen Dr Johnson with me when I was last abroad, enquired much for him: Mrs Fermor, the Prioress, niece to Belinda in the Rape of the Lock, taking occasion to tell me, comically enough, 'That she believed there was but little comfort to be found in a house that harboured *poets*; for that she remembered Mr Pope's praise made her aunt very troublesome and conceited, while his numberless caprices would have employed ten servants to wait on him; and he gave one' (said she) 'no amends by his talk neither, for he only sate dozing all day, when the sweet wine was out, and made his verses chiefly in the night; during which season he kept himself awake by drinking coffee, which it was one of the maids business to make for him, and they took it by turns.'

These ladies really live here as comfortably for aught I see as peace, quietness, and the certainty of a good dinner every day can make them. Just so much happier than as many old maids who inhabit Milman Street and Chapel Row, as they are sure not to be robbed by a treacherous, or insulted by a favoured servant in the decline of life, when protection is grown hopeless and resistance vain; and as they enjoy at

least a moral certainty of never living worse than they do
to-day: while the little knot of unmarried females turned
fifty round Red Lion Square *may* always be ruined by a
runaway agent, a bankrupted banker, or a roguish steward;
and even the petty pleasures of sixpenny quadrille may
become by that misfortune too costly for their income.—*Au
reste*, as the French say, the difference is small: both coteries
sit separate in the morning, go to prayers at noon, and read
the chapters for the day: change their neat dress, eat their
little dinner, and play at small games for small sums in the
evening; when recollection tires, and chat runs low.[8]

A few yards further along, at 67 rue du Cardinal-Lemoine, is
the site of the house where the mathematician and philosopher
Blaise Pascal died on 19 August 1662. He had been living here
at his sister's house, at the sign of the Golden Lion. Just beyond
this point an alleyway opens up to give access to the pleasant
courtyard of apartments at no. 71. This was where the French
writer Valéry Larbaud went to live in 1920. Later, James Joyce
borrowed his apartment and completed *Ulysses* here.

It is more than chance that takes Jake Barnes and Bill
Gorton up the rue du Cardinal-Lemoine. For Hemingway this
was a street with personal associations. In his early days in
Paris he himself had lived at no. 74 in the third-floor apartment he describes in *A Moveable Feast* (1964):

> Home in the rue du Cardinal Lemoine was a two-room flat
> that had no hot water and no inside toilet facilities except an
> antiseptic container, not uncomfortable to anyone who was
> used to a Michigan outhouse. With a fine view and a good
> mattress and springs for a comfortable bed on the floor, and
> pictures we liked on the walls, it was a cheerful, gay flat.[9]

On the ground floor of the same building was the *bal musette*
mentioned at the start of *The Sun Also Rises*, in which Ford
Madox Ford gave his Friday parties for contributors to the
Transatlantic Review. 'Inside,' wrote Ford's wife, Stella
Bowen, 'the rough tables and wooden benches were painted
scarlet and the walls around the dance floor were set with
mirrors and painted pink, with garlands, all done by hand!'[10]

There are few parts of Paris still so redolent of the atmosphere evoked by the writers of the twenties and thirties as the area round the place de la Contrescarpe. As you walk into it from the rue du Cardinal-Lemoine, it is not difficult to get the impression that you have suddenly come upon the square of a small provincial town. This was the corner of Paris which to the end of his life Hemingway remembered with most affection. In 'The Snows of Kilimanjaro' (1938) the dying writer thinks back to the time in his youth when he had been living on the edge of the place de la Contrescarpe:

... where the flower sellers dyed their flowers in the street and the dye ran over the paving where the autobus started and the old men and the women, always drunk on wine and bad marc; and the children with their noses running in the cold; the smell of dirty sweat and poverty and drunkenness at the Café des Amateurs and the whores at the Bal Musette they lived above. The Concierge who entertained the trooper of the Garde Republicaine in her loge, his horse-hair-plumed helmet on a chair. The locataire across the hall whose husband was a bicycle racer and her joy that morning at the Cremerie when she had opened *L'Auto* and seen where he placed third in Paris-Tours, his first big race. She had blushed and laughed and then gone upstairs crying with the yellow sporting paper in her hand. The husband of the woman who ran the Bal Musette drove a taxi and when he, Harry, had to take an early plane the husband knocked upon the door to wake him and they each drank a glass of white wine at the zinc of the bar before they started. He knew his neighbours in that quarter then because they all were poor.
    Around that *Place* there were two kinds: the drunkards and the sportifs. The drunkards killed their poverty that way; the sportifs took it out in exercise. They were the descendants of the Communards and it was no struggle for them to know their politics. They knew who had shot their fathers, their relatives, their brothers, and their friends when the Versailles troops came in and took the town after the Commune and executed anyone they could catch with calloused

hands, or who wore a cap, or carried any other sign he was a working man. And in that poverty, and in that quarter across the street from a Boucherie Chevaline and a wine-co-operative he had written the start of all he was to do. There never was another part of Paris that he loved like that, the sprawling trees, the old white plastered houses painted brown below, the long green of the autobus in that round square, the purple flower dye upon the paving, the sudden drop down the hill of the rue Cardinal Lemoine to the River, and the other way the narrow crowded world of the rue Mouffetard. The street that ran up toward the Pantheon and the other that he always took with the bicycle, the only asphalted street in all that quarter, smooth under the tyres, with the high narrow houses and the cheap tall hotel [39 rue Descartes] where Paul Verlaine had died. There were only two rooms in the apartments where they lived and he had a room on the top floor of that hotel that cost him sixty francs a month where he did his writing, and from it he could see the roofs and chimney pots and all the hills of Paris.[11]

Orwell in the rue du Pot-de-Fer

At the corner of the rue Mouffetard and the rue Blainville there was once the cabaret of the Pomme de Pin,[12] frequented in the 16th century by Ronsard and the other poets of the Pléiade. Here Hemingway's walkers turn right into the rue Blainville and follow it round into the rue Tournefort, past the house at no. 25 where Prosper Mérimée lived as a young man. At the intersection with the rue du Pot-de-Fer their path crosses that of another writer, who, though he was Hemingway's contemporary, cuts a quite different figure in the Paris of the time.

George Orwell went over to Paris in the spring of 1928. Unconnected with any literary group, he lived a fairly solitary life in a cheap hotel at 6 rue du Pot-de-Fer. For a time he gave English lessons and wrote; later, as we have seen, he was reduced to washing dishes in the luxurious Hotel Lotti on the corner of the rue Saint-Honoré. *Down and Out in Paris and London* opens with a morning scene in the rue du Pot-de-Fer. Like the rest of the area, it is a street which has managed to

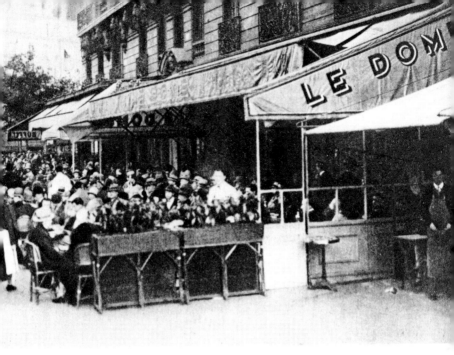

10 The *terrasse* of the café du Dôme between the wars

11 The Hotel Edgar Quinet in Montparnasse by Foujita, 1950

retain something of its earlier appearance. Orwell gives it the name of rue du Coq d'Or:

The rue du Coq d'Or, Paris, seven in the morning. A succession of furious, choking yells from the street. Madame Monce, who kept the little hotel opposite mine, had come out on to the pavement to address a lodger on the third floor. Her bare feet were stuck into sabots and her grey hair was streaming down.

Madame Monce: '*Salope*! *Salope*! How many times have I told you not to squash bugs on the wallpaper? Do you think you've bought the hotel, eh? Why can't you throw them out of the window like everyone else? *Putain*! *Salope*!'

The woman on the third floor: '*Vache*!'

Thereupon a whole variegated chorus of yells, as windows were flung open on every side and half the street joined in the quarrel. They shut up abruptly ten minutes later, when a squadron of cavalry rode past and people stopped shouting to look at them.

I sketch this scene, just to convey something of the spirit of the rue du Coq d'Or. Not that quarrels were the only thing that happened there—but still, we seldom got through the morning without at least one outburst of this description. Quarrels, and the desolate cries of street hawkers, and the shouts of children chasing orange-peel over the cobbles, and at night loud singing and the sour reek of refuse-carts, made up the atmosphere of the street.

It was a very narrow street—a ravine of tall, leprous houses, lurching towards one another in queer attitudes, as though they had all been frozen in the act of collapse. All the houses were hotels and packed to the tiles with lodgers, mostly Poles, Arabs and Italians. At the foot of the hotels were tiny *bistros*, where you could be drunk for the equivalent of a shilling. On Saturday nights about a third of the male population of the quarter was drunk. There was fighting over women, and the Arab navvies who lived in the cheapest hotels used to conduct mysterious feuds, and fight them out with chairs and occasionally revolvers. At night the policemen would only come through the street two together. It was a fairly rackety place. And yet amid the noise and dirt lived the usual respectable French shopkeepers, bakers and laundresses and the like, keeping themselves to themselves and quietly piling up small fortunes.[13]

The Maison Vauquer

If we break for a while with Hemingway's route and continue a few yards down the rue Tournefort to the point where it joins the rue Lhomond, we reach the spot (30 rue Tournefort/45 rue Lhomond) where Balzac placed the Maison Vauquer in *Le père Goriot*. His description of the boarding house in which Rastignac and Vautrin lived reflects the meagre quality of life in these streets in the early 19th century. The date is 1819, just a year before Mérimée went to live in the same street, then called the rue Neuve-Sainte-Geneviève:

The lodging-house is Madame Vauquer's own property. It stands at the lower end of the rue Neuve-Sainte-Geneviève where it slopes so abruptly towards the rue de l'Arbalète that carriages rarely use it. The absence of wheeled traffic deepens the stillness which prevails in these streets cramped between the domes of the Val-de-Grâce and the Panthéon, two buildings that overshadow them and darken the air with the leaden hue of their dull cupolas. In this district the pavements are dry, the gutters have neither mud nor water, grass grows along the walls. The most carefree passer-by feels depressed where even the sound of wheels is unusual, the houses are gloomy, the walls like a prison. A Parisian straying here would see nothing around him but lodging-houses or institutions, misery or lassitude, the old sinking into the grave or the cheerful young doomed to the treadmill. It is the grimmest quarter of Paris and, it may be said, the least known. [...]The front of the lodging-house gives on a little garden and it is placed at right-angles to the rue Neuve-Sainte-Geneviève from which you see it, as it were, in section. [...]

The house itself, three storeys high without counting the attics, is built of hewn stone and washed with that yellow shade which gives a mean look to nearly every house in Paris. The five windows at the front on each floor have small panes, and their blinds are all drawn up to different levels so that the lines are at sixes and sevens. At the side there are two windows, and those on the ground floor are barred with an iron grille. A yard about twenty feet square lies behind the building, inhabited by a happy family of pigs, hens and rabbits, and beyond that there is a shed for fire-wood. The meat-safe is hung up between this shed and the kitchen window, and the greasy water from the sink flows below it. The cook sweeps all the refuse of the house into the rue Neuve-Sainte-Geneviève through a little door in the yard, and uses floods of water to clean it up for fear of an epidemic.[14]

A missed execution in the place Saint-Jacques

In Balzac's time the streets around the Maison Vauquer were on the unsavoury fringes of the city. The southern reaches of the rue Saint-Jacques and the rue du Faubourg-Saint-Jacques led out to the ill-famed square which became the site of the guillotine when it was moved from the place de Grève in 1832. Today the tree-ringed place Saint-Jacques could scarcely be more inoffensive, but in the twenty years during which the guillotine was sited there, the surrounding taverns and cabarets were a favourite resort of the criminal underworld. Thackeray describes how he set out at first light one morning to catch the execution of Giuseppe Fieschi, who had taken part in a plot against the life of Louis-Philippe. His account has a weird surrealism which points up the nightmarish aspects of the scene:

It was carnival time, and the rumour had pretty generally been carried abroad that he was to die on that morning. A friend, who accompanied me, came many miles, through the mud and dark, in order to be in at the death. We set out before light, floundering through the muddy Champs Elysées; where, besides, were many other persons floundering, and all bent upon the same errand. We passed by the Concert of Musard, then held in the Rue St Honoré: and round this, in the wet, a number of coaches were collected. The ball was just up, and a crowd of people, in hideous masquerade, drunk, tired, dirty, dressed in horrible old frippery, and daubed with filthy rouge, were trooping out of the place: tipsy women and men, shrieking, jabbering, gesticulating, as French will do; parties swaggering, staggering forwards, arm in arm, reeling to and fro across the street, and yelling songs in chorus: hundreds of these were bound for the show, and we thought ourselves lucky in finding a vehicle to the execution place, at the Barrière d'Enfer. As we crossed the river and entered the Enfer Street,* crowds of students, black workmen, and more drunken devils from more carnival balls, were filling it; and on the grand place there were thousands of these assembled, looking out for Fieschi and his cortège. We waited and waited; but alas! no fun for us that morning: no throat-cutting; no august spectacle of satisfied justice; and the eager spectators were obliged to return, disappointed of their expected breakfast of blood. It would have been a fine scene, that execution, could it but have taken place in the midst of the mad mountebanks and tipsy strumpets who had flocked so far to witness it, wishing to wind up the delights of their carnival by a *bonne-bouche* of a murder.[15]

The 13th arrondissement

To find a 20th-century equivalent of the place Saint-Jacques as it was in the days of the public guillotine would hardly be possible, but one might do worse than make an excursion into the neighbouring 13th arrondissement—according to Henry Miller's friend Alfred Perlès. This was his vision of south-eastern Paris in 1931:

The hour to visit the Gobelins district—that is to say, the 13th Arrondissement—is toward le *crépuscule*. It would be better still to go when you have a nightmare, but then you

---

* The rue d'Enfer ran along what is now the line of the boulevard Saint-Michel, the rue Henri-Barbusse and the avenue Denfert-Rochereau.

might forget your *carte d'identité* and your revolver. And you might walk into a hospital by mistake and have your insides removed before you woke up.

There may be quarters in Paris more hoary, but it would be difficult to find another more sinister, more terrifying. Around the Place Paul Verlaine there is perhaps only a consumptive melancholy aura, but when you come to the Place Nationale the life of the 13th Arrondissement burgeons into cancerous loveliness. If you have come by way of the Boulevard de la Gare, along the Rue Nationale, you will already have had a foretaste.

I have always noticed that where the hotels have the most high sounding names the streets are most dismal and decrepit. The hotels themselves are apt to be morgues or infirmaries. Take the Grand Hotel de la Paix, for example. Which Grand Hotel de la Paix? Any one. Nine times out of ten, the roof is collapsing, or the clients are standing in front of the door with bloody aprons, or there is a dead canary swinging from the window ledge.

But the Place Nationale! Well, in the first place, the Place Nationale is not Red—it is Surrealist! Part of it belongs to Paris, the rest has been filched from Poland, the Ruhr, Williamsburg, Monaco ... The sky is made of zinc, the walls are burnt milk, the people are prisoners, the cats lie on the low roofs like houris after the bath. When the bus comes dashing around the corner, dragging its anchor, the urinal lurches like a drunken pedestrian. [...]

The Place Jeanne d'Arc is not precisely disappointing—it is simply different from what you expect it to be. It has an air of tranquillity, but it is a heavy tranquillity, as of turbines going to sleep. All about it is death, desolation and despair. Coming along the Rue Jeanne d'Arc, from the Boulevard de la Gare, you pass through a veritable Purgatory. The charred tenements, arranged like prison blocks, are almost terrifying; they are separated from one another by gloomy courts barred at each end by enormous iron gates. What you expect to happen happens. People emerge from their dwellings garbed in black, their shoulders stooped, their limbs bloated or broken, their voices raucous and malign;

now and then you see a face with a nose missing, or an eye. Their gestures are heavy and repetitive, as if they were still attached to the machine. Wherever there are factories and mills, wherever there are ghettos and almshouses, wherever there are clinics and madhouses, you will see these sorrowful, bent figures, these worn coins that have circulated so long that they are beyond recognition.[16]

The boulevard du Montparnasse

The charred tenements of Perlès's description have gone, duly replaced by modern equivalents even more hideous than their predecessors. So there are few tourists to be found taking an after-dinner stroll in the 13th arrondissement. The 14th, which includes Montparnasse, is another matter. This was the direction that Hemingway's characters were taking when we left them at the corner of the rue du Pot-de-Fer. After returning to the rue Saint-Jacques,[17] they follow the short stretch of the boulevard de Port-Royal and then continue along the boulevard du Montparnasse. The roll-call of cafés they pass is a sufficient indication of the literary focus of this boulevard. At the end of the First World War the café de la Rotonde virtually monopolised the literary and artistic life of the neighbourhood, but in the early twenties it was superseded—at least among the expatriates—by the Dôme. According to Montparnasse legend, the shift in popularity began when the manager of the Rotonde one day refused to serve a young American girl who was sitting on the *terrasse* without a hat, smoking a cigarette. Across the road, the manager of the Dôme had no such scruples; and the incident proved the making of his fortunes. Whatever the truth of the matter, it is certain that the Rotonde tended to be regarded with suspicion by the expatriate community. In *Exile's Return* (1934) Malcolm Cowley describes the fracas which resulted when he and some friends entered the Rotonde to denounce its proprietor as a police spy.

The extent to which Montparnasse life revolved around the cafés is suggested by Jimmie Charters, barman of the Dingo, in the reminiscences he passed on to Morrill Cody in 1937:

The Dôme, as I have said, was the focal point for the English and Americans. In the normal course of events you went there in the morning, or whenever you got up, for a breakfast of *croissants* and coffee, to read the morning paper, and to rehash with your friends the events of the night before. That finished, you wandered off to your occupation of the day. If you were an artist you might attend classes at one of the art academies nearby; if a writer, you returned to your apartment, or with a friend or two you might go off on some excursion to other parts of Paris, to a museum or the races, to your bank for mail, or to luncheon with a Right-Banker on the Champs Elysées. But by afternoon, you would be back again on the terrace of the Dôme drinking your *apéritif*, that stimulating forerunner of the night to come.

For dinner you would collect your friends and depart to some 'little' restaurant where they served some speciality of which you or they were particularly fond. This restaurant might be nearby, but more than likely it was in another quarter. Dinner would last for a couple of hours, but nine or ten o'clock would almost surely see you back on the Dôme terrace again!

There you would meet a new set of friends, your original party would break up and a new one form. Suddenly someone would say, 'Let's go round to the Dingo,' or it might be the Falstaff or the Trois et As or the Jockey. Those were a few of the smaller, more intimate bars where the management catered exclusively to foreigners and the few internationally-minded French. [...] And so, night after night, these smaller bars would be packed to the mouldings with groups of Anglo-Saxons of all kinds. [...] Finally, forced out by the management, many would simply move over to the Dôme again, which stayed open all night. There, between four and five, they would meet the stragglers returning from the Montmartre 'dancings' and there would be a final nightcap all around preparatory to going home.[18]

Not everyone viewed this agreeable life-style so indulgently. Sinclair Lewis (1885–1951) had visited Paris in the early 1920s as the respected author of *Babbitt* and *Main Street*, and he felt that the city's posturing expatriates had given him less than his due. His comments in an article for the *American Mercury* of October 1925 were no doubt jaundiced, but they probably contained a measure of truth:

> Among the other advantages of the Dôme, it is on a corner charmingly resembling Sixth Avenue at Eighth Street, and all the waiters understand Americanese, so that it is possible for the patrons to be highly expatriate without benefit of Berlitz. It is, in fact, the perfectly standardized place to which standardized rebels flee from the crushing standardization of America.[19]

Most of the literary cafés of Montparnasse were—and in many cases still are—strung out along the same stretch of the boulevard. As well as the Dôme and the Rotonde, they include the Closerie des Lilas, where Hemingway wrote much of *The Sun Also Rises*, the Coupole, and the Select. Although references to them abound in the work of American writers such as Dos Passos, Malcolm Cowley and Hemingway himself, they were not entirely expatriate preserves. These cafés were also a focus for the intellectual life of French writers. And the French of course stayed on when the Americans went home. The volume of Simone de Beauvoir's autobiography which deals with the thirties continually brings us back to the terraces of the Dôme and the Coupole. At the end of this period, as the Second World War envelops Paris, the changing life of the city is measured partly in terms of the atmosphere and clientèle of the cafés. On 2 September 1939 Sartre leaves for the army, while Simone de Beauvoir remains in Paris:

> The alarm goes off at 3 a.m. We walk down to the Dôme; night air very mild. The Dôme and the Rotonde are feebly lit. The Dôme is noisy; lots of uniforms. Out on the *terrasse* two tarts are sitting with their arms round a couple of officers; one of the girls is singing mechanically. The officers take no notice of them. Inside, shouts and laughter. We take a taxi to the place Hébert through this mild and empty night. Find the square bathed in moonlight, but deserted except for two gendarmes. It's like something out of a Kafka novel ...[20]

The intimate role played by these cafés is suggested by the entry de Beauvoir makes in her journal five days later: 'I have a fond attachment to this carrefour Montparnasse: the half-empty sidewalk cafés, the expression of the switchboard girl at the Dôme; I have the sense of being part of a family and that protects me against depression.'[21]

Jean Rhys and Henry Miller in Montparnasse

By the time Jake Barnes and Bill Gorton reach the Select, which was the first of the Montparnasse cafés to stay open all night, they have walked almost to the Gare Montparnasse. The route is one that Hemingway himself must have followed many times, for the Dingo bar was situated just to the left, at 10 rue Delambre, in the building which is now the Auberge du Centre. It was in this bar, described by Jimmie Charters in *This Must Be the Place* (1937), that Hemingway and Scott Fitzgerald first met in April 1925.

The rue Delambre opens onto the boulevard Edgar Quinet a few yards from the Montparnasse cemetery, where Baudelaire, Sainte-Beuve, Maupassant, Huysmans, Sartre and Simone de Beauvoir are all buried. Parallel to the western edge of the cemetery, and almost opposite the rue Delambre, is the rue de la Gaîté, in which George Moore talks of enjoying the company of thieves and house-breakers. At the centre of Montparnasse's *quartier louche*, it is still the site, at no. 26, of the Théâtre de la Gaîté Montparnasse, where Colette performed her 'poses plastiques'. 'Oh! soirs un peu chauds de la rue de la Gaîté!' writes the poet André Salmon. 'Nights when we more or less risked our lives, albeit cheerfully, eating chips, wolfing *crêpes*, licking ices, gulping oysters *aux Iles Marquises* or guzzling mussels in the open air and sharing *gauffres*, all of them washed down with *gaillac* and given an edge by small glasses of marc.'[22]

Across the two ends of the rue de la Gaîté, the boulevard Edgar Quinet and the avenue du Maine converge on the Gare Montparnasse. The building programme of the past few years has brought a number of changes to the area round the station, but the quiet, defeated melancholy of Jean Rhys strikes a chord which not even the newest buildings can quite eliminate from this region. Jean Rhys had crossed from England to Europe after the First World War and she spent much of the twenties in Paris, associated for part of that time with Ford Madox Ford. The experience of her heroines in *Quartet* (1928) and *Good Morning Midnight* (1939) is rarely far from her own. This is one of Marya Zelli's many temporary homes in *Quartet*:

> The Hotel du Bosphore looked down on Montparnasse station, where all day a succession of shabby trains, each trailing its long scarf of smoke, clanked slowly backwards and forwards.
>
> Behind the trains a background of huge advertisements: A scarlet haired baby Cadum: *Exigez toujours du Lion Noir.* A horrible little girl with a pigtail: *Evitez les contrefaçons.*
>
> An atmosphere of departed and ephemeral loves hung about the bedroom like stale scent, for the hotel was one of unlimited hospitality, though quietly, discreetly and not more so than most of its neighbours. The wallpaper was vaguely erotic—huge and fantastically shaped mauve, green and yellow flowers sprawling on a black ground. There was one chair and a huge bed covered with a pink counterpane. It was impossible, when one looked at that bed, not to think of the succession of *petites femmes* who had extended themselves upon it, clad in carefully thought out pink or mauve chemises, full of tact and savoir faire and savoir vivre and all the rest of it.[23]

But it would be unjust to leave Montparnasse on quite such a falling note. In the autumn of 1930 Henry Miller's wife June* came over to Paris to join him there, and the early pages of *Tropic of Cancer* are sprinkled with memories of that visit. Miller walks the same streets as Jean Rhys, but his response to them could hardly be more different. Michelet once noted in his Journal that Paris was for him not a question of particular monuments or works of art; his love for it was to do with something more essential: 'Ce qu'il y a de plus beau en elle:

---

* The Mona of *Tropic of Cancer*.

ce n'est ni Notre-Dame ni tel édifice, c'est *elle-même*.' Few writers can convey this relish for the texture of Paris more persuasively than Miller:

It is a little after daybreak. We pack hurriedly and sneak out of the hotel. The cafés are still closed. We walk, and as we walk we scratch ourselves. The day opens in milky whiteness, streaks of salmon-pink sky, snails leaving their shells. Paris. Paris. Everything happens here. Old, crumbling walls and the pleasant sound of water running in the urinals. Men licking their mustaches at the bar. Shutters going up with a bang and little streams purling in the gutters. *Amer Picon* in huge scarlet letters. *Zigzag*. Which way will we go and why or where or what?

Mona is hungry, her dress is thin. Nothing but evening wraps, bottles of perfume, barbaric earrings, bracelets, depilatories. We sit down in a billiard parlor on the Avenue du Maine and order hot coffee. The toilet is out of order. We shall have to sit some time before we can go to another hotel. Meanwhile we pick bedbugs out of each other's hair. Nervous. Mona is losing her temper. Must have a bath. Must have this. Must have that. Must, must, must ...

'How much money have you left?'

Money! Forgot all about that.

Hôtel des Etats-Unis. An *ascenseur*. We go to bed in broad daylight. When we get up it is dark and the first thing to do is to raise enough dough to send a cable to America. [...] Meanwhile there is the Spanish woman on the Boulevard Raspail—she's always good for a warm meal. By morning something will happen. At least we're going to bed together. No more bedbugs now. The rainy season has commenced. The sheets are immaculate ... [24]

The rue Notre-Dame-des-Champs and rue de Fleurus

Just beyond the place Bienvenue, the avenue du Maine runs down into the seemingly interminable rue de Vaugirard, the longest street in Paris. A few minutes' walk from here is the western end of the rue Notre-Dame-des-Champs, a street which today has little beyond its literary ghosts (now for the most part accommodated in modern buildings of striking ugliness) to attract the passer-by. Victor Hugo and Sainte-Beuve both came to live here in 1827, having previously been neighbours in the rue de Vaugirard. Hugo's house, where he wrote *Hernani*, was later demolished to make way for the boulevard Raspail; at the time of his occupancy it was no. 11. Sainte-Beuve moved into the house which stood on the site of the present no. 19. Both writers were still young men at this stage. In the early 19th century the rue Notre-Dame-des-Champs was not a street for those who had already won success. When Godefroid comes to live here in Balzac's *Madame de la Chanterie* (1848), it is in spite of the warnings of an aged neighbour:' "Are you aware," he said, "that the district in which you want to live is deserted by eight o'clock in the evening and that robbery is the least of the dangers one encounters there?" '[25]

This was scarcely true a hundred years later, but the street seems to have retained its attraction for young writers. In 1920 we find Ezra Pound moving into a studio at no. 70 bis to be followed four years later by Hemingway, who took a flat above the saw-mill at no. 113. It is the place he recalls in a passage of random memories in *Green Hills of Africa* (1935). He and his wife Hadley had been considering a flat on the boulevard du Temple, but instead

> ... we had taken the upstairs of the pavilion in Notre Dame des Champs in the courtyard with the sawmill (*and the sudden whine of the saw, the smell of sawdust and the chestnut tree over the roof with a mad woman downstairs*) and the year worrying about money (*all of the stories back in the mail that came in through a slit in the saw-mill door, with notes of rejection that would never call them stories, but always anecdotes, sketches, contes, etc. They did not want them, and we lived on poireaux and drank cahors and water*) and how fine the fountains were at the Place de L'Observatoire (*water sheen rippling on the bronze of horses' manes, bronze breasts and shoulders, green under thin-flowing water*) and when they put up the bust of

Flaubert in the Luxembourg on the short cut through the gardens on the way to the rue Soufflot (*one that we believed in, loved without criticism, heavy now in stone as an idol should be*).[26]

In these early days, when rejection slips outnumbered notes of acceptance, Hemingway was a frequent visitor to the neighbouring rue de Fleurus. Gertrude Stein had moved into no. 27 with her brother Leo back in 1903, and she went on living there with Alice Toklas when she and Leo later parted company. For years the flat in the rue de Fleurus was a place of pilgrimage for younger writers arriving in Paris. Stein gives a description of the building, which was later marked by a plaque, in her *Autobiography of Alice B. Toklas*:

> 'The house at 27 rue de Fleurus consisted then as it does now of a tiny pavillon of two storeys with four small rooms, a kitchen and a bath, and a very large atelier adjoining. Now the atelier is attached to the pavillon by a tiny passage added in 1914 but at that time the atelier had its own entrance, one rang the bell of the pavillon or knocked at the door of the atelier, and a great many people did both, but more knocked at the atelier. I was privileged to do both. I had been invited to dine on Saturday evening which was the evening when everybody came ...'[27]

But Gertrude Stein was a jealous goddess and the *Autobiography* was amongst other things a way of paying off the many writers and artists who had given her cause for offence. Hemingway, who had outgrown his early discipleship, was one of them, and he came in for some finely calculated malice. ('Ninety percent Rotarian' was one of the comments that cannot have delighted him.) He later took effective revenge in *A Moveable Feast*.

The Luxembourg Gardens

At its eastern end the rue de Fleurus meets the edge of the Jardin du Luxembourg. These Renaissance gardens take their name from the palace which Marie de Médicis, wife of

Henri IV, had built in the 17th century. She wanted a replica of the Pitti Palace in Florence—which the Luxembourg certainly is not—and paid for it by the simple expedient of driving round to the Bastille one night and robbing it of the money which Henri IV had stored there for a future war.

Visiting Paris a few years after the Gardens had been completed, John Evelyn commented:

> In summ, nothing is wanting to render this Palace, & Gardens perfectly beautyfull & magnificent; nor is it one of the least diversions, to behold the infinite numbers of Persons of quality, & Citizens, & strangers who frequent it, and to whom all accesse is freely permitted: so as you shall meete some walkes & retirements full of Gallants & Ladys, in others melancholy Fryers, in others studious Scholars, in others jolly Citizens; some sitting & lying on the Grasse, others, running, & jumping, some playing at bowles, & ball, others dancing & singing; and all this without the least disturbance, by reason of the amplitude of the place; & what is most admirable, you see no Gardners or people at Worke in it, and yet all kept in such exquisite order, as if they did nothing else but worke; It is so early in the mornings that all is dispatch'd, and don without the least confusion: I have been the larger in the description of this Paradise, for the extraordinary delight I have taken in those sweete retirements.[28]

Later responses to the Gardens have tended to sound a more muted note. In 1840 Thackeray writes of walking to the Luxembourg, 'where bonnes, students, grisettes, and old gentlemen with pigtails love to wander in the melancholy, quaint old gardens.'[29] The melancholy and the consciousness of age go together. The sense of it as a place haunted by its historical past is echoed by Edmond Texier in his *Tableau de Paris* (1852): 'The soul still feels an involuntary impulse of sadness, a something melancholy and subdued in the air you breathe there. One does not move, as in the Tuileries, with completely unfettered spirits; one feels oneself pursued by the ghosts of the past.'[30]

By bringing together the very old and the very young, public gardens will always invite an element of retrospection, but this seems particularly true of the Luxembourg. It was something that Alfred de Musset was aware of in *La confession d'un enfant du siècle* (1836), the novel which recounts his affair with George Sand. Octave, the character based on de Musset himself, has supped with the beautiful Marco and been taken by her to her apartment overlooking the Luxembourg Gardens. While she waits for him on the bed, he lingers by the window, looking out over the Gardens in the light of the early morning:

> The appearance of the avenues of the Luxembourg made my heart leap; every other thought vanished. How many times, playing truant on these little knolls, I had stretched out in the shade, brimming with wild poetry. For alas! this was the scene of my childhood debaucheries. Among the leafless trees and the withered plants of the flower-beds I found all these memories again. It was there, when I was ten, that I had walked with my brother and my tutor, throwing bread to a few poor birds that were numb with cold; it was there, sitting in a corner, that I had watched for hours the little girls dancing in a ring and listened to my naive heart beating to the refrains of their childish songs; there, coming home from school, that I had crossed the same avenue a thousand times, kicking along a pebble and lost in a line of Virgil. 'Oh, my childhood!' I cried. 'There you are! Oh, my God! There you are in this place!'[31]

It is a relief to turn from this weight of nostalgia to the blithe figure of George Moore. Regrets were far from his mind when he came here after breakfast one morning in the 1870s. 'I threw myself on a bench,' he recalls, 'and began to wonder if there was anything better in the world worth doing than to sit in an alley of clipped limes smoking, thinking of Paris and of myself.'[32]

The place Saint-Sulpice

The visitor who walks from the corner of the Luxembourg Gardens down the rue Bonaparte will see rising above the nearby buildings the twin towers of Saint-Sulpice. 'One of the noblest structures in Paris,' Gibbon called it. The poet Raoul Ponchon was less enthusiastic:

> Je hais les tours de Saint-Sulpice!
> Quand par hazard je les rencontre,
>   Je pisse
>   Contre.*

Perhaps the most exhaustive celebration of the place Saint-Sulpice comes from the Polish French writer Georges Perec in his *Tentative d'épuisement d'un lieu parisien* (1975). His aim, he tells us, was to describe 'what is generally unremarked, what doesn't get noticed, what has no significance—what is going on when nothing is going on, apart from the weather, the people, the cars and the clouds.' For three days in October 1974 he divided his time between the café de la Mairie, the Tabac Saint-Sulpice and the now defunct Fontaine Saint-Sulpice (café), recording the trivial details that entered his field of vision. The result conveys the feel of the Paris streets with curious resonance. In this extract from the fourth section Perec is in the café de la Mairie late on the afternoon of Friday 18 October. Lights are going on in the café, dusk is gathering:

> It's five to six
>
> From a blue van a man has taken out a porter's trolley which he has loaded with various sorts of cleaning equipment and which he has pushed into the rue des Canettes.
> Outside it's practically impossible to distinguish faces any more
>
> Colours melt into one another: Shades of grey occasionally lit up
>
> Spots of yellow. Glowings of red
>
> A 96 goes by almost empty
>
> A police car goes by and turns in front of the church

---

* I hate the towers of Saint-Sulpice! When I chance upon them, I piss upon them.

An 86 goes by empty, an 87 reasonably full

The bells of Saint-Sulpice begin to ring

A 70 full, a 96 empty, another 96 even more empty

Umbrellas up

The motor vehicles put on their lights
A 96 without many people in, a 63 full

The wind seems to be blowing in rainy gusts, but few cars
are using their windscreen-wipers

The bells of Saint-Sulpice stop ringing
(was it vespers?)

A 63 goes by almost empty

Night, winter: unreal aspect of the passers-by

A man carrying carpets

A lot of people, a lot of shadows, a 63 empty; the ground is
shining, a 70 full, the rain seems heavier. It is six-ten. Sound
of horns; start of traffic jam

I can scarcely see the church, but on the other hand, I see
almost the whole café (and myself as I write) reflected in the
café's own windows

The jam has cleared
The headlamps alone mark the passage of the cars

The street-lamps light up one by one

Right at the bottom (hôtel Récamier?) there are now several
lighted windows

[...]

It is 18–45

Cars go by

a yellow postal van stops in front of the letter-box which a
postman relieves of its contents (Pairs/Hors-Paris, banlieue
comprise)

It's still raining

I drink a gentiane de Salers.[33]

Saint-Germain-des Près

From Saint-Sulpice the rue Bonaparte leads down to the boulevard Saint-Germain and the place Saint-Germain-des-Près. Opposite the church is the café des Deux Magots; next to the Deux Magots, the café de Flore; across the road, the Brasserie Lipp. The Deux Magots and the Flore, in particular, were two of the main meeting-places of French intellectuals in the years leading up to the Second World War. Today they tend to be meeting-places of the fashionable and the well-to-do. But tradition dies hard. The lovely Deux Magots has for some time glossed its high prices with a note at the bottom of the menu identifying it, for anyone who might not have guessed, as 'le Rendez-Vous de l'élite intellectuelle'.

In the war years, however, it was the café de Flore that attracted most of the intellectuals, at least those associated with existentialism and the arts. Jean-Paul Sartre describes how this came about:

> From 1930 to 1939 I went regularly to the 'Dôme' in Montparnasse. As I was a teacher and hadn't much money I lived in a hotel; and like all people who live in hotels I spent most of the day in cafés. In 1940 the 'regulars' of the Dôme began to go elsewhere, for two reasons: the Métro station 'Vavin' was closed, and we had to make our way to the Dôme in the evenings, in complete darkness and on foot from the Gare de Montparnasse. Besides, the Dôme was overrun with Germans, and these Germans were tactless enough to bring their own tea and coffee, and to have these prepared and served in front of us Frenchmen, who were already reduced to drinking some anonymous and ghastly substitute.
>
> The fortunes of the Café de Flore at that time were made by the fact that it was just across the road from the station of St. Germain des Près. It had previously been merely an annexe of the Deux Magots, but in 1939 or thereabouts

Picasso, Léon-Paul Fargue, and André Breton began to go to the Flore. A lot of cinema people followed their example, and a lot of successful painters and celebrities of one sort or another. I was only a shabby little teacher at that time and I was too shy to go in.

But in 1940 the clientèle became quite different, for the reasons I've just given, and Simone de Beauvoir and I more or less set up house in the Flore. We worked from 9 a.m. till noon, when we went out to lunch. At 2 we came back and talked with our friends till four, when we got down to work again till eight. And after dinner people came to see us by appointment. It may seem strange, all this, but the Flore was like home to us: even when the air-raid alarm went we would merely feign to leave and then climb up to the first floor and go on working ... [34]

Another perspective on the café is given by Simone de Beauvoir in *La force de l'âge*:

The Flore had its own mores, its private ideology; the little band of regulars who met there daily were neither wholly Bohemian nor wholly bourgeois, but belonged for the most part, in a vague sort of way, to the world of films or the theatre. They lived on unspecified private incomes, from hand to mouth, or on their expectations. Their God and oracle, the source of all their opinions, was Jacques Prévert: they worshipped his films and poetry, doing their best to ape his language and attitudes. We too found Prévert's verses and lyrics very much to our taste: his dreamy, somewhat inconsequential anarchism suited us perfectly. [...] But the sympathy we felt for the young idlers in the Flore was tinged with impatience: the main object of their nonconformism was to justify their inactivity, and they were very, very bored. Their chief means of distraction was the Shock Brigade*, with each member of which they all in turn had an affair of varying length—generally pretty short. Once they had gone the rounds they started off again at the beginning,

---

* 'But the most common type of woman was what we nicknamed the Shock Brigade: pale-haired creatures, all to a greater or lesser extent ravaged by drugs (or alcohol, or just life), with sad mouths and shifty, restless eyes.'

which induced a certain monotony after a while. They spent the whole day venting their spleen with blasé little aphorisms, uttered in between yawns. They were forever complaining about *la connerie humaine*.[35]

This atmosphere of bored and reckless youth outlasted the war to become a feature of life in the bars and cabarets of Saint-Germain-des-Près in the late forties and early fifties. Its self-destructive tones are finely caught in the photographs of Ed van der Elsken.

Alongside the Flore and the Deux Magots, on the edge of the boulevard, stands the oldest church in Paris. Saint-Germain-des-Près, which from the Middle Ages onwards was the centre of the extensive territories of the Abbaye Saint-Germain, has survived the city's changing fortunes for eight centuries. In his *Pays parisiens* (1932) Daniel Halévy suggests the influence it exerts on the surrounding area. Having walked along the rue Saint-André-des-Arts and the rue de Buci, he stands in the little place de Fürstenberg:

It is so strange, this square *place* with its ten trees correctly aligned, its intimate and exact proportions. At the bottom, very high, the Abbey, brick and stone, magnificent in its robust simplicity. How far I was from this architecture in the rue Saint-André-des-Arts and the carrefour de Buci! Surely it must be from the abbey that we get these new impressions, this sense of total displacement? from the abbey, from its dominating, indestructible spirit? from its abbots and its monks? That must be it. We are walking on holy ground where the laity has only recently been admitted. Until the Revolution, the abbey of Saint-Germain-des-Près possessed these places, inhabited them. And had done for so many centuries! A hundred years of modern commotion do not wipe out a thousand years of Benedictine tranquillity. Here, before 1789, were living those men to whom we owe so much, the writers of the *Histoire littéraire de la France*. Their imprint lives on. The square form of the place de Fürstenberg is that of their demolished cloister. The building has fallen, the outline remains. The Revolution has dispersed the men and the papers, but it has not broken the silence favourable to thought. When a taxi crosses the place de Fürstenberg, you wonder what on earth it is doing there.[36]

A Parisian apartment

The final section of the rue Bonaparte, which runs down from Saint-Germain-des-Près to the river, covers what used to be the rue des Petits-Augustins. It was in this street, at about the site of the present no. 13, that William Cole came to stay in 1765. After a seventeen-hour coach journey from Roye he arrived in Paris at seven o'clock in the evening. His troubles began almost at once:

> In the Custom House Yard, as soon as I had paid, & been dispatched at the Bureau, I was accosted by a French Valet, who offered his Services to me [...]. However, though I told the Man over & over that I had no Occasion for him, yet he was so officious about me, that I could not get rid of him: & getting me an Hackney Coach to carry me to my Lodgings, in the Rue des Petits Augustins, at the *Hôtel d'Orléans*, in the Fauxbourg St Germain, he jumped up behind the Coach, where I should not have known that he had been, had it not happened, that the Portmanteaus being put into the Coach with me, one of the Doors of the Coach flew open, & let one of them fall into the Street, & upon my calling out to the Coachman to stop, he was ready to pick it up. In short, there was no saying him Nay; for he would follow me to my Lodgings, where, finding it absolutely necessary to have a French Servant, as my own knew not a word of the Language, I consented, thro' his Perseverance, to accept of his Service.[37]

The relationship was not entirely happy. Within a week the man was trying to extort more than his agreed wages, and Cole was only persuaded to keep him on by the hotel proprietress's refusal to find anyone else—'though,' Cole adds, 'I had no opinion of him, nor did I at all like his drunkenness; which was very Disagreeable, especially when I was out with him, in looking over Churches and going about the City, (as he was to go about with me, and to inform me of such Particulars as I wanted to be informed about.)' Cole seems to have had trouble with drunken servants. Horace Walpole's servant, who accompanies him round the Church and Convent of St Denis, casts a shadow over the trip by throwing in impertinent observations at every opportunity, 'which he would not [have] presumed to have done, had he been sober'.

It is not long before Cole's landlady too starts trying to swindle him. He records the fact with a wealth of circumstantial detail—'to show how alert the French are to take all Opportunities to cheat, and make the most of the English, (& other Foreigners, no doubt), who come to make but a short Stay among them.' For all that, he acquired comfortable lodgings within sound of the clock of Saint-Germain-des-Prés and with a view across the neighbouring roofs to the dome of the collège des Quatre-Nations on the quai de Conti. His description of them gives us an interesting glimpse of how an Englishman in easy circumstances would expect to live in the Paris of the mid-18th century:

> The Apartment I chose was up two Pair of Stairs; it consisted of a little Bedchamber for my Servant in the Passage, or little Gallery to my own, where an elegant & lofty Crimson Damask Bed was at the further End, raised on a Step, & floored with Oak, & had an Extempory Partition, if I chose it, to divide it off from the other Part of the Room; which was paved with neat small octagon red Bricks, never washed, but frequently rubbed with a waxed Brush to keep them polished: the common Flooring both above & below Stairs in Paris, & thro'out all France. The Room was furnished with a Bureau, half a Dozen elegant & sumptuous elbow-Chairs & a Sopha of the same Sort, of the Tapestry of their own Manufacture, a *Cuvette* or flat-bottomed awkward Bason to wash Hands in, with the Fire Furniture, as Shovel, Tongs, & Pair of Dogs to burn Wood on; which with a Towel to wash your Face with, & another for Breakfast, & a miserable little Deal Table, was all the Furniture I found in the Room: the Rest, as a Glass to shave with, Tea Equipage of all Sorts, even to the Kettle to boil the Water in,

Glasses to drink out of, &c, I was forced to purchase on the next Morning: together with Tea, Sugar & other Necessaries, which the French Valet was very expert in procuring. The Apartment was beautifully situated just above the Duke de la Rochefaucault's Garden, which was very large & elegant, with a small oval Pond, in which was a single Swan ...[38]

The rue des Beaux-Arts, rue Visconti, rue de Seine

Between Cole's lodgings and the boulevard Saint-Michel are clustered some of the most interesting streets in Paris. An idea of the range of their literary associations can be gained from the rue Jacob, which has accommodated writers as diverse as Stendhal and Samuel Johnson, Hemingway and Laurence Sterne, Mérimée and Colette. On the other side of the rue de Seine the Restaurant Magny[39] has long since disappeared from the rue Mazet but the café Procope,[40] now a restaurant, still serves its customers in the rue de l'Ancienne-Comédie, and at 25 rue des Grands-Augustins you can still find the house where La Bruyère was living in 1688 when the *Caractères* appeared—the same building that Heinrich Heine moved into a century and a half later. Those streets which managed to survive the construction of the boulevard Saint-Germain have preserved a character which does much to explain why the 6th arrondissement has drawn to itself so many writers over the past hundred years.

Most of these writers no doubt came here by choice, but the case of Oscar Wilde was slightly different. If you turn from the rue Bonaparte into the rue des Beaux-Arts, you will see at no. 13 the former Hotel D'Alsace, now simply called l'Hôtel. It was here that at the age of forty-six, exiled from England and broken by his imprisonment, Wilde died on 30 November 1900. At the turn of the century the hotel was a less tasteful establishment than it has since become. 'I can't stand this wall-paper,' Wilde is supposed to have remarked shortly before his death. 'One of us will have to go.'

Parallel to the rue des Beaux-Arts is the extraordinary rue Visconti, where Balzac lived from 1826 to 1828 in the house at no. 17. In the first of his many disastrous commercial enterprises he set up a printing press on the ground floor while himself living in the flat above it. His biographer André Maurois describes the arrangement:

> The big printer's shop, on the ground floor, had windows looking onto the street. An iron circular staircase led up to Balzac's living quarters—lobby, sitting-room, bedroom with alcove. Latouche,* who had good taste and enjoyed bargain-hunting, helped him to furnish the last of these rooms, of which the walls were draped with blue muslin.[41]

It was the failure of this venture that was indirectly responsible for Balzac's future career. He had dabbled in fiction before, but now, desperate for money, he turned to it seriously, and in 1829 *Les chouans*, his first novel, was published.

On the other side of the street, at no. 24, the house still stands in which Jean Racine spent the last seven years of his life and where he died on 21 April 1699 at the age of sixty.

At its eastern end the rue Visconti meets the rue de Seine. It was in this street that Baudelaire, stricken by debt, leaving the house only at night, lived for a few wretched months at no. 57. Reflecting on this period of the poet's life, Francis Carco is put in mind of Baudelaire's prose poem 'À une heure du matin':

> Alone at last! Not a sound to be heard but the rumbling of some belated and decrepit cabs. For a few hours we shall have silence if not repose. At last the tyranny of the human face has disappeared, and I myself shall be the only cause of my sufferings. At last, then, I am allowed to refresh myself in a bath of darkness! First of all, a double turn of the lock. It seems to me that this twist of the key will increase my solitude and strengthen the barricades which at this instant separate me from the world ... Horrible life! Horrible town! ... [42]

Further up the street, 60 rue de Seine is the address of the Hotel La Louisiane. It was in the years between the wars that Cyril Connolly came to know it, and he recalls the happiness of those times in *The Unquiet Grave*:

* A writer and critic who had given some support to Balzac.

Then came the days of ferrets with ribs like wish-bones for whom we bought raw liver from the horse-butcher in the Rue de Seine while they tunnelled round the octagonal room in the Hôtel de la Louisiane. They pursued oranges, eggs and ping-pong balls and wore harness with little bells; and from their number came forth a queen, the tawny, docile Norfolk beauty whom we named the English rose, who performed her cycle of eating, playing, sleeping and relieving herself and who saw three continents from a warm sleeve. She hunted the rue Monge and the Rue Mouffetard, the courts of the Val de Grâce and the gardens of the Observatoire, the Passage des Princes and the Place de Fürstenberg. She searched the Parc Montsouris and the Buttes-Chaumont, the doss-houses of the Rue Quincampoix and the Boulevard de la Chapelle; she visited the tattered buildings in the Rue de la Goutte d'Or and heard the prostitutes calling to each other from their beds in the Rue de la Charbonnière; she explored the gilt, the plush, the columns and flaking ceilings of the Deuxième Arrondissement, the arcades of the Palais-Royal and the Place des Victoires, the corner-houses, razor-sharp, in the Rue de la Lune. She sniffed at all the gates of Paris: Porte Saint-Denis, Porte d'Orléans, Porte des Lilas; pocket gardens of the Gobelin workers along the Bièvre, exposed tendons of the Nord railway by the boulevard Barbès and warehouses on the Saint-Martin Canal. Yet most she loved, a short walk from her couch of straw, the stony public garden by Saint-Germain-des-Prés.[43]

In the closing years of the war the same hotel became for a while the home of Sartre and Simone de Beauvoir:

I had sworn I would not spend a second year on the Rue Dauphine; and well before the holidays I applied to the proprietors of the Hôtel de la Louisiane, on the Rue de Seine, where many of the Flore's regulars lived. I moved in during October. My room contained a divan, several book-shelves, a large and massive table, and a poster on the wall representing an English Lifeguardsman. The day I arrived, Sartre upset a bottle of ink over the moquette carpet, with the result that the proprietress instantly removed it; but the

parquet flooring suited me as well as any carpet would have.
I also had a kitchen of my own. From my window I looked
out over a great sea of rooftops. None of my previous
retreats had come so close to being the apartment of my
dreams, and I felt like staying there for the rest of my life.
Sartre had a tiny room at the other end of the corridor: its
bareness more than once surprised his visitors. He did not
even own any books; any we bought we lent to people, who
never returned them.[44]

The Louisiane, which has mercifully resisted any temptation
to cash in on its past, remains today a modest, friendly hotel.

Shakespeare and Company

The literary figures who have inhabited the streets around the
carrefour de l'Odéon are numerous enough to fill a book of
their own, but one person in particular, who played an oblique
but important role in the literary life of Paris between the wars,
deserves a mention. According to Hemingway, Sylvia Beach
'had a lively, sharply sculptured face, brown eyes that were as
alive as a small animal's and as gay as a young girl's, and wavy
brown hair that was brushed back from her fine forehead and
cut thick below her ears and at the line of the collar of the
brown velvet jacket she wore. She had pretty legs and she was
kind, cheerful and interested, and loved to make jokes and
gossip. No one that I ever knew was nicer to me.'[45]

Shakespeare and Company, which was the bookshop Sylvia
Beach founded and ran, first at 8 rue Dupuytren, then at 12 rue
de l'Odéon, had an importance far beyond that of simply
selling the work of British and American authors. It was a
meeting-place, postal address and general first-aid station for
a wide range of writers. 'On a cold windswept street, this was a
warm, cheerful place with a big stove in winter, tables and
shelves of books, new books in the window, and photographs
on the wall of famous writers both dead and living. The
photographs all looked like snap-shots and even the dead
writers looked as though they had really been alive.'[46]

So Hemingway described the shop at 12 rue de l'Odéon.

But it was in the earlier days at 8 rue Dupuytren, where the doors opened triumphantly on 19 November 1919, that Shakespeare and Company embarked on its most spectacular project. This was the publication of *Ulysses*. Sylvia Beach had met Joyce one Sunday at a party on the second floor of 34 rue du Bois de Boulogne. She urged him to call on her in the rue Dupuytren:

> The very next day, Joyce came walking up my steep little street wearing a dark blue serge suit, a black felt hat on the back of his head, and, on his narrow feet, not so very white sneakers. He was twirling a cane, and, when he saw me looking at it, he told me that it was an ashplant stick from Ireland, the gift of an Irish officer on a British man-of-war that had stopped at the Port of Trieste. ('Stephen Dedalus,' I thought, 'still has his ashplant.') Joyce was always a bit shabby, but his bearing was so graceful and his manner so distinguished that one scarcely noticed what he had on. Everywhere he went and on everyone he met, he made a deep impression.
>
> He stepped into my bookshop, peered closely at the photographs of Walt Whitman and Edgar Allan Poe, then at the two Blake drawings; finally, he inspected my two photographs of Oscar Wilde. Then he sat down in the uncomfortable little armchair beside my table.
>
> He told me again that Pound had persuaded him to come to Paris. Now he had three problems: finding a roof to put over the heads of four people; feeding and clothing them; and finishing *Ulysses*.[47]

The third problem, at least, was solved. *Ulysses* was finished and Sylvia Beach finally managed to publish it to coincide with Joyce's fortieth birthday on 2 February 1922. Meanwhile, Shakespeare and Company had moved in the summer of 1921 to its new site in the rue de l'Odéon, just opposite the bookshop run by Sylvia Beach's friend Adrienne Monnier.[48] Here it remained through the twenties and thirties, lending and selling books, arranging readings, offering a refuge from the cold Paris winters. These were the years commemorated by Hemingway.

After the war Shakespeare and Company did not reopen.[49] The great days of the expatriate generation were over. The Latin Quarter, Montparnasse and the streets around the Odéon were given back to the Parisians and the tourists.

CHAPTER 5

Western Paris

The place de la Concorde

In the early pages of *The Tragic Muse* (1890) Henry James's hero, Nick Dormer, stands at the edge of the place de la Concorde and looks out over 'the great square, the opposite bank of the Seine, the steep blue roofs of the quay, the bright immensity of Paris'.[1] From no other point does one get so lively an impression of the expansive sweep of the city. The broad prospect of the Champs-Elysées is balanced by the tree-lined avenues of the Tuileries, while alongside runs the slow curve of the Seine.

From the start it was an inviting site for popular celebrations. The square, then called place Louis XV, was still being completed when in 1770 a splendid firework display was held in honour of the marriage of Marie Antoinette and the future Louis XVI. A fallen fuse ignited some of the heaped up fireworks and in the ensuing blaze 133 of the panic-stricken spectators were killed. It was an inauspicious opening both for the marriage and for the square. But the firework disaster was a trifle compared to the grim celebrations that followed some twenty years later when the guillotine made its first appearance on the same spot, which had by then been renamed place de la Révolution. Such was the carnage that the residents of the nearby rue Saint-Honoré appealed to have the place of execution changed, claiming that the stench of stale blood which rose from the stones of the square was damaging their health and devaluing their property.

It was here that on 21 January 1793 Louis XVI mounted the

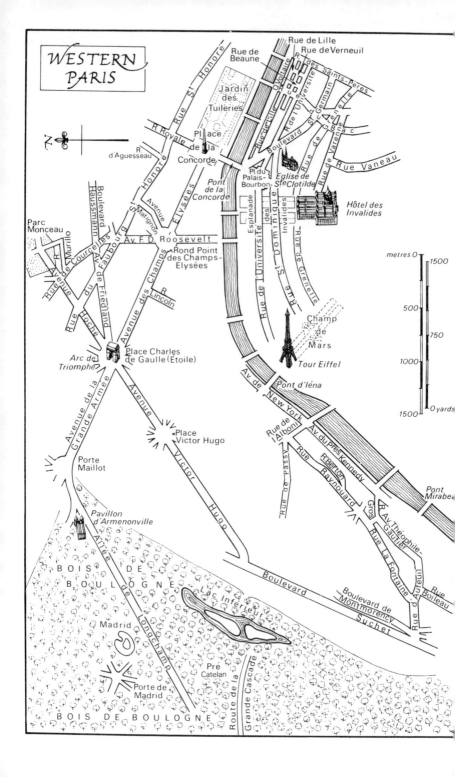

scaffold, leaning on the arm of the Abbé Edgeworth, uncle of Maria Edgeworth. Louis-Sébastien Mercier was one of those who had voted for the execution, but he had little relish for the event itself: 'His blood flows, and there are people who dip a fingertip, a quill, a scrap of paper in it. There is one who tastes it, and says: "It is vilely salt!" An executioner at the scaffold side sells small bundles of his hair; people buy the ribbon that tied it. Everyone carries off a small fragment of his clothing or some other blood-stained remnant from the tragic scene. I saw the populace go by, arm in arm, laughing, talking, as if returning from some festivity.'[2]

But the Revolution was already beginning to prey on its own. Within a year, the shadows of suspicion were gathering around one of its most popular leaders, Georges Jacques Danton. Of all the deaths in the place de la Révolution, it is perhaps his that has made the deepest appeal to the imagination. This is how Hilaire Belloc sets the scene:

> It was close on six, and the sun was nearly set behind the trees of the Étoile; it reddened the great plaster statue of Liberty which stood in the middle of the Place, where the obelisk is now, and to which Madame Roland delivered her last phrase ['Oh Liberty, what crimes are committed in thy name']. It sent a level beam upon the vast crowd that filled the square, and cast long shadows, sending behind the guillotine a dark lane over the people. The day had remained serene and beautiful to the last, the sky was stainless, and the west shone like a forge.[3]

The one-time hero for whom the crowd was waiting was a heavily built man, scarred and pock-marked, whose passionate speeches in the cafés and meeting-places of the Revolution had led him to be hailed as the 'tribune of the people'. A successful lawyer at the outset, Danton had risen to become Minister of Justice and a powerful figure on the Committee of Public Safety. But his extravagant life-style and his uncompromising bluntness had also made him enemies. When he turned against the Terror and began to advocate a measure of clemency, he left himself fatally vulnerable. Once Robespierre had deserted him, he was lost.

Late in the afternoon of 16 Germinal (6 April) 1794, the three red tumbrils set out from the prison of the Conciergerie along the usual route: across the Pont Neuf to the quai du Louvre, then down the rue Saint-Honoré to the rue Royale and finally into the place de la Révolution. Outside the café de la Régence, on the *terrasse*, the painter David, who had once been Danton's friend, sketched them as they went past.

By chance, a poet called Arnault was crossing the rue Saint-Honoré as the tumbrils made their way towards the guillotine. Danton was known to him by sight and he doubled back through the Gardens of the Tuileries. From the railings at the western end, surrounded by the crowd, he watched Danton and his associates brought forward to the guillotine, which stood mid-way between the statue of Liberty and the entrance to the Tuileries. Towards the end of his life Arnault set down an account of Danton's final moments:

> Danton was the last to appear on the platform, soaked with the blood of his friends. Night was falling. At the foot of the horrible statue whose mass stood out against the sky in a dreadful silhouette, I saw, like a shade from Dante, the tribune standing, dimly lit by the dying sun, as though emerging from the tomb instead of about to enter it. Nothing more striking [...] than the expression of that head which, on the point of falling, seemed to be dictating laws. Time cannot erase the horrible pantomime from my memory. I recall the full force of my feeling at Danton's last words, which I did not hear myself but which were passed round with horror and admiration: 'Make sure you show my head to the people: it's worth seeing'.[4]

A few months later, as Danton had predicted, Robespierre made the same journey. The tumbril stopped for a moment in front of his house, at 398 rue Saint-Honoré, so that he could see the front door splattered with bull's blood by the exulting crowd. Altogether, 1119 people were executed in the place de la Révolution in the course of three fearful years from 1792 to 1795.

The Champs-Elysées

By 1796 things were changing. First the guillotine was re-moved, then the statue of Liberty. During the first half of the 19th century the square gradually acquired its present aspect, regaining in 1830 the name of place de la Concorde, which it had already enjoyed for a short time during the Revolution. Over the next few years the obelisk from Luxor was mounted in the centre and the lumpish allegorical statues of French towns were disposed around the edge. By the 1880s its bloody associations were far in the past. It had become by then the square that Proust remembered from his childhood. He de-scribes a typical scene in *Du côte de chez Swann* (1913). The snow has finally stopped and Marcel's mother has sent him off with the maid, Françoise, to play in the Champs-Elysées. His life at the time revolves around his meetings there with Swann's daughter, Gilberte:

That day we found no one there, or else a solitary girl, on the point of departure, who assured me that Gilberte was not coming. The chairs, deserted by the imposing but uninspir-ing company of governesses, stood empty. [...]

Françoise found it too cold to stand about, so we walked to the Pont de la Concorde to see the Seine frozen over, on to which everyone, even children, walked fearlessly, as though upon an enormous whale, stranded, defenceless, and about to be cut up. We returned to the Champs-Elysées; I was growing sick with misery between the motionless wooden horses and the white lawn, caught in a net of black paths from which the snow had been cleared, while the statue that surmounted it held in its hand a long pendent icicle which seemed to explain its gesture. [...] Suddenly the sky was rent in two: between the punch-and-judy and the horses, against the opening horizon, I had just seen, like a miraculous sign, Mademoiselle's blue feather. And now Gilberte was run-ning at full speed towards me, sparkling and rosy beneath a cap trimmed with fur, enlivened by the cold, by being late, by her anxiety for a game; shortly before she reached me, she slipped on a piece of ice and, either to regain her balance, or because it appeared to her graceful, or else pretending that she was on skates, it was with outstretched arms that she smilingly advanced, as though to embrace me.[5]

The Champs-Elysées are home ground for the heroes of both Balzac and Flaubert. On the point of leaving the provinces for Paris, Flaubert's Frédéric Moreau has a final meeting with his closest friend, Deslauriers, who gives him the classic advice to become a rich woman's lover—'Remember Rastignac in *La comédie humaine*. You'll succeed, I'm sure of it!' The process of disillusionment which *L'éducation sentimentale* charts with such precision finds one of its many images in Frédéric's changing attitude to the glittering cavalcades along the Champs-Elysées. New to Paris and already in love with Mme Arnoux, he walks, on days of sunshine, to the end of the Champs:

> Women, seated at ease in barouches, their veils floating in the breeze, passed close to him, while the horses paced steadily along with a scarcely perceptible swaying, that made the polished harness creak. More and more carriages appeared. Beyond the Rond-Point, where they slowed down, they filled the entire roadway. Mane brushed mane, lamp grazed lamp; steel stirrups, silver curb chains, and brass buckles flashed scattered points of light among knee breeches, white gloves and furs drooping over the crests on the carriage doors. He felt as though he were lost in a remote world. He let his eyes wander over the faces of these women; and vague resemblances recalled Mme Arnoux to his mind. He pictured her among them in a little brougham, like Mme Dambreuse's brougham. But now the sun was setting, and a cold wind stirred up eddies of dust. The coachmen thrust their chins down into their neckcloths, the wheels turned faster, the asphalt grated; and all the carriages swept down the long avenue at a brisk trot, jostling, swerving, overtaking; then at the Place de la Concorde they scattered. The sky behind the Tuileries took on the hue of its slate roof. The trees in the gardens became two solid masses, tinged with purple at the top. The lamps were lit; and the pale green expanse of the Seine broke into shot silver against the piles of the bridges.[6]

In time, Frédéric himself comes to be part of this 'monde lointain'. At the end of an afternoon's horse-racing on the Champ-de-Mars he drives back down the Champs-Elysées with Rosanette, who is later to become his mistress. It is again the characteristic 19th-century scene in which carriages of every sort jam the avenue, but Frédéric's perspective has changed:

> The setting sun, piercing the vapour, cast through the Arc de Triomphe an almost horizontal beam of reddish light, which glittered on the wheel hubs, the door handles, the butts of the shafts, and the rings of the axle-trees. The great avenue was like a river carrying on its current the bobbing manes of horses and the clothes and heads of men and women. On either side rose the trees, like two green walls, glistening after the rain. Above, patches of blue as soft as satin appeared here and there in the sky.
>
> Then Frédéric remembered those days, already distant, when he had coveted the unspeakable delight of riding in one of these carriages, beside one of these women. That delight he now possessed, yet he had no joy in it.[7]

One of the imposing private houses past which Frédéric and Rosanette would have driven on their way down the Champs-Elysées was the hôtel Choiseul-Gouffier at nos. 71–9, later demolished to make way for the rue Lincoln. It was here, during the years covered by *L'éducation sentimentale*, that the great financier Emile Girardin lived. Early in 1856 Charles Dickens went there to dine. The account of his entertainment which he sent back to his friend Forster gives an amusing image of the scale of life behind the doors of rich men's houses in the days of the Second Empire:

> No man unacquainted with my determination never to embellish or fancify such accounts, could believe in the description I shall let off when we meet, of dining at Emile Girardin's—of the three gorgeous drawing rooms with ten thousand wax candles in golden sconces, terminating in a dining room of unprecedented magnificence with two enor-mous transparent plate-glass doors in it, looking (across an

ante-chamber full of clean plates) straight into the kitchen, with the cooks in their white paper caps dishing the dinner. From his seat in the midst of the table, the host (like a Giant in a Fairy story) beholds the kitchen, and the snow-white tables, and the profound order and silence there prevailing. Forth from the plate-glass doors issues the Banquet—the most wonderful feast ever tasted by mortal: at the present price of Truffles, that article alone costing (for eight people) at least five pounds. On the table are ground glass jugs of peculiar construction, laden with the finest growth of Champagne and the coolest ice. With the third course is issued Port Wine (previously unheard of in a good state on this continent), which would fetch two guineas a bottle at any sale. The dinner done, Oriental flowers in vases of golden cobweb are placed upon the board. With the ice is issued Brandy, buried for 100 years. To that succeeds Coffee, brought by the brother of one of the convives from the remotest East, in exchange for an equal quantity of Californian gold dust. The company being returned to the drawing-room—tables roll in by unseen agency, laden with Cigarettes from the Hareem of the Sultan, and with cool drinks in which the flavour of the Lemon arrived yesterday from Algeria, struggles voluptuously with the delicate Orange arrived this morning from Lisbon. That period past, and the guests reposing on Divans worked with many-coloured blossoms, big table rolls in, heavy with massive furniture of silver, and breathing incense in the form of a little present of Tea direct from China—table and all, I believe; but cannot swear to it, and am resolved to be prosaic. All this time the host perpetually repeats 'Ce petit dîner-ci n'est que pour faire la connaissance de Monsieur Dickens; il ne compte pas; ce n'est rien'. And even now I have forgotten to set down half of it—in particular the item of a far larger plum pudding than ever was seen in England at Christmas time, served with a celestial sauce in colour like the orange blossom, and in substance like the blossom powdered and bathed in dew, and called in the carte (carte in a gold frame like a little fish-slice to be handed about) 'Hommage à l'illustre écrivain d'Angleterre.' That illustrious man staggered out at the last drawing-room door, speechless with wonder, finally; and even at that moment his host, holding to his lips a chalice set with precious stones and containing nectar distilled from the air that blew over the fields of beans in bloom for fifteen summers, remarked 'Le dîner que nous avons eu, mon cher, n'est rien—il ne compte pas—il a été tout-à-fait en famille—il faut dîner (en vérité, dîner) bientôt. Au plaisir! Au revoir! Au dîner!'[8]

The avenue Matignon and the rue du Faubourg-Saint-Honoré

From the Rond-Point at the centre of the Champs-Elysées the avenue Matignon leads up towards the rue du Faubourg-Saint-Honoré. On the left-hand side, at no. 3, a plaque records that this was the site of the house in which the German poet Heinrich Heine, who had been living in Paris since 1831, died on 17 February 1856. Only fifty-eight at the time of his death, he had contracted syphilis back in his student days in Götting-en and by the time he moved into the avenue Matignon his condition was desperate. It was in this flat on the fifth floor that he was sought out by Camille Selden, the mysterious admirer whose visits brightened the last months of his life. In her memoir of their relationship Camille, whose real name was Elise von Krienitz, gives a brief description of the setting:

His windows, overlooking the Avenue, opened on to a narrow balcony, covered in hot weather with a striped linen awning, such as appear in front of small cafés. The apartments consisted of three or four rooms—the dining-room and two rooms used by the master and the mistress of the house. A very low couch, behind a screen encased in wall-paper, several chairs, and opposite the door a walnut-wood secretary, formed the entire furniture of the invalid's chamber.[9]

For the rest of his life Heine was confined to this small room, where he was visited by Camille and looked after by Mathilde, the wife whom he had originally found working in a glove shop in the passage Choiseul. When the autumn days were warm enough, Heine's mattress would be laid out on the balcony, and from there he was able to catch his last glimpses of the streets of Paris.

At its northern end the avenue Matignon meets the fashionable and expensive rue du Faubourg-Saint-Honoré, where at no. 29 Coco Chanel had her town house, frequented in the twenties by writers such as Jean Cocteau and Max Jacob. A few doors further along at no. 39, just opposite the rue d'Aguesseau, stands the British Embassy, bought by George III from the Princess of Borghese. It was here that Thackeray was married and that Dickens gave readings from his books; here, too, that on 25 January 1874 W. Somerset Maugham was born. Maugham's father was a prosperous lawyer who had no direct link with the Embassy, but in the wake of France's crushing defeat by the Prussians in 1870 a new law had been proposed, which was to make anyone born on French soil liable to conscription into the French army. In response to this, one wing of the Embassy had been turned into a makeshift maternity ward for British nationals resident in Paris.

For the first few years of his life Maugham lived in the family home at 25 avenue d'Antin (today the avenue Franklin D. Roosevelt). Then the death of his mother in 1882 and of his father two years later left him an orphan, to be packed off to the grey shores of England, the austere hospitality of a clergyman uncle and the uncongenial rigours of an English public school. Paris was the repository of all that was sweetest in his childhood and it retained its place in his affections. His milieu was that of the 8th and 16th arrondissements, and that is the area of Paris in which his characters tend to be most at home. If we find them further east, then they have probably been lunching at the Ritz.

It is a curious reflection that Somerset Maugham, who was still alive in the 1960s, should have been an earlier inhabitant of the rue du Faubourg-Saint-Honoré than Gustave Flaubert. For the ageing Flaubert, who came here the year after Maugham's birth, it was an unfortunate move. His niece had a flat at no. 240, at the far end of the street from the British Embassy, and Flaubert decided to join her in the same building. He was already in low spirits and within a few weeks he was faced with the news of his financial ruin through the improvidence of his niece's husband. There was little to make him fond of the new apartment. Nonetheless, he worked on through the crisis, and it was here that he completed the *Trois contes* (1877).

Before long he was again receiving his friends on Sunday afternoons. Zola remembers the group of them—Turgenev, Goncourt, Daudet and himself—in a room filled with the smoke from Flaubert's various pipes: 'from 3 o'clock to 6 o'clock we went at a gallop through different subjects'. On the mantelpiece was Flaubert's large gilded statue of the Buddha, and in front of it would stand the novelist himself:

> When we think of Flaubert, those of us who knew him well in his final years, it is in this white and gold drawing-room that we see him, planting himself in front of us with that characteristic movement of the heels, huge and silent, with his large blue eyes—or else bursting with tremendous paradoxes and shaking his two fists at the ceiling.[10]

Dickens in the rue de Courcelles

Just to the north of this stretch of the rue du Faubourg Saint-Honoré is the rue de Courcelles. It is a street which has attracted more literary inhabitants than most—amongst them Proust, Colette and Henri Barbusse[11]—but its most distinguished British resident was Dickens. In November 1846, having settled matters with the agent ('a French Mrs Gamp'), he moved into a house at no. 48. In its place there now stands a museum of Asian art, but we can get an impression of what it must have been like from one of Dickens's letters:

> I will merely observe that it is fifty yards long and eighteen feet high, and that the bedrooms are exactly like opera-boxes. It has its little courtyard and garden, and porter's house and cordon to open the door, and so forth; and is a Paris mansion in little. There is a gleam of reason in the drawing-room. Being a gentleman's house, and not one furnished to let, it has some very curious things in it; some of

the oddest things you ever beheld in your life; and an infinity of easy chairs and sofas. . . . Bad weather. It is snowing hard. There is not a door or window here—but that's nothing! there's not a door or window in all Paris—that shuts; not a chink in all the billions of trillions of chinks in the city that can be stopped to keep the wind out.[12]

The weather seems to have caused Dickens something of a problem here. 'Cold intense', he writes on 6 December. 'The water in the bedroom jugs freezes into solid masses from top to bottom, bursts the jugs with reports like small cannon, and rolls out on the table and wash-stands hard as granite.'[13]

Just south of the parc Monceau the rue de Courcelles is met by the rue Murillo, where at no. 4 stands the house overlooking the park in which Flaubert had lived from 1869 to 1875. When he was not at his family home in Croisset near Rouen, Flaubert occupied the fourth-floor apartment here, dispensing hospitality on Sundays and working during the week on *La tentation de Saint Antoine* (1874).

It was only three years after Flaubert left the area that late one night, in the spring of 1878, after crossing from Dover to Calais, the twelve-year-old Rudyard Kipling 'came to a boarding house full of English people at the back of the Parc Monceau'. His father was in charge of the Indian Section of part of the Paris Exhibition that year, and Kipling's holiday provided the substance of the early pages of his *Souvenirs of France* (1933). Among other excursions, he climbed up into the head of Bartholdi's Statue of Liberty, which was in Paris at the time, awaiting transportation to America. This childhood visit laid the foundations of an enduring affection for France which later transmitted itself through Kipling's enthusiasm for French literature.

The arc de Triomphe and Bois de Boulogne

From the parc Monceau—or, as Baedeker used to call it, 'the small but highly elegant parc Monceau'—there is a clear view along the avenue Hoche to Napoleon's arc de Triomphe. The arch itself has tended to inspire literature that is patriotic rather than memorable. J. F. Destigny's image of it as 'l'anneau conjugale de la France et des cieux' (the wedding ring of France and the heavens) is more flamboyant than most, but it conveys the characteristic tone. Less startlingly, Victor Hugo resorts to an image that seems to have been close to his heart:

> Entre tes quatre pieds toute la ville abonde
> Comme une fourmilière aux pieds d'un éléphant.*

As Hugo was no doubt aware, this image at one time had a shadowy reality in the mind of Louis XV's engineer. In 1758 he proposed the erection of a huge triumphal elephant on this site, surmounted by a statue of the King. Disappointingly, this was another of Paris's elephant projects which never matured.

The arc de Triomphe remained a focus for patriotism into the 20th century, and it was here that on 11 November 1923 the flame was lit to mark the tomb of the unknown warrior. The symbolic significance of the arch has more than once made it the centre of political demonstrations—of the kind, for example, that the American poet e.e. cummings attended one afternoon in 1924:

> 16 heures
> l'Etoile
>
> the communists have fine Eyes
>
> some are young some old none
> look alike the flics rush
> batter the crowd sprawls collapses ...[14]

But the arc de Triomphe has not been monopolised by the literature of patriotism and politics. As often as not, it figures in a purely social context, for it was through the triumphal arch that the elegant processions of the 19th century passed on their way from the centre of Paris to the Bois de Boulogne. In pre-Revolutionary days, before the arch was built, one of the high points of the social year had been the annual pilgrimage of the *beau monde* to the convent at Longchamp to hear the Easter services. Since this was the important occasion on

---

* Between your four feet the whole city abounds,
  like an ant-hill at the feet of an elephant.

which all the latest fashions in clothes and carriages were displayed, the destruction of the convent during the Revolution seemed an inadequate reason for putting a stop to it. So the Passion week excursions continued—to the satisfaction of Mrs Trollope, who witnessed one of them in 1835. It was, she wrote afterwards, 'an extremely pretty spectacle, rivalling a spring Sunday in Hyde Park as to the number and elegance of the equipages, and greatly exceeding it in the beauty and extent of the magnificent road on which they show themselves.'[15]

At other times men and women repaired to the Bois for duels and for dinners, for country outings, horse-riding and polite promenades. To dine on the island with moonlight playing across the lake was already to be half-way towards a world of fiction. No writer has been more sensitive to the wood's elusive social charm than Marcel Proust. The closing pages of *Du côté de chez Swann* are an elegy for the Bois as it used to be. One November morning Marcel, now in middle age, sets out to walk across it:

> The different parts of the Bois, so easily confounded in summer in the density and monotony of their universal green, were now clearly divided. A patch of brightness indicated the approach to almost every one of them, or else a splendid mass of foliage stood out before it like an oriflamme. I could make out, as on a coloured map, Armenouville, the Pré Catelan, Madrid, the Race Course and the shore of the lake. Here and there would appear some meaningless erection, a sham grotto, a mill, for which the trees made room by drawing away from it, or which was borne upon the soft green platform of a grassy lawn. I could feel that the Bois was not really a wood, that it existed for a purpose alien to the life of its trees; my sense of exaltation was due not only to the admiration of the autumn tints but to a bodily desire.[16]

What he longs for is a vanished social world for which the Bois had provided a perfect context. But in place of the coach and pair there is now the motor car; the slender horses have gone; the men stroll round with bare heads and the women in vulgar hats piled high with fruits and flowers. Of the beauties who walked here when he was young there is scarcely a trace:

Alas! in the acacia-avenue—the myrtle-alley—I did see some of them again, grown old, no more now than grim spectres of what once they had been, wandering to and fro, in desperate search of heaven knew what, through the Virgilian groves. They had long fled, and still I stood vainly questioning the deserted paths. The sun's face was hidden. Nature began again to reign over the Bois, from which had vanished all trace of the idea that it was the Elysian Garden of Woman; above the gimcrack windmill the real sky was grey; the wind wrinkled the surface of the Grand Lac in little wavelets, like a real lake; large birds passed swiftly over the Bois, as over a real wood, and with shrill cries perched, one after another, on the great oaks which, beneath their Druidical crown, and with Dodonaic majesty, seemed to proclaim the unpeopled vacancy of this estranged forest, and helped me to understand how paradoxical it is to seek in reality for the pictures that are stored in one's memory, which must inevitably lose the charm that comes to them from memory itself and from their not being apprehended by the senses. The reality that I had known no longer existed. It sufficed that Mme Swann did not appear, in the same attire and at the same moment, for the whole avenue to be altered. The places that we have known belong now only to the little world of space on which we map them for our own convenience. None of them was ever more than a thin slice, held between the contiguous impressions that composed our life at that time; remembrance of a particular form is but regret for a particular moment; and houses, roads, avenues are as fugitive, alas, as the years.[17]

Since the days of Mme Swann the character of the Bois, particularly at night, has perhaps changed even more than Proust allows. *Paris insolite* (1952) is Jean-Paul Clébert's tribute to the seedier aspects of the city as he experienced them in the years after the Second World War. These are his reflections on more modern frequenters of the Bois:

It's impossible to sleep in the woods of Paris, either Boulogne or Vincennes. All the same it's a pity. Even in winter when the cold shrinks the light from the street lamps. Impossible to bed down. For they are there. And when you start dreaming, stretched out nice and peacefully in the grass, looking at the stars, there's always a character dressed all in grey who comes along and walks to and fro near you, stops a few yards away, takes out a cigarette, uses up a box of matches, and comes to ask you for a light. Then the piercing blue eyes (nothing more creepy than that hollow look, too clear, empty, haunted by the impossible). And you have all the trouble in the world explaining to him that you're not there for pleasure (you can say that again!) but to get some kip. You have to threaten him with mugging, beating up, even murder before he regretfully pushes off. There are countless numbers of them who trot along after dinner to the porte Maillot, bicycle in hand, and go up the avenues or circle the lake, walking slowly down the alleys, their eyes straining towards the shade. They have a perfect knowledge of the slightest thicket and stop as soon as they see a couple on a bench or lying on the grass, then they make a wide circle, closing in again with the cunning of a Red Indian, past-masters of the art of the silent approach over dead leaves and broken branches, hiding behind a tree and wrapping the lovers in a soft yet attentive look, concentrating most closely on the progress of the hands rather than the meeting of the mouths, imagining the curves of the bodies, divining the play of shadows. [...] I know these bastards— I chose to make my home for a good while behind the Longchamp waterfall with two or three like-minded vagabonds ...[18]

The seizième

Flanking the Bois de Boulogne are the streets of the seizième. In no other quarter of the city does the number of the arrondissement carry such a wealth of implication. This is not the address of Paris's down and outs. An apartment here tends to be one of the more tangible rewards of artistic success, as a glance at the roll-call of writers and musicians who have died in this district over the past hundred years will confirm. The tone of the area is described with affectionate irony by Léon-Paul Fargue in *Le piéton de Paris* (Passy and Auteuil are the two rich suburbs situated in the seizième):

> Passy-Auteuil is a large province in which the families know one another, keep an eye on one another—and sometimes hate one another, if one of them happens to have a few more guests, a few more politicians or poets than the other at its weekly, monthly, annual tea-party; or if so and so's son has passed the baccalauréat with or without a distinction. Patissiers, butchers, dry-cleaners and concierges know all about the family quarrels, divorces and inheritances.
>
> They are almost foster brothers, almost cousins; they mourn at the funerals, rejoice at the Christenings, send their daughters to English classes at the Institute, just as their customers do, wear gloves on Sunday. Neither the working class nor the poor have any place in this perpetual garden party which goes on year in year out between the place Victor Hugo and the Seine. All the ceremonial occasions of Passy-Auteuil see the same troop of guests returning to church or to the luncheon parties; they confer on the social events of the seizième arrondissement a slight air of comic opera which is not without charm.[19]

The lure of this sort of retreat was summed up by Colette, who herself went to live just alongside the Bois de Boulogne in 1916, at 69 boulevard Suchet:

> To live in Auteuil means that one is in flight from the crowds and the noise of the city, that one is clinging to that skirt of verdure whose hem recedes further to the west with every year that passes, eaten away along its borders ...[20]

Of those who have moved out here in the past hundred years or so, the Goncourt brothers were among the first. In 1868 they left the rue Saint-Georges and came to the house which still stands at 67 boulevard de Montmorency, and which is now the headquarters of the Académie Goncourt.[21] It was here that Jules died of syphilis two years later and here, on the second floor, that writers such as Zola, Daudet, Maupassant, Huysmans and Gautier met together in Goncourt's so-called 'Grenier', the literary salon he started in 1885.

But the vogue for retreating to Auteuil goes back far beyond the 19th century. Just off the rue d'Auteuil is the rue Boileau, where the poet himself bought a house in 1685 on the site of the present no. 26. Here, in declining health, he looked after his garden and received his friends, 'happy as a king', said Racine, 'in his fastness, or rather in his hostelry at Auteuil'.

The sense of this as a privileged region, foreign ground to the Parisian masses, is caught in a brief anecdote which André Gide set down in his *Journal* for 2 June 1930:

> I remember that one day, on my way to see my poor niece shortly before her end, I took a taxi.
>
> 'To the hospital in rue Boileau,' I say to the driver. He asks me:
>
> 'What number?'
>
> 'I don't know. But you must know it ... After all!—the hospital ...' Then, turning round and in a tone of voice that mingled hatred, scorn, irony, and rancour:
>
> 'For us, it's Lariboisière.'*
>
> And these innocent syllables, pronounced with the drawl of the Paris street-urchin, took on the ring of a death-knell.
>
> 'Go on!' I told him. 'People die in private hospitals just the same as in the wards.'
>
> But his remark had sent a cold shiver down my back.[22]

The rue Boileau was not alone in providing a refuge for 17th-century writers weary of the city. A short way off, in what is now the avenue Théophile-Gautier, Molière lived for six years on the site of the present no. 62, where he rented a first-floor apartment in 1667 and moved in with his baby daughter. It was here, towards the end of the same year, that he wrote *Amphytrion*.

The house was a meeting place for many of Molière's friends, including Boileau, La Fontaine, Racine and La Bruyère. One more than usually convivial evening, recorded in

* The public hospital on the boulevard de la Chapelle. See p. 197.

the memoirs of the actor Baron, later became known as the 'souper d'Auteuil'. Towards the end of it most of Molière's guests, drunk on wine and philosophy ('Que notre vie est peu de chose ... qu'elle est remplie de traverses!'), decided to commit suicide and left *en masse* for the river. Molière finally dissuaded them on the grounds that 'un si beau projet' should properly be carried out during the day when all the world could witness it. The would-be suicides agreed on reflection that between eight and nine the following morning would perhaps be a better time, and so retired to bed.

Three centuries later the tone of literary evenings in Auteuil no doubt tends to be less extravagant, but the avenue Théophile-Gautier has not entirely lost its appeal to men of letters. For forty years, until his death in 1970, another of its residents was François Mauriac, author of such books as *Thérèse Desqueyroux* (1927) and *Le mystère Frontenac* (1933) and winner of the Nobel prize for literature in 1952. The house in which he lived can still be seen at no. 38.

It is an unlovely building, particularly when compared with the pretty house in which Balzac once lived in the nearby rue Raynouard. Much the most interesting literary monument in the area, this has now become the musée Balzac (47 rue Raynouard). It was the writer's home for five and a half years. In flight, as usual, from his creditors, and less than eager to do service in the National Guard, Balzac moved here in September 1841 under the name of M. de Brugnol. In these circumstances, it was one of the attractions of the house that it had two exits, one onto the rue Raynouard, the other onto the rue du Roc (now rue Berton). Working his usual manic schedule and sustained by endless cups of coffee, Balzac managed to write some of his finest novels during this period, including *La rabouilleuse* (1841–2), *Splendeurs et misères des courtisanes* (1843), *La cousine Bette* (1846), *Le cousin Pons* (1847). To do this he had to follow a regime which would have killed anyone with less stamina: rising at midnight, he worked for eight hours, took quarter of an hour for a meal, went back to work until five in the afternoon, dined, then took six hours sleep in preparation for the same round on the following day.

The museum which has been established inside his house

contains a number of pictures, letters and editions of the novelist's work, as well as cherished objects like the famous turquoise cane and a handsome pair of embroidered braces. The red and white *cafetière de Balzac*, in which he used to heat up his coffee, is displayed in the study.

The Eiffel Tower

Sitting in the garden of Balzac's house one catches a glimpse across the river of what has become Paris's most famous landmark—a sight that Balzac himself never saw. In a remarkably short space of time the Eiffel Tower has become throughout the world a symbol of Paris more powerfully evocative than any other. With characteristic flair the cultural critic Roland Barthes set out to examine this phenomenon:

> Maupassant often lunched at the restaurant in the Tower, though he didn't care much for the food: *It's the only place in Paris*, he used to say, *where I don't have to see it*. And it's true that you must take endless precautions, in Paris, not to see the Eiffel Tower; whatever the season, through mist and cloud, on overcast days or in sunshine, in rain—wherever you are, whatever the landscape of roofs, domes, or branches separating you from it, *the Tower is there*. [...]
> The Tower is also present to the entire world. First of all as a universal symbol of Paris, it is everywhere on the globe where Paris is to be stated as an image; from the Midwest to Australia, there is no journey to France which isn't made, somehow, in the Tower's name, no schoolbook, poster, or film about France which fails to propose it as the major sign of a people and of a place: it belongs to the universal language of travel. Further: beyond its strictly Parisian statement, it touches the most general human image-repertoire: its simple, primary shape confers upon it the vocation of an infinite cipher: in turn and according to the appeals of our imagination, the symbol of Paris, of modernity, of communication, of science or of the 19th century, rocket, stem, derrick, phallus, lightning rod or insect, confronting the great itineraries of our dreams, it is the inevit-

The Place de la Concorde in 1829

A nineteenth-century view of the Longchamp waterfall in the Bois de Boulogne

15 The cabaret of the Chat Noir; Rodolphe Salis standing

able sign; just as there is no Parisian glance which is not compelled to encounter it, there is no fantasy which fails, sooner or later, to acknowledge its form and to be nourished by it. [...]

Like the devil Asmodeus, by rising above Paris, the visitor to the Tower has the illusion of raising the enormous lid which covers the private lives of millions of human beings; the city then becomes an intimacy whose functions, i.e., whose connections he deciphers; on the great polar axis, perpendicular to the horizontal curve of the river, three zones stacked one after the other, as though along a prone body, three functions of human life: at the top, at the foot of Montmartre, pleasure; at the centre, around the Opera, materiality, business, commerce; toward the bottom, at the foot of the Panthéon, knowledge, study; then, to the right and left, enveloping this vital axis like two protective muffs, two large zones of habitation, one residential, the other blue-collar; still farther, two wooded strips, Boulogne and Vincennes. [...]

For the tourist who climbs the Tower, however mild he may be, Paris laid out before his eyes by an individual and deliberate act of contemplation is still something of the Paris confronted, defied, possessed by Rastignac. Hence, of all the sites visited by the foreigner or the provincial, the Tower is the first obligatory monument; it is a Gateway, it marks the transition to a knowledge: one must sacrifice to the Tower by a rite of inclusion from which, precisely, the Parisian alone can excuse himself: the Tower is indeed the site which allows one to be incorporated into a race, and when it regards Paris, it is the very essence of the capital it gathers up and proffers to the foreigner who has paid to it his initiational tribute.[23]

Built for the Exposition Universelle of 1889, the tower excited considerable opposition among the artists and writers of the time, several of whom, including Maupassant, Leconte de Lisle and Dumas fils, signed a petition against it. 'A hollow candlestick' was Huysmans' phrase. It is surprising in this context that the attitude of Edmond de Goncourt was by no means one of unmixed disdain. He would have had little time for Cocteau's later claim that it was the Notre-Dame of the left bank, but he was nonetheless sensitive to a certain eerie beauty in the unfamiliar structure. Walking back on the evening of 6 May 1889 from the rue d'Amsterdam to his house in Auteuil, he was caught up in the celebrations to mark the opening of the Exhibition:

> A mauve sky, which the illuminations filled with something like the glow of an enormous fire—the sound of countless footsteps creating the effect of the rushing of great waters—the crowds all black, that reddish, burnt-paper black of present-day crowds—a sort of intoxication on the faces of the women, many of whom were queuing up outside the lavatories, their bladders bursting with excitement—the Place de la Concorde an apotheosis of white light, in the middle of which the obelisk shone with the rosy colour of a champagne ice—the Eiffel Tower looking like a beacon left behind on earth by a vanished generation, a generation of men ten cubits tall.[24]

Some two months later he returned to have dinner there, and afterwards walked round the exhibits set up on the Champ-de-Mars, amongst them a replica of an Egyptian village—the rue du Caire:

> This evening I dined on the platform of the Eiffel Tower with the Charpentiers, the Hermants, the Dayots, the Zolas, etc. Going up in the lift, I had a feeling in the pit of my stomach as if I were on a ship at sea, but no dizziness. Up there, we were afforded a realization, beyond anything imaginable on ground level, of the greatness, the extent, the Babylonian immensity of Paris, with odd buildings glowing in the light of the setting sun with the colour of Roman stone, and among the calm, sweeping lines of the horizon the steep, jagged silhouette of Montmartre looking in the dusky sky like an illuminated ruin.
> We talked about the Javanese women, and when I mentioned their rather repulsive yellow flesh, Zola said: 'It has a softness you don't find in European flesh.' And he finished

his sentence by squeezing his nose, which in the grip of his sensual fingers took on the appearance of a piece of indiarubber.

A peculiar sensation, rather like that of taking a header into space, the sensation of coming down those open-work steps in the darkness, plunging every now and then into an infinite void, and one feels like an ant coming down the rigging of a man-of-war, rigging which has turned to iron.

And there we were in the Rue du Caire, where every evening all the erotic curiosity of Paris is concentrated, in the Rue du Caire, with its obscene-looking ass-drivers, with its big Africans in lascivious postures, gazing lecherously at the women who go by, with its excited crowds reminding one of cats pissing on hot coals—the Rue du Caire, a street which could be called Rutting Street.[25]

The Faubourg Saint-Germain

The Eiffel Tower stands on the margin of the 7th arrondissement, the heart of which is the Faubourg Saint-Germain. Rue de Grenelle, rue de Varenne, rue du Bac—it is around these streets that one finds the sober hôtels which for the past two centuries have sheltered the Parisian nobility. When William Cole visited the city in 1765, it was already well established as the most fashionable quarter of Paris. His friend Horace Walpole, son of the British Prime Minister and author of *The Castle of Otranto* (1764) was living in the faubourg at the time of Cole's arrival. The newcomer hurried round to see him, but found him practically immobile, half-crippled by gout:

> At Noon he was disposed to take an Airing, in order to better his Health, & to show me about the City of Paris; so wrapping his Legs in Flannel, & being helped into his Coach, or as they call them half-Coaches, which hold but 2 Persons, who set opposite one to the other, (his *Vis-a-Vis*), he carried me all over that whole Quarter of the City which is called the Faubourg St Germain, reckoned the politest Part of the Town, & where all the Hôtels of any Consequence are situated, & where all the Foreigners of any Distinction are lodged ...[26]

Unable to get out of his coach, Walpole sends in cards to a number of resident Englishmen, including the British ambassador and the politician and pamphleteer John Wilkes who, Cole reminds us, was living in banishment at the time 'for seditious and blasphemous writings'. (His exile had been enforced by issue no. 45 of his anti-Government journal *The North Briton* and by the publication of his *Essay on Woman*, judged obscene.)

Amongst the dwellings of the rich and noble, discretion can command a higher price than elsewhere. It was probably for this reason that an earlier visitor to Paris, Dr Martin Lister, could note the prevalence of bills advertising unobtrusive medical services for the common affliction:

> The *Pox* here is the great Business of the Town; a Disease which in some measure hath contributed to the ruin of Physick here, as in *London*. This secret Service hath introduced little contemptible Animals of all sorts into Business, and hath given them occasion to insult Families, after they had once the Knowledge of these Misfortunes. And it is for this Reason the Quacks here, as with us, do thrive vastly into great Riches beyond any of the Physicians, by treating privately these Calamities.

> It was a pleasant Diversion to me to read upon the Walls every where about the Town, but more particularly in the *Fauxbourg* of St. *Germain*, the Quacks Bills printed in great Uncial Letters.

As,

De par l'Ordre du Roy.
Remede infallible & commode pour la
gerison des maladies secretes sans
gardar la chambre.

Another,

Par permission de Roy.
Manniere tres aisee & tres sure pour guerir
sans incommodite, & sans que persone en
appercoive, les maladies veneriennes, &c.

[...]

By these Bills it is evident, there is yet a certain Modesty and Decorum left in the Concealing this Disease, even amongst the *French*; They would be Cured secretly, and as though nothing were doing; which those Wretches highly promote.[27]

Lister's irreverent amusement is a far cry from the tone of a later writer who became literature's high priest of the Faubourg Saint-Germain. For Marcel Proust it was an enchanted region, the magic circle within which all life's fugitive goals seemed to be contained. At the start of *Le côté de Guermantes* (1920–21) Marcel and his family have come to live in a flat that forms part of the hôtel de Guermantes. For Marcel the nearness of the exalted Guermantes family is intoxicating:

How could their dining-room, their dim gallery upholstered in red plush, into which I could see sometimes from our kitchen window, have failed to possess in my eyes the mysterious charm of the Faubourg Saint-Germain, to form part of it in an essential fashion, to be geographically situated within it, since to have been entertained to dinner in that room was to have gone into the Faubourg Saint-Germain, to have breathed its atmosphere, since the people who, before going to table, sat down by the side of Mme. de Guermantes on the leather-covered sofa in that gallery were all of the Faubourg Saint-Germain. [...]
As for the tiny strip of garden that stretched between high walls at the back of the house, where on summer evenings Mme de Guermantes had liqueurs and orangeade brought out after dinner, how could I not have felt that to sit there of an evening, between nine and eleven, on its iron chairs— endowed with a magic as potent as the leathern sofa— without inhaling the breezes peculiar to the Faubourg Saint-Germain was as impossible as to take a siesta in the oasis of Figuig without thereby being necessarily in Africa. Only imagination and belief can differentiate from the rest certain objects, certain people, and can create an atmosphere. Alas, those picturesque sites, those natural accidents, those local

curiosities, those works of art of the Faubourg Saint-Germain, never probably should I be permitted to set my feet among them. And I must content myself with a shiver of excitement as I sighted, from the deep sea (and without the least hope of ever landing there) like an outstanding minaret, like the first palm, like the first signs of some exotic industry or vegetation, the well-trodden doormat of its shore.[28]

When at last he does make shore, Marcel inevitably finds that it is not the magic circle of his imagination, for this, by definition, remains always a hair's breadth beyond reach. But his vision of the Faubourg Saint-Germain was not altogether eccentric; the strain of religious imagery with which he imbues it had already suggested itself to another writer much preoccupied with the nuances of social intercourse. In *The American* (1877), Henry James's hero, Christopher Newman, makes his way to one of the hôtels in the rue de l'Université to see the woman whom a friend has fixed on as a prospective bride for him. If you have wandered through these streets in the dead hours of a Sunday afternoon, you will recognise the atmosphere that James describes:

He walked across the Seine, late in the summer afternoon, and made his way through those gray and silent streets of the Faubourg St. Germain, whose houses present to the outer world a face as impassive and as suggestive of the concentration of privacy within as the blank walls of Eastern seraglios. Newman thought it a queer way for rich people to live; his ideal of grandeur was a splendid façade, diffusing its brilliance outward too, irradiating hospitality. The house to which he had been directed had a dark, dusty, painted portal, which swung open in answer to his ring. It admitted him into a wide, gravelled court, surrounded on three sides with closed windows, and with a doorway facing the street, approached by three steps and surmounted by a tin canopy. The place was all in the shade; it answered to Newman's conception of a convent.[29]

Sainte-Clotilde

For many of the inhabitants of these hallowed streets the local church is the église de Sainte-Clotilde, which stands in a small square opposite what was once the house of Walpole's friend Mme du Deffand and is now the Ministry of War. Worship here can never have been quite the same for some of them after one particular service in January 1932. Henry Miller was on the point of leaving Paris to take up an unlikely post as *répétiteur d'anglais* at a lycée in Dijon:

> The night before I left we had a good time. About dawn it began to snow: we walked about from one quarter to another taking a last look at Paris. Passing through the Rue St. Dominique we suddenly fell upon a little square and there was the Eglise Ste.-Clotilde. People were going to mass. Fillmore, whose head was still a little cloudy, was bent on going to mass too. 'For the fun of it!' as he put it. I felt somewhat uneasy about it; in the first place I had never attended a mass, and in the second place I looked seedy and felt seedy. Fillmore, too, looked rather battered, even more disreputable than myself; his big slouch hat was on assways and his overcoat was still full of sawdust from the last joint we had been in. However, we marched in. The worst they could do would be to throw us out.
>
> I was so astounded by the sight that greeted my eyes that I lost all uneasiness. It took me a little while to get adjusted to the dim light. I stumbled around behind Fillmore, holding his sleeve. A weird, unearthly noise assailed my ears, a sort of hollow drone that rose up out of the cold flagging. A huge, dismal tomb it was with mourners shuffling in and out. A sort of antechamber to the world below. Temperature about 55 or 60 Fahrenheit. No music except this undefinable dirge manufactured in the subcellar—like a million heads of cauliflower wailing in the dark. People in shrouds were chewing away with that hopeless, dejected look of beggars who hold out their hands in a trance and mumble an unintelligible appeal.
>
> That this sort of thing existed I knew, but then one also

knows that there are slaughterhouses and morgues and dissecting rooms. One instinctively avoids such places. [...]

We were moving about from one spot to another, surveying the scene with that clearheadedness which comes after an all-night session. We must have made ourselves pretty conspicuous shuffling about that way with our coat collars turned up and never once crossing ourselves and never once moving our lips except to whisper some callous remark. Perhaps everything would have passed off without notice if Fillmore hadn't insisted on walking past the altar in the midst of the ceremony. He was looking for the exit, and he thought while he was at it, I suppose, that he would take a good squint at the holy of holies, get a close-up on it, as it were. We had gotten safely by and were marching towards a crack of light which must have been the way out when a priest suddenly stepped out of the gloom and blocked our path. Wanted to know where we were going and what we were doing. We told him politely enough that we were looking for the exit. We said 'exit' because at the moment we were so flabbergasted that we couldn't think of the French for exit. Without a word of response he took us firmly by the arm and, opening the door, a side door it was, he gave us a push and out we tumbled into the blinding light of day. It happened so suddenly and unexpectedly that when we hit the sidewalk we were in a daze.[30]

The rue de Lille and quai Voltaire

A couple of minutes walk from the church, just off the rue Saint-Dominique, is the place du Palais-Bourbon, where Maria Edgeworth stayed when she visited Paris in 1820: 'Our apartments here are in the house of a Russian Countess whom I have never yet had the time to see notwithstanding a multitude of civil messages ... Being at the corner of the Place Bourbon the two windows give varieties of view—it is just opposite the beautiful Palais Bourbon ...' .[31]

On her previous trip in 1802 Maria Edgeworth had stayed a short distance down the road from the Palais Bourbon in the rue de Lille. It was a street in which both Stendhal and Mérimée were later to take up residence. Stendhal lived here only briefly,[32] but Prosper Mérimée made his home on the second floor of no. 52 for the last eighteen years of his life. A fortnight before his death, bitterly disappointed by the course of France's humiliating war with Prussia, he went down to Cannes where he died on 23 September 1870. Within a few months his home in the rue de Lille had been soaked in petrol and fired by the *pétroleuses* of the Commune. All his papers and belongings were destroyed. The arson was probably a revenge of sorts for the close connections Mérimée had maintained with the government of Napoleon III and the Empress Eugénie.

From the rue de Lille it is only a step to the historic quai Voltaire. A stroll past the elegant line of galleries and antique shops will also take you past the house at no. 25 lived in first by Alfred de Musset and later by the novelist Henri de Montherlant (1896–1972). A few doors further along is the Hotel du Quai Voltaire at no. 19, where Baudelaire lived from 1856 to 1858 while working on *Les fleurs du mal* and where Oscar Wilde later stayed for a few weeks in February 1883. Finally, at no. 9, stands the hôtel where the father of Anatole France had his bookshop. It was here that France spent much of his early life. 'I have preserved,' he wrote afterwards, 'a charming memory of this fine quai Voltaire where I developed a taste for the arts.' Twenty years later Rudyard Kipling occasionally ventured across to the left bank, where he too made early contact with the book-boxes of the quai Voltaire, 'then filled with savage prints and lithographs of the war of '70'.

As often as not, those Paris streets which are named after eminent men of letters have little prior connection with their patrons, but on the wall of 27 quai Voltaire a plaque records that it was in this house that Voltaire himself died on 30 May 1778. He had originally moved into an apartment here in 1723 but was soon driven out by the noise. Half a century later, when he returned to Paris in February 1778, he again came to live here for the few weeks that remained to him. He died in the first-floor apartment overlooking the courtyard, opposite the door which opens onto the rue de Beaune. The plaque is not alone in recording his passage; today the ground floor of the building is occupied by the Restaurant Voltaire.

Saul Bellow in the rue Vaneau

The antique shops which line the quai Voltaire, like the high-tech shops of the nearby boulevard, are a symptom of modern Paris. For the American novelist Saul Bellow they are also a symptom of Paris in decline. Revisiting the places he had known in the late forties, when he lived on the rue Vaneau, he was led to meditate gloomily on the changes that have overtaken this part of the city:

> High rents have done for the family bistros that once served delicious, inexpensive lunches. A certain decrepit loveliness is giving way to unattractive, over-priced, over-decorated newness. Dense traffic—the small streets make you think of Yeats's 'mackerel-crowded seas'—requires an alertness incompatible with absent-minded rambling. Dusty old shops in which you might lose yourself for a few hours are scrubbed up now and sell pocket computers and high-fidelity equipment. Stationers who once carried notebooks with excellent paper now offer a flimsy product that lets the ink through. Very disappointing. Cabinet-makers and other small artisans once common are hard to find.
>
> My neighbour, the *emballeur* on the rue de Verneuil, disappeared long ago. This cheerful specialist wore a smock and beret and, as he worked in an unheated shop, his big face was stung raw. He kept a cold butt-end in the corner of his mouth—one seldom sees the *mégots* in this new era of prosperity. A pet three-legged hare, slender in profile, fat in the hindquarters, stirred lopsidedly among the crates. But there is no more demand for hand-hammered crates. Progress has eliminated all such simple trades. It has replaced them with boutiques that sell costume jewellery, embroidered linens or goosedown bedding. In each block there are three or four *antiquaires*. Who would have thought that Europe contained so much old junk? Or that, the servant class having disappeared, hearts nostalgic for the bourgeois epoch would hunt so eagerly for Empire breakfronts, Récamier sofas and curule chairs? ...'[33]

CHAPTER 6

Northern Paris

The rue d'Amsterdam and rue de Rome

'A mad affair, drenched in absinthe and given a dramatic touch every now and then by a few knife-thrusts.'[1] This, according to Goncourt, was the relationship between Alphonse Daudet and Marie Rieu. Its scene was the rue d'Amsterdam, and it has the hallmarks of northern Paris.

Daudet had arrived at the Gare d'Austerlitz, cold and hungry, in November 1857. Though living on the left bank in the rue de Tournon, he tramped nightly across the city to enjoy the literary atmosphere of the Brasserie at 9 rue des Martyrs. In this somewhat dissolute setting the delicate beauty of the youth from Provence quickly attracted notice. Amongst the women who hung around the Brasserie there was one whose attention was caught immediately: 'Regardez-moi, voyons ... J'aime la couleur de vos yeux ... Comment vous appelez-vous?'[2]

To the displeasure of Daudet's wife he later described the whole relationship in a novel of thinly veiled autobiography called *Sapho* (1884). Subtitled 'Parisian Manners', it is a bitter-sweet elegy for the writer's youth and for the intimately Parisian context of the relationship.

Marie Rieu was already in her mid-thirties when they met, Daudet was still in his teens. They needed somewhere inexpensive to live and the cluster of streets, named after European cities, which had grown up around the Gare Saint-Lazare seemed an obvious area to choose. Together they set up house just beside the station at 24 rue d'Amsterdam. The zinc canopy over the balcony has gone and a new floor has been added, but

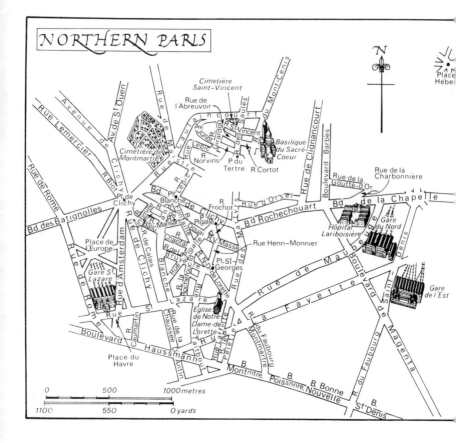

otherwise the building remains much as Daudet described it in *Sapho*. The first to see it was Marie—or Fanny, as she becomes in the novel:

> 'This time, I think I've found it ... rue d'Amsterdam, just opposite the station ... Three rooms and a big balcony ... It's a tall building, five floors ... but you can carry me up.'
> [...]

The flat was rented at once and pronounced charming, in spite of the arrangement of its rooms which resulted in the kitchen and the sitting-room opening onto a back courtyard where the smell of slops and chlorine rose from a tavern, in spite of the bedroom which gave onto the noisy, sloping street and which was shaken day and night by the jolting of wagons, dray carts, cabs and omnibuses, in spite of the piercing whistle of trains arriving and departing, along with all the din of the Gare Saint-Lazare which across the road unfurled its huge glass roofs the colour of dirty water. But there was the advantage of knowing that the train was at hand, and with it Saint-Cloud, Ville-d'Avray, Saint-Germain. The green refuges along the banks of the Seine were almost under their terrace. For they had a terrace, a wide and convenient one, which thanks to the munificence of the previous tenants was furnished with a striped zinc canopy. Under the drumming of the winter rain it was sad, but in summer it would be just the spot for dinner in the open air—like being in a mountain chalet.[3]

Later no. 24 gained a different sort of literary distinction when it became 'la Taverne anglaise', a restaurant frequented by Huysmans in the 1880s and depicted by him in À rebours. Des Esseintes sits waiting here to catch the boat-train to London; but then he finds that the typical English atmosphere of the place—robust women stuffing themselves with pie, sombrely dressed men discussing the weather, gross portions of food served with pints of ale—has in itself been enough to satisfy his thirst for foreign travel. He returns home weary but contented.

The rue d'Amsterdam seems to have tempted writers from the start. In its early days both Heinrich Heine and the elder Dumas lived there,[4] and in 1860, a year before the arrival of Daudet and Marie Rieu, Baudelaire had been living next door in the third-floor apartment at no. 22, depressed and still struggling with his translation of the tales of Edgar Allan Poe.

Along the other side of the Gare Saint-Lazare the rue de Rome runs up beside the railway track and follows it out towards the north-west of the city. It is an uninspiring street and to reach no. 89 you must walk far enough to cross the boulevard des Batignolles. Beside a sober building which overlooks the railway cutting a large plaque records that the symbolist poet Stéphane Mallarmé (1842–98) lived in this house from the year 1875. It was here on the fourth floor that he held his famous 'mardis', the Tuesday gatherings which over the years attracted most of the central figures of late 19th-century French literature, as well as a number of Englishmen such as

Swinburne, Oscar Wilde and George Moore. ('Our age has grown too noisy', wrote André Gide in 1925, 'for it to be easy now to imagine the calm and almost religious atmosphere of that place.')[5] For most of this period Mallarmé was teaching English at the lycée Condorcet (65 rue Caumartin), where one of his pupils was the writer Daniel Halévy:

> Mallarmé came from his small flat in the rue de Rome, where he had perhaps left the young Claudel or the young Valéry, and then crossed the place and the pont de l'Europe. Each day, he told George Moore, he was gripped by the temptation to throw himself from the top of the bridge onto the tracks, in order finally to escape the mediocrity in which he was imprisoned. [...]
>
> He sat there in the teacher's chair; and we, in front of him, sat there on our benches, and we had the impression that, just as we did, he came to class with no great taste for it and no great repugnance, driven by the force of circumstance, and that he remained as uncommitted, as much an outsider, as we ourselves, quick, like us, to introduce in secret mysterious, fruitful absences. Throughout the daily schedule, the explanations of grammar, the short exercises (with him they were always short) dictated in a low, musical voice, he continued (as we did ourselves) obstinately to follow some dream, similar perhaps to our own.[6]

Notre-Dame de Lorette

In his walk to the lycée Condorcet, Mallarmé must have daily passed the entrance of the Restaurant Trapp. At 109 rue Saint-Lazare, it stood more or less opposite the rue d'Amsterdam on the edge of the place du Havre. A bystander on the evening of 16 April 1877 could have seen most of the major French novelists of the day entering its doors, for the Restaurant Trapp was holding an unusual dinner.* Those present included Flaubert, Zola, Maupassant, Huysmans and Gon-

---

* Amongst other items on the menu were Potage purée Bovary, Truite saumonée à la fille Elisa, and Liqueurs de l'Assommoir, each in honour of one of the most celebrated novels by Flaubert, Goncourt and Zola.

court, and the occasion marked the founding of the Naturalist Movement in literature.

The site was well chosen. If there is a sense in which the Marais belongs to the 17th century or Montparnasse to the generation between the wars, then this area of Paris which makes up the 9th arrondissement belongs to the authors associated with Naturalism. It is not a part of the city much talked of in Michelin or the Guide Bleu; there are few museums, fewer monuments; its history is brief and unremarkable. And yet it had an obvious appeal for those writers who were deliberately turning towards the murkier underside of Paris life.

Walk north from the boulevard Haussmann at dusk, when the lights come on and the evening shoppers take to the streets. This was the time at which, from the mid-years of the 19th century, the girls of the *quartier Bréda* (the neighbourhood of the rue Frochot and the rue Henri-Monnier) came down to ply their trade on the Grands Boulevards, their nightly passage marked by 'the chink of jade, the scent of musk, the rustle of silk'. It is the world of Nana, Zola's superb courtesan. Born in poverty in the rue de la Goutte-d'Or, she grows up to become a creature of devastating sexual power. Exploiting her one talent with naive ruthlessness, she cuts a path through every level of Parisian society, moving at will between the *beau monde* of the boulevards and the *demi-monde* that Zola brilliantly evokes in the streets which radiate north from Notre-Dame de Lorette. In one of the lulls in her career, she and her lesbian friend Satin take to spending their nights on the streets, using as a base Satin's little room on the rue La Rochefoucauld:

Along both sides of the rue Notre-Dame-de-Lorette, two lines of women, keeping close to the shops, holding up their skirts, their heads bent forward, hastened towards the boulevards with a businesslike air, bestowing not a glance on the displays in the windows. It was the hungry onslaught of the *quartier Bréda* in the first flare of the gas-lamp. Nana and Satin always passed close to the church and continued along the rue Le Peletier. Then, a hundred yards from the café Riche, they would let fall the trains of their dresses, which until that moment they had held carefully in their hands. After that, regardless of the dust, sweeping the pavement and swinging their hips, they would walk slowly along, moving slower still whenever they came into the flood of light from some large café. Holding their heads high, laughing loudly, and looking back after the men who turned to glance at them, they were in their element. Their whitened faces, set off by the red of their lips and the black of their eye-lashes, assumed in the shadow the disturbing charm of some imitation Eastern bazaar held in the open street.

Until twelve o'clock, in spite of the jostling of the crowd, they promenaded gaily along, merely muttering 'stupid fool!' now and again behind the backs of the awkward fellows whose heels caught in their flounces. They exchanged familiar nods with the café waiters, lingered sometimes to talk at the tables, accepting drinks which they swallowed slowly, while waiting till the people came out of the theatres. But, as night advanced, if they had not made one or two trips to the rue La Rochefoucauld, their pursuit became more eager—they no longer picked and chose. Beneath the trees of the now gloomy and almost deserted boulevards, ferocious bargains were made, and occasionally the sound of oaths and blows could be heard; whilst fathers of families, with their wives and daughters, used to such encounters, would pass sedately by without hastening their footsteps.

Later, Nana and Satin would adjourn to the rue du Faubourg Montmartre. There, until two o'clock in the morning, the lights of the restaurants, the brasseries and the pork butchers, blazed away, whilst a swarm of women hung about the doors of the cafés; it was the last bright and animated corner of nocturnal Paris, the last market for the contracts of a night, where business was openly transacted among the various groups, from one end of the street to the other, as though along the open corridor of a brothel. And on nights when they returned home unsuccessful, they wrangled with each other. The rue Notre-Dame-de-Lorette stretched out dark and deserted, with only the occasional

The Lapin Agile in 1872

Interior of the Lapin Agile shortly before the First World War, showing
the plaster crucifix and the painting by Picasso to the left of it. Frédé
plays the guitar

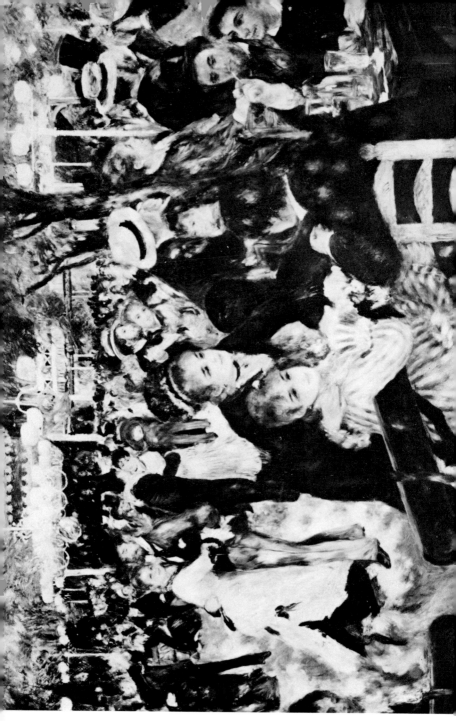

18 The Moulin de la Galette (1876) by Renoir

shadow of some woman dragging herself along; it was the belated return of the girls of the neighbourhood, exasperated by an evening of enforced idleness, and still looking for custom as they argued in a hoarse voice with some drunk who had lost his way, and whom they detained at the corner of the rue Bréda or the rue Fontaine.[7]

Strangely, these were not the women who were primarily responsible for the notoriety of this new area. By 1840 the word 'lorette' had slipped into the language as a synonym for a rather different type of person. It was in the 1830s that the rue Notre-Dame-de-Lorette was constructed, and in an article written a few years later Théophile Gautier described how the new houses had been let at low rent—usually to the sort of young girls who would not be too fastidious about the damp walls—on the one condition that the tenants put curtains in their windows in order to give the false impression of an area already well populated. The girls who took up the offer and settled here came to be known as *lorettes*. The typical *lorette*, Gautier suggests, was aged between fifteen and twenty-nine; she had no job and disdained the restricted life of the kept woman. She preferred instead 'to take the chances of a life of complicated adventures and multiple loves'.[8] For the provincial bourgeois whose son was destined for Paris, this represented a threat far more insidious than the straightforward commerce of Nana and Satin, as the author of *Paris inconnu* (1861), Privat d'Anglemont, was well aware:

As soon as one mentions the name of Notre-Dame de Lorette in the provinces, maidens lower their eyes, mothers cross themselves, girls of marriageable age look at you askance. If you have the misfortune to say in conversation: I went to see a friend living in the rue Notre-Dame-de-Lorette, you are finished. The prefect closes his doors to you, the mayor no longer greets you, the priest will never accept you as his partner at cards, the justice of the peace forbids his son to hunt with you. By contrast, at these words, the young men will surround you, seeking your friendship, trying to make you talk, hoping that you will read them in secret a few pages of that mysterious book called Notre-Dame de Lorette.[9]

Not surprisingly, it was only the more raffish of the English travellers who found their way up to this part of Paris—or at least who admitted in print to having done so. When Thackeray went to live in Paris in 1833 he was still only twenty-two, but he had already gambled away a good part of his fortune and lost the rest in a business failure. At the time the future author of *Vanity Fair* saw himself as a painter and accordingly chose to settle in the area round Notre-Dame de Lorette:

> The life of the young artist here is the easiest, merriest, dirtiest existence possible. He comes to Paris, probably at sixteen, from his province; his parents settle forty pounds a year on him, and pay his master; he establishes himself in the Pays Latin, or in the new quarter of Notre Dame de Lorette (which is quite peopled with painters); he arrives at his atelier at a tolerably early hour, and labours among a score of companions as merry and poor as himself. Each gentleman has his favourite tobacco-pipe; and the pictures are painted in the midst of a cloud of smoke, and a din of puns and choice French slang, and a roar of choruses, of which no one can form an idea who has not been present at such an assembly.[10]

Details of this kind were the beginnings of a mythology of Bohemian Paris which, in such books as George Du Maurier's *Trilby* (1894), survived almost unchanged to the end of the century.

Zola in the rue Ballu

Yet there was more to it than myth. A striking number of the streets around the rue Notre-Dame-de-Lorette were in the last half of the century inhabited by writers. (Gautier, de Nerval, Heine, Maupassant, Murger, Dumas, Hugo all at some time lived in the area.) It was in one of these streets, in the building at 23 rue Ballu, that Emile Zola took an apartment to supplement his country property at Médan. Edmond de Goncourt attended the house-warming on Wednesday 3 April 1878:

House-warming dinner at Zola's.

A study in which the young master works on a massive Portuguese throne in Brazilian rosewood, a bedroom with a carved four-poster bed and twelfth-century stained-glass in the window, tapestries showing greenish saints on the walls and ceilings, altar frontals over the doors, a whole houseful of ecclesiastical bric-à-brac: all this makes a somewhat eccentric setting for the author of *L'assommoir*.

He gave us a very choice, very tasty dinner, a real gourmet's dinner, including some grouse whose scented flesh Daudet compared to an old courtesan's flesh marinaded in a bidet.

Flaubert, stimulated by the food and a little drunk, reeled off, to the accompaniment of oaths and obscenities, the whole series of his ferocious, truculent truisms about the *bôrgeois*. And while he was speaking, I saw an expression of melancholy surprise on the face of my neighbour, Mme Daudet, who seemed pained, upset and at the same time disillusioned by the man's gross, intemperate unbuttoning of his nature. [...]

In the evening, the band of toadies invaded the little flat; and the archaic knick-knacks in the drawing-room and bedroom soon disappeared in the smoke of the cigars and cigarettes of the Naturalist school.[11]

Arnold Bennett in the rue de Calais

Parallel to the rue Ballu, a block north of it, is the rue de Calais, where Arnold Bennett lived while he was working on *The Old Wives' Tale* (1908). The flat he occupied was in the building in which Berlioz had died and which still stands today at no. 4. Bennett moved in here towards the end of 1903 and stayed until December 1906. 'Every afternoon', he recalls in *Sketches for Autobiography*, 'and sometimes in the evening a distant violin used to play, very badly, six bars—no more—of an air of Verdi's over and over again; never any other tune! The sound was too faint to annoy me, but it was the most melancholy thing that I have ever heard.'[12]

It was perhaps playing on the afternoon in 1905 when he received a visit from another English writer, who was at the time living on the far side of the city in Montparnasse:

> Friday, March 3rd.
> Somerset Maugham came up for tea. He has a very calm almost lethargic demeanour. He took two cups of tea with pleasure and absolutely refused a third; one knew instantly from his tone that nothing would induce him to take a third. He ate biscuits and *gaufrettes* very quickly, almost greedily, one after the other without a pause, and then suddenly stopped. He smoked two cigarettes furiously, in less time than I smoked one, and solidly declined a third. I liked him. He said he had sold a play to Liebler through Fred Kerr, on the terms of £300 down, and £100 every quarter until they produced it—in advance of royalties. I asked him if he liked the Quartier Montparnasse and he said, 'Yes; the atmosphere of it is rather like Oxford.'[13]

Bennett's journal makes no reference to a later meeting with Somerset Maugham, which Maugham himself records in *The Vagrant Mood* (1952):

> One night after we had been dining together and were sitting amid the Empire furniture* of his apartment, he said:
> 'Look here, I have a proposal to make to you.'
> 'Oh?'
> 'I have a mistress with whom I spend two nights a week. She has another gentleman with whom she spends two other nights. She likes to have her Sundays to herself and she's looking for someone who'll take the two nights she has free. I've told her about you. She likes writers. I'd like to see her nicely fixed up and I thought it would be a good plan if you took the two nights that she has vacant.'
> The suggestion startled me.
> 'It sounds rather cold-blooded to me,' I said.
> 'She's not an ignorant woman, you know,' Arnold insisted. 'Not by any manner of means. She reads a great deal,

---

* 'It was certainly not genuine,' Maugham assures us, 'but this he did not know, and he was exceedingly proud of it.'

Madame de Sévigné and all that, and she can talk very intelligently.'

But even that didn't tempt me.[14]

Dickens and George Sand in the rue de Douai

An English writer who had made his way through the same streets in the previous century was Charles Dickens. On 10 January 1856 he paid a visit to the hôtel Viardot at 50 rue de Douai. Situated almost exactly opposite the rue Vintimille, this hôtel was the home of the opera singer Pauline Viardot and her husband. Dickens had been invited there to meet George Sand,[15] but the occasion proved something of a disappointment:

> I suppose it to be impossible to imagine anybody more unlike my preconceptions than the illustrious Sand. Just the kind of woman in appearance whom you might suppose to be the Queen's monthly nurse. Chubby, matronly, swarthy, black-eyed. Nothing of the blue stocking about her, except a little final way of settling all your opinions with hers, which I take to have been acquired in the country, where she lives, and in the domination of a small circle. A singularly ordinary woman in appearance and manner. The dinner was very good and remarkably unpretending. [...] The Viardots have a house away in the new part of Paris, which looks exactly as if they had moved into it last week and were going away next. Notwithstanding which, they have lived in it eight years. The opera the very last thing on earth you would associate with the family. Piano not even opened. Her husband is an extremely good fellow, and she is as natural as it is possible to be.[16]

There is no mention in this account of another novelist who for over thirty years was also an occupant of the hôtel Viardot. The Russian writer Turgenev had formed a lifelong attachment to Pauline Viardot and from 1847 he had his own apartment on the third floor of the hôtel. Towards the end of Turgenev's life, Daudet went to visit him there:

The hôtel was furnished with tasteful luxury, a great concern both for art and for comfort. Crossing the hallway I glimpsed a picture gallery through an open door. Sweet voices, the voices of young girls, could be heard through the hangings. They alternated with the impassioned contralto voice singing *Orphée* which rose with me, filling the staircase as I climbed.

Upstairs, on the third floor, was a small apartment, draught-proofed, upholstered, as crowded with objects as a boudoir.

Turgenev had borrowed the artistic tastes of his friends: music from the wife, painting from the husband.

He was stretched out on a couch.

I sat down near him. And immediately we picked up the conversation we had been having a few days earlier.[17]

Proust in the rue Fontaine

A hundred yards or so from the site of the hôtel Viardot, the rue de Douai is intersected by the rue Fontaine. Remote from the world of *À la recherche du temps perdu*, this street nonetheless witnessed an epic moment in the sentimental education of the young Marcel Proust. In his *Pays parisiens* Daniel Halévy has left an engaging record of it. He was at the time a school-friend of Proust at the lycée Condorcet:

In the rue Fontaine, just about half-way between the rue Chaptal and the rue Mansart, there was a little dairy and in the dairy, as might be expected, a dairy-maid, but one whose proud and alluring beauty surpassed all expectation. She was called Madame Chirade, and wherever her life is drawing to a close today, I am willing to bet that she is still beautiful, so firm and pure were the features of her face and the lines of her body. Everyone admired, even respected her: surrounded by the *Moulin Rouge*, the *Rat Mort* and the *Truie qui file*, Madame Chirade was a glorious image of Montmartre at its most virtuous.

I had sung her praises to Proust; he wanted to see her. I took him to the rue Fontaine and there we stood, both of us motionless in front of the shop, looking into the interior. Madame Chirade came and went, busy serving her customers: her forearms were covered by that sort of white arm-sheath which dairy-maids wear; and her black dress and her black hair added still more to the brilliance of her face. I had not exaggerated: she was magnificent. I can still hear Proust's voice murmuring in my ear:

'How beautiful she is!'

And he added, literature rarely being far from our thoughts:

'As beautiful as Salammbô.'

Then, after a silence no doubt devoted to brief and fervent admiration, turning to me again:

'Do you think it would be possible to sleep with her?' he asked.

The idea was entirely new to me, and it both disconcerted me and inspired me with a sudden and rapid respect for the boldness of its originator. I had to confess my ignorance on the question. When we had looked our fill, we started walking again, slightly distracted, slightly thoughtful. Marcel was evidently mulling over a project and looking for some way to realize it.

'We shall need to take her some flowers,' he suggested at length.

We agreed a day and a time. Together we left the lycée, avoiding our friends; at the bottom of the rue Pigalle, a woman was selling roses; we bought an armful from her and continued on our way, slightly solemn, like soldiers preparing themselves for a difficult and dangerous mission. A few yards further and we were on the doorstep of the shop. Madame Chirade was there, standing by the counter. It was just a question of taking the plunge. My own role, I must admit, was modest; I participated as guide, spectator; neither the perils nor the hopes nor the glories of the enterprise were mine. Would Proust dare? I had my doubts. He did dare. Bravely holding out his bouquet, he walked straight up to the goddess who, somewhat startled, looked at him, allowing him to come forward. Motionless on the footpath, my wide eyes fixed on the scene, I watched the outcome. I

saw Proust approach Madame Chirade. Did he say anything, did he stammer out a sentence? I do not know, I only
remember seeing a smile cross the woman's face, and at the
same time as it smiled, the handsome face said *no*, moving
gently but firmly from right to left, left to right. Proust, I
suppose, with a look if not with a word, insisted, and
Madame Chirade, still smiling and determined, took one,
two, three steps forward, obliging Proust to retreat the same
distance. From where I stood I could only see his back and,
over his shoulder, the white paper around the flowers. But *la
belle Chirade*—what must she have seen? the moving expression of a disappointed cherub, afflicted, desolated, sup-
pliant; I can imagine the huge eyes, the lips half-open. And
indeed, there was no severity in the face of Madame Chirade; there was even a certain gentleness, but a gentleness
combined, alas, with extreme resolution. Smiling, she continued to advance, inexorably, with small, measured steps,
and Proust, defeated step by step, was soon on the pavement
beside me. I can think of no more graceful way of being put
to flight.[18]

The rue des Martyrs

Running up towards Montmartre at an angle to the rue Notre-
Dame-de-Lorette is the rue des Martyrs. For many years this
street was as notorious as its neighbour. It was dotted with
dubious bars, disreputable hotels and the sort of private apartments that were rented out for the conduct of more or less
illicit liaisons, both heterosexual and homosexual. The latter
were something of a speciality of Montmartre, which for the
last two decades of the 19th century was recognised as the
lesbian centre of Paris. Cafés like Le Rat Mort, opposite La
Nouvelle Athènes in the place Pigalle, and Le Hanneton in the
rue Pigalle were well known for a clientèle which included
women briskly attired in jacket and tie, who danced with one
another under the lights of the neighbouring *bals musette*. It
was here that Colette and her lover the marquise de Belbeuf,
'Missy', came to savour the atmosphere of life on the social
margins. The rue des Martyrs was an appropriate site for the
lesbian table d'hôte to which Satin takes Nana in Zola's novel.

But from a literary point of view the most important land-mark in the street was the Brasserie des Martyrs, where Daudet had met Marie Rieu. Of all Paris's literary cafés none has inspired more intense devotion from its patrons than the Brasserie. Situated at no. 9, about fifty yards up from the church of Notre-Dame de Lorette, decorated with mirrors and gilt, and brilliantly lit with new gas-lamps, it was one of the intellectual centres of mid-19th-century Paris and a magnet to those who had come to the city with literary aspirations.

However ambivalent he may have felt about his relationship with Marie Rieu, Daudet looked back on the Brasserie with evident nostalgia: 'How many memories are brought back by that one name, the Brasserie; how many faces seen there for the first time through the smoke, in the light of the glasses of beer.'[19] Among the habitués, he recalls, were the painter Gustave Courbet, Murger, the author of *Scènes de la vie de bohème*, Baudelaire, correct and cold, drinking English liqueurs with the designer Constantin Guys:

It would take a volume to describe the Brasserie table by table. Here, the table of thinkers—bare heads, tumbling beards, a scent of coarse tobacco, cabbage soup and phi-losophy. Further on, dark blue jackets, berets, animal cries, jokes, witticisms; these are the artists, painters and sculp-tors. [...] And then there are the women, former models, faded beauties, with strange names like Titine de Barrancy and Louise Coup-de-Couteau. They are unusual women, who have a curious refinement, having passed from hand to hand and preserved from each of their innumerable liaisons a residue of artistic knowledge. They have opinions about everything, proclaiming themselves realists or fantasists, catholics or atheists, in conformity with their lover of the moment. It is touching and absurd.[20]

Absinthe in Montmartre

The Brasserie des Martyrs was a place of intellectual fer-ment, but also, as Daudet goes on to emphasise, a place of disappointed ambitions and broken lives. A clue to some of this desolation is provided by Daudet's remark to Goncourt that his relationship with Marie Rieu was *suant d'absinthe*. Before it was banned in 1915, the enticing drink, made from an infusion of wine and wormwood, cast a powerful spell over this part of Paris. It is notable how many descriptions of the area place it in darkness or dusk or the half-light of dawn. Montmartre was no longer just the Butte—the hill, with its sleepy village at the top—it was also this night-time world that was growing up on the boulevards and side-streets around the base of the hill. At the close of the last century an Englishman, H. P. Hugh, noted this development in an article called 'The Two Montmartres':

> As the night closes in you watch with fascination the gradual streaks of light that crawl out, as avenue after avenue is lighted up, and the whole city is lined out in fire at your feet. The red sails of the Moulin Rouge swing round, the flash light from the Tour Eiffel touches the Sacré-Coeur and whitens the thousand-year-old church of Saint-Pierre. The other Montmartre awakens while the quiet inhabitants of the hill go to sleep.
>
> It is a strange grey study in nature, this midnight Montmartre. It is the doing and the done, and the done and the doing. Artists with hope before them, poets with the appreciation of some girl only, and side by side with these the hurried anxious faces of unkempt women and tired-eyed men.
>
> The sickly odour of absinthe lies heavily on the air. The 'absinthe hour' of the Boulevards begins vaguely at half-past-five, and ends just as vaguely at half-past-seven; but on the hill it never ends. Not that it is a home of the drunkard in any way; but the deadly opal drink lasts longer than anything else, and it is the aim of Montmartre to stop as long as possible on the *terrasse* of a café and watch the world go by. To spend an hour in a really typical haunt of the Bohemians is a liberal education. There is none of the reckless gaiety of the Latin quarter, but at the same time there is a grim delight in chaffing at death and bankruptcy.[21]

Hugh's description is redolent of the *fin de siècle*. Absinthe had become part of the texture of a particular life-style that flourished in Montmartre. References to it pervade the literature of the period. Zola's sketch of Nana and Satin gossiping the afternoon away in Satin's squalid little room in the rue La Rochefoucauld, while drinking absinthe to overcome depression—'pour oublier, disaient-elles'—must have represented a typical scene: around them the detritus of Satin's life; her skirts slung over the chairs, still encrusted with mud from the night before; Satin herself sunk in lethargy, waiting for the evening again, for *l'heure du gaz*.

It was to this milieu that absinthe owed its gloomy reputation, summed up in Degas' painting of the two hopeless drinkers sitting in the café de la Nouvelle Athènes at 9 place Pigalle. Yet as Daudet's memories of the Brasserie des Martyrs suggest, there was more to Montmartre cafés than the inevitable haze of absinthe. 'A liberal education' was Hugh's phrase, and it is the same image that underlies George Moore's account of café-life in the 1870s. For him the scene of Degas' painting was not just a drinking place:

> I did not go to either Oxford or Cambridge, but I went to the 'Nouvelle Athènes'. [...] With what strange, almost unnatural clearness do I see and hear—see the white face of that *café*, the white nose of that block of houses, stretching up to the Place, between two streets. I can see down the incline of those two streets, and I know what shops are there; I can hear the glass door of the *café* grate on the sand as I open it. I can recall the smell of every hour. In the morning that of eggs frizzling in butter, the pungent cigarette, coffee and bad cognac; at five o'clock the fragrant odour of absinthe; and soon after the steaming soup ascends from the kitchen; and as the evening advances, the mingled smells of cigarettes, coffee, and weak beer. A partition rising a few feet or more over the hats, separates the glass front from the main body of the *café*. The usual marble tables are there, and it is there we sat and aestheticized till two o'clock in the morning.[22]

Thackeray's arrival in Paris

The growth of this new Montmartre had only been made possible by the formation of the outer boulevards in 1864. An English visitor entering Paris in the first half of the 19th century would have seen no more than the usual trailing outskirts of a large city. Before the days of the train, the customary route lay down the rue du Faubourg Saint-Denis, between the sites of what have now become the Gare du Nord and the Gare de l'Est. Along the present line of the outer boulevards, dividing the city from the open country, was an octroi wall of white roughstone, ten feet high and three feet thick. It was at one of the barriers in this wall, at almost exactly the spot where the métro station of La Chapelle stands today, that Thackeray was stopped for inspection as he entered Paris in the 1830s:

> But, behold us at Paris! The Diligence has reached a rude-looking gate, or *grille*, flanked by two lodges; the French kings of old made their entry by this gate; some of the hottest battles of the late revolution were fought before it. At present, it is blocked by carts and peasants, and a busy crowd of men, in green, examining the packages before they enter, probing the straw with long needles. It is the Barrier of St. Denis, and the green men are the customs'-men of the city of Paris. If you are a countryman who would introduce a cow into the metropolis, the city demands twenty-four francs for such a privilege; if you have a hundred-weight of tallow candles, you must, previously, disburse three francs; if a drove of hogs, nine francs per hog. [...] In the present instance, after a momentary pause, one of the men in green mounts by the side of the conductor, and the ponderous vehicle pursues its journey.
>
> The street which we enter, that of the Faubourg St. Denis, presents a strange contrast to the dark uniformity of a London street, where everything, in the dingy and smoky atmosphere, looks as though it were painted in India-ink—black houses, black passengers, and black sky. Here, on the contrary, is a thousand times more life and colour. Before you, shining in the sun, is a long glistening line of *gutter*,—

not a very pleasing object in a city, but in a picture invaluable. On each side are houses of all dimensions and hues; some but of one storey; some as high as the tower of Babel. From these the haberdashers (and this is their favourite street) flaunt long strips of gaudy calicoes, which give a strange air of rude gaiety to the street. Milk-women, with a little crowd of gossips round each, are, at this early hour of the morning, selling the chief material of the Parisian *café-au-lait*. Gay wine-shops, painted red, and smartly decorated with vines and gilded railings, are filled with workmen taking their morning's draught. That gloomy-looking prison on your right is a prison for women; once it was a convent for Lazarists: a thousand unfortunate individuals of the softer sex now occupy that mansion: they bake, as we find in the guide-books, the bread of all the other prisons; they mend and wash the shirts and stockings of all the other prisoners; they make hooks and eyes and phosphorus boxes, and they attend chapel every Sunday—if occupation can help them, sure they have enough of it. Was it not a great stroke of the legislature to superintend the morals and linen at once, and thus keep these poor creatures continually mending?—But we have passed the prison long ago, and are at the Port St. Denis itself.[23]

Morning in the boulevard de la Chapelle

A short way along the boulevard de la Chapelle from the point at which Thackeray was stopped by customs men stand the walls of Lariboisière. Work began on the hospital only a few years after Thackeray's triumphal entry, and its sombre presence features again and again in newspaper reports of the 19th century chronicling the troubled nights of the quarter. As Louis Chevalier has remarked,[24] it is usually an *affaire de nuit*, usually a crime—a belated passer-by caught on the corner of the rue de la Chapelle and the boulevard or the corner of the rue d'Aubervilliers and the boulevard: 'The wounded man was taken to Lariboisière'.

It was at the period of the hospital's construction that Zola chose to set *L'assommoir* (1876). One of his finest novels, it is also one of the most detailed literary documents about Paris. Working-class life in the streets of northern Paris has never been more vividly realised. The desire of the Naturalists to achieve scientific objectivity in their novels was never likely to be fulfilled, but it gave a sharp focus to much of their descriptive writing. At the start of *L'assommoir*, Gervaise wakes in the early morning to find that Lantier, her man, has not returned to their hotel room:

> The hotel was in the boulevard de la Chapelle, to the left of the Barrière Poissonnière.* It was a tumbledown two-storey building, painted purple halfway up, with rotting, rainsodden shutters. Above a cracked glass lantern you could descry 'Hotel Boncoeur, Proprietor Marsouillier', painted between two windows in big yellow lettering with bits missing where damp had eaten away the plaster. The lantern bothered Gervaise, so she straightened up, still holding the handkerchief to her mouth. She looked to the right towards the boulevard de Rochechouart, where butchers in bloodstained aprons were standing about in groups in front of the slaughterhouse, and now and again the fresh breeze wafted an acrid stench of slaughtered animals. To the left her eyes ran along a stretch of avenue and stopped almost opposite at the white mass of the Lariboisière hospital, then being built. She let her gaze travel slowly along the octroi wall from one horizon to the other; behind that wall she sometimes heard in the night the screams of men being done to death. And now she stared into secluded angles and dark corners, black with damp and refuse, terrified of discovering Lantier's body lying there dead with its belly stabbed through and through. When she looked up and beyond the unending grey wall which girdled the city like a belt of desolation, she saw a great light, the golden dust of sunrise filled already with the morning roar of Paris. [...]

For two hours longer, until eight o'clock, Gervaise made

---

* i.e. just opposite the present site of the Barbès-Rochechouart mètro station. A desolate Salvation Army building stands there now; barely legible across its flaking walls are the words, written in rust-coloured paint, JESUS T'AIME. VIENS A LUI.

herself stay at the window. The shops had opened and the torrent of workmen's smocks coming down from the heights had dried up; only a few laggards were now hurrying past the barrier. The same men were still standing in the bars, drinking, coughing and spitting. After the workmen came the workgirls—polishers, dressmakers, florists, huddled up in their thin dresses, tap-tapping along the outer boulevards in threes and fours, chattering away and giggling, darting keen glances about them. Now and then there was one quite alone, thin, pale and sad-looking, staying close to the octroi wall so as to keep clear of the rivulets of muck ...[25]

Lantier returns, but the prospect of happiness can rarely be more than a dream in the world that Zola creates. His vision of these infested streets is essentially bleak.

The Gare du Nord

Next to Lariboisière, between the rue de Maubeuge and the rue du Faubourg-Saint-Denis, is the Gare du Nord. Built in the 1860s along with the Gare de l'Est, it did little to dispel a certain element of dreariness in the region. The penumbra of melancholy that gathers round the railway stations of big cities was already apparent when George Moore arrived in Paris in 1873 to study art. The scene will still be familiar to anyone who has stepped stiffly onto the platform after a night-crossing from Dover:

We all know the great grey and melancholy Gare du Nord at half past six in the morning; and the miserable carriages, and the tall, haggard city. Pale, sloppy, yellow houses; an oppressive absence of colour; a peculiar bleakness in the streets. The *ménagère* hurries down the asphalt to market; a dreadful *garçon de café*, with a napkin tied round his throat, moves about some chairs, so decrepit and so solitary that it seems impossible to imagine a human being sitting there. Where are the Boulevards? where are the Champs-Elysées? I asked myself; and feeling bound to apologize for the appearance of the city, I explained to my valet that we were passing through some by-streets, and returned to the study of a French vocabulary.[26]

Cabarets and dance-halls on the boulevard de Rochechouart

When Marya Zelli moves to a hotel near the Gare du Nord in Jean Rhys's *Quartet*, she already has memories of an earlier stay:

> ... she remembered the dingy streets, the vegetable shops kept by sleek-haired women, the bars haunted by gaily dressed little prostitutes who seemed to be perpetually making the gesture of opening their bags to powder their noses. Over the whole of the quarter the sinister and rakish atmosphere of the Faubourg Montmartre spread like some perfume.[27]

The lines catch a mingling of tones which is characteristic of the area, for if the note of melancholy recurs in the history of Montmartre, so also does the note of gaiety and colour, the note we associate with the theatres and cabarets and dance-halls. It was just to the west of Gervaise's hotel that in 1881 the painter Rodolphe Salis opened his cabaret at 84 boulevard Rochechouart. Almost at once Le Chat Noir became a resort of the literary and artistic population of the area—amongst them, the poets Verlaine and Moréas. But the cabaret had also started a new vogue among the people of fashion, who began for the first time to turn to Montmartre for their pleasures. The *beau monde* of Paris vied for the honour of being insulted by Salis. And when in 1885 Aristide Bruant took over the site, his cabaret, Le Mirliton, continued the same tradition. Striding to and fro in the red scarf and broad-brimmed felt hat immortalised by Lautrec's poster, he treated his well-bred audience with scathing contempt. In 1892 the aged Goncourt went to hear him at a private party given by the publisher Charpentier. His fierce disgust with what he saw prompted him to one of the finest portraits in the *Journal*:

> He appeared wearing a blood-red silk shirt, with a velvet jacket and long polished leather gaiters. Beneath a centre

parting, fine, regular features, dark, velvety eyes in the shadows of deep brows, a short, straight nose, a dark, matt complexion, and on this face something half feminine, half cynical male, which produces an overall impression of an enigmatic androgyne.

What he sang before the society women who were there was quite indescribable. This ignoble lyricism consisted of foul adjectives, dirty words, purulent slang, the vocabulary of sordid brothels and clinics for venereal diseases.

You had to see Bruant belching this out in his brassy voice, see him as I saw him, in profile, the look in the sinister shadow of his perfidiously gentle eye, the coal-black nostril of the tip-tilted nose, and the movements of the facial muscles, reminiscent of the jaw movements of a wild beast eating carrion.

Meanwhile I, for all that I am no prude, had the impression that I was attending a prison concert [...] And to think that those society women, without the protection of a fan, without even a blush on their cheeks, listening to the man from close to, smiled and clapped their pretty aristocratic hands at words no different from the obscene scribblings on walls from which they avert their eyes.

Oh, Bruant's songs in society drawing-rooms and dynamite in carriage entrances! These are two warning signs of the approaching end of the bourgeois age.[28]

Goncourt's reaction is consciously at odds with the spirit of the time. Bruant's songs of backstreet love and the glories of death on the guillotine, his abuse of the audience and his unashamed hustling for their money were all expressive of a vital strand of Montmartre culture, and his cabaret, which later moved down to the rue des Martyrs, remained one of the most fashionable in Paris.

The world of cabarets and dance-halls is a side of Montmartre life that has perhaps been better captured by the artists than the writers. It is the world of Renoir and Manet, of Steinlen's posters and Lunel's drawings. It is, pre-eminently, the world of Toulouse Lautrec and the dancers of the Elysée-Montmartre, the Moulin de la Galette and the Moulin Rouge.

From Bruant's cabaret it was only a step to 72 boulevard Rochechouart, the entrance to the Elysée-Montmartre. This was the prototype of all the great dance-halls of the late 19th century. With its gilded stucco, velvet hangings, crimson plush and brilliant globes of light, it had enjoyed its heyday in the mid-years of the century under Napoleon III.[29] But then in the 1880s it achieved a brief resurgence with the introduction of the can-can. The well-publicised audacity of the new dance was enough to draw a stream of pleasure-seekers out to the fringes of the city to see stars like 'Nini Patte en l'Air', Jane Avril and La Goulue.

One of the graduates of this world was George Moore's friend Marie Pellegrin. He had come across her portrait at the studio of his friend Octave Barrès and been bewitched by it. Barrès gives him a brief account of her past:

> She had run away from home at fifteen, had danced at the Elysée Montmartre.
>
> > Sa Jupe avait des trous,
> > Elle aimait des voyous,
> > Ils ont les yeux si doux.
>
> But one day a Russian prince had caught sight of her, and had built her a palace in the Champs-Elysées; but the Russian prince and his palace bored her.[30]

Nonetheless, it is to Russia that she is about to travel. At a party in Montmartre, the day before she leaves, Moore finally meets her—a young woman dressed in black, coming across the garden. His description of their meeting and of her last days communicates precisely that hectic mixture of gaiety and despair which is the keynote of the Parisian demi-monde in the 19th century and which we recognise again and again in the scenes of *La dame aux camélias*, *Nana*, or *L'éducation sentimentale*. The enduring image of *Gay Paree* which still haunts the pages of the travel brochures has its origin here on the outer boulevards in the years of the can-can. Moore has a delicate sense both of the fragile beauty of this world and of the realities which threaten to engulf it:

It was she, Marie Pellegrin.

She wore a dress similar to the one she wore in her portrait, a black silk covered with lace, and her black hair was swathed about her shapely little head. She was her portrait and something more. Her smile was her own, a sad little smile that seemed to come out of a depth of her being, and her voice was a little musical voice, irresponsible as a bird's, and during dinner I noticed how she broke into speech abruptly as a bird breaks into song, and she stopped as abruptly. [...]

As we went towards the house where coffee was being served, Marie asked me if I played cards, but I excused myself, saying that I would prefer to sit and look at her [...] The game was baccarat, and in a little while I saw that Marie was losing a great deal of money, and a little later I saw La Glue[31] trying to persuade her away from the card-table.

'One more deal.' That deal lost her the last louis she had placed on the table. 'Someone will have to pay my cab,' she said.

We were going to the Elysée-Montmartre, and Alphonsine lent her a couple of louis, *pour passer sa soirée*, and we all went away in carriages, the little horses straining up the steep streets; the plumes of the women's hats floating over the carriage hoods. Marie was in one of the front carriages, and was waiting for us on the high steps leading from the street to the *bal*.

'It's my last night,' she said, 'the last night I shall see the Elysée for many a month.'

'You'll soon be back again?'

'You see, I have been offered five hundred thousand francs to go to Russia for three years. Fancy, three years without seeing the Elysée,' and she looked round as an angel might look upon Paradise out of which she is about to be driven. 'The trees are beautiful,' she said, 'they're like a fairy-tale'; and that is exactly what they were like, rising into the summer darkness, unnaturally green above the electric lights. In the middle of a circle of white globes the orchestra played upon an *estrade*, and everyone whirled his partner as if she were a top. 'I always sit over there under the

trees in the angle,' she said; and she was about to invite me
to come and sit with her, when her attention was distracted
from me; for the people had drawn together into groups,
and I heard everybody whispering, 'That's Marie Pellegrin.'
Seeing her coming, her waiter with much ostentation began
to draw aside tables and chairs, and in a few minutes she was
sitting under her tree, she and La Glue together, their friends
about them, Marie distributing absinthe, brandy, and
cigarettes. A little procession suddenly formed under the
trees and came towards her, and Marie was presented with a
great basket of flowers, and all her company with bouquets;
and a little cheer went up from different parts of the *bal,
Vive Marie Pellegrin, la reine de l'Elysée.*[32]

Some time later Moore hears at a dinner party that she has
returned from Russia and is ill. He hurries to her lodgings
on the corner of the rue des Martyrs. She receives him
gracefully—'*Comme les anglais sont gentils. Dès qu'on est
malade ...*'—but next day he hears that she is dead. She had
died on her balcony in a new gown, having gone out to watch
the fireworks.

By this time the days of the Elysée-Montmartre were numbered. It was on 5 October 1889, just over six months after the
inauguration of the Eiffel Tower, that Charles Zidler opened
his Moulin Rouge. On the corner of the place Blanche and
the rue Lepic, at 90 boulevard de Clichy, it rapidly took over
both the dancers and clientèle of its rival. Among the can-can
dancers who assured its success were two of Lautrec's most
famous models, Jane Avril and La Goulue. Jane Avril was the
illegitimate daughter of an Italian nobleman. Her slightly
mournful grace touched a chord in Lautrec and she became a
close friend. Meanwhile La Goulue, who had been his earlier
favourite, sank into wretchedness. A child of the streets, La
Goulue had worked, like Zola's Gervaise, in a laundry in the
rue de la Goutte-d'Or, dancing by night in the *bals musette* of
the neighbouring streets. At her peak she could command huge
fees. She was the undisputed mistress of the Moulin Rouge,
even on one occasion flipping off the Prince of Wales's top-hat
with her foot as he watched from the edge of the stage. But

then alcohol and obesity took over. Her steady decline from
side-show attraction to waitress in a brothel to rag-picker
along the boulevards perhaps suggests that Marie Pellegrin's
was not an unkind fate.

Pigalle

From the place Blanche the boulevard runs in one direction
towards the place Pigalle, in the other towards the place de
Clichy. This is the heart of night-time Montmartre.

It has always tended to be the more sordid aspects of life
along the outer boulevards that have attracted writers. In this
George Moore, with his enthusiasm for the glitter of Montmartre, was an exception. More typical, and more ambiguous,
is the response of Jean Rhys's heroine as she looks out from
another of her cheap hotel rooms:

> From the balcony Marya could see one side of the Place
> Blanche. Opposite, the Rue Lepic mounted upwards to the
> rustic heights of Montmartre. It was astonishing how signi-
> ficant, coherent and understandable it all became after a
> glass of wine on an empty stomach.
>
> The lights winking up at a pallid moon, the slender
> painted ladies, the wings of the Moulin Rouge, the smell of
> petrol and perfume and cooking.
>
> The Place Blanche, Paris. Life itself. One realised all sorts
> of things. The value of an illusion, for instance, and that the
> shadow can be more important than the substance. All sorts
> of things.[33]

The writer who, more than any other, made this shady
half-world of Montmartre his own was Francis Carco. In his
description of the view down the boulevard Clichy from the
place Pigalle we can recognise many of the most evocative
elements:

> The trees along the boulevard Clichy stood out against the
> weeping clouds of a low October sky. Pools of water re-
> flected the light, and belated pedestrians hurried along the
> narrow footpath in the middle.

Close to the shuttered windows of the shops moved a sad tide of shadows, alert and mistrustful. Two policemen kept an eye on the girls who were walking up and down. [...] Sometimes, in the light of the gas-lamp, the appearance of their faces was so tragic that they might have been dead souls raised up by the wind. And far off, at the end of this wide boulevard, the place Blanche displayed its rows of lights.[34]

This is the setting of *Jésus-la-Caille* (1914), Carco's bitter, sentimental tale of prostitutes and apaches in Montmartre. The dreary poetry of these haunts of pleasure can still be felt along the boulevards today. The twilight of a rainy autumn afternoon seems to offer the quintessential imaginative context for this quarter of the city.

In the years between the wars it was the singers and cabaret performers—heirs of Aristide Bruant—rather than the dancers who embodied the spirit of the area. Then as now in Montmartre the night worlds of criminal and entertainer frequently overlapped. In the memoirs of her early years Edith Piaf tells how she arrived in Pigalle in 1930 when she was eighteen and fell in love with a pimp called Albert. Since she refused to go on the streets for him, she was given another role:

> From then on my job was to prospect for rich women. While I was singing in the streets, I had to check out the dance-halls where there were prosperous-looking women, wearing necklaces and rings. In the evening I made my report to Albert. He took down all my information in a little notebook, then on Saturday evenings and Sundays he went off in his best suit to the dance-halls I had indicated. Since he was very handsome and self-assured, he always managed to seduce one of the women who were dancing there. At dawn he would suggest taking her back to her home, 'because,' he explained, 'the district has a bad reputation.' Without fail, he would take every one of them into the impasse Lemercier,* a sombre and deserted cul-de-sac. He then clamped his left hand brutally across their mouth to stop them crying

---

* About five minutes' walk from the place de Clichy, off the rue Lemercier.

out. With his right hand he gave them a series of quick slaps, then seized their necklaces, rings and money. Meanwhile, I was waiting in the café de la Nouvelle Athènes. Often, when things had gone well, I would see him come in with bulging pockets and a wide smile of triumph on his lips. He would buy me champagne the whole night.[35]

This kind of episode has a familiar ring. In his history of the area Louis Chevalier quotes a string of newspaper articles from the early years of the century describing *faits divers* in which figures like Albert and his women play a recurring role. A bar in the rue Lepic, a hotel room in the rue des Martyrs, a dance-hall in the place Blanche, a room rented for a mistress in the rue La Bruyère—these are the characteristic stage-sets for Montmartre's unglamorous crimes of passion.

Sacré-Coeur

Writers in English have known these doubtful places by repute, but rarely more than that. Only one could perhaps have claimed to know them as intimately as Piaf herself. In this passage from *Black Spring* (1936) Henry Miller has walked up from the boulevard Clichy, following the rue Caulaincourt through the edge of the Montmartre cemetery. He then takes the sudden turn into the rue de Maistre:

> The sharp swing to the right plunges me into the very bowels of Paris. Through the coiling, sliding intestines of Montmartre the street runs like a jagged knife-wound. [...]
>
> At that point where the rue Lepic leans over on its side for a breathing spell, where it bends like a hair-pin to renew the steep ascent, it seems as if a flood-tide had receded and left behind a rich marine deposit. The dance-halls, the bars, the cabarets, all the incandescent lace and froth of the electrical night pales before the seething mass of edibles which girdle the base of the hill. [...]
>
> Along the rue d'Orsel, the sun is sinking. Perhaps it's the sun sinking, perhaps it's the street itself dismal as a vestibule. Over the sorrow-bitten façades a thin scum of grease, a thin green film of fadedness, a touch of dementia. And then

suddenly, presto! all is changed. Suddenly the street opens wide its jaws and there, like a still white dream, like a dream embedded in stone, the Sacré-Coeur rises up. A late afternoon and the heavy whiteness of it is stifling. A heavy, somnolent whiteness, like the belly of a jaded woman. Back and forth the blood ebbs, the contours rounded with soft light, the huge billowy cupolas taut as savage teats. On the dizzy escarpments the trees stick out like spiny thorns whose fuzzy boughs wave sluggishly above the invisible current that moves trance-like beneath the roots. Pieces of sky still clinging to the tips of the boughs —soft, cottony wisps dyed with an eastern blue. [...]

Night is coming on, the night of the boulevards, with the sky red as hell-fire and from Clichy to Barbès a fretwork of open tombs. The soft Paris night, like a ladder of toothless gums and the ghouls grinning behind the rungs. All along the foot of the hill the urinals are gurgling, their mouths choked with soft bread. It's in the night that Sacré-Coeur stands out in all its stinking loveliness. Then it is that the heavy whiteness of her skin and her humid stone breath clamps down on the blood like a valve.[36]

The Montmartre cemetery

From the outer boulevards the course of Miller's walk takes us first through the edge of the cemetery. Here, among the trees, are the graves of Stendhal and de Vigny, the Goncourts and the Dumas, of Murger and Feydeau and Théophile Gautier. It is a place which has over the years won from the inhabitants of northern Paris a curious affection. Daniel Halévy pays tribute to it in his *Pays parisiens*:

The Montmartre cemetery is not a magnificent or heroic place like the Père Lachaise. It would be unreasonable to ask so much of it. But it is still a fine cemetery; it has kept faith with what Montmartre used to be, with what it hoped to remain. Of course, it has not survived unscathed. Over the tombs they have built (what brutality, what baseness) an iron and concrete bridge with its incessant din of trams and lorries. Stendhal lies beneath; Stendhal, *milanese*, says the inscription. It seems that this bridge was necessary to bring the Butte Montmartre closer to the centre of Paris. The uncrossable cemetery protected the gardens up there on the heights, and so to destroy the gardens the cemetery had to be humiliated.

The destiny by which cities are degraded has great power, but all power finds its limit. When nobility or beauty has alighted somewhere, its traces cannot be so quickly effaced, and our cemetery, inclined, like Montmartre itself, towards Paris and towards the sun, remains beautiful. Its trees, which will soon be a hundred years old, cover it with their shade. It is not well known, but those who do know it and will inhabit it one day, are attached to it. One must not, I repeat, think of Père Lachaise when walking there. Père Lachaise is the whole of Paris. Montmartre is a moment of it—three or four decades—a rapid flowering of artistic, republican Paris, the Paris of Louis-Philippe king of the French, of Napoleon III emperor. Here lie the remains of Cavaignac, Stendhal, the Dumas: how much spirit, courage, honour![37]

The streets of the Butte Montmartre

Halévy's reference to republican Paris is apt. It was in the days of the Commune that the Butte first began to figure largely in the annals of the city. In the summer of 1870 Napoleon III had initiated a disastrous war against Prussia. Seven weeks later the French were humiliatingly defeated at Sedan. In the wake of this defeat the Paris mob declared a Republic and the Prussian army laid siege to the city. Paris surrendered and an armistice followed, but the republicans and revolutionaries, hostile to the new Versailles government, refused to disarm. Here on the Butte Montmartre the Commune which they formed centred its resistance.

The brush with revolution was turbulent but short-lived. After the bloody suppression of the Commune—a shameful episode for which the building of the Sacré-Coeur was partly intended to atone—the Butte continued to remain essentially remote from the life of the city. Even at the turn of the century

H. P. Hugh could report that 'One of the inhabitants of the hill told me that it was five years since he had been to "Paris", and chatted of passing events as if he was a thousand miles from that throbbing, hysterical and wayward city.'[38]

A year or two later the novelist Roland Dorgelès found what was still a rural scene when he came to visit the streets to the north and west of Sacré-Coeur. He was a student at the time at the Ecole des Arts décoratifs on the left bank, and with a group of friends he decided to cross Paris in order to taste 'the joys of the country' in Montmartre. Having paused to look out over the strange city sprawling beneath them, they turn back to the Butte:

> ... Continuing our expedition, we reached the place du Tertre: we could have been a hundred miles from Paris. The old houses had roofs like tiled bonnets and finches nested in the acacias. The people too were of another kind. On the rue du Mont-Cenis a young girl was looking after some geese; further down, a housewife was hanging out her washing. [...]
>
> This was the village of my dreams, so perfect that it seemed unreal. It was a village from fairy-tale with its calvary, its old cemetery [Saint-Vincent] overgrown with brambles, the little bells of the convent, a well with a rusty chain, the scent of the stable, a wagoners' inn. It lacked neither the street-fountain surrounded by girls with bare arms, nor the orchard where a nun was picking pears, nor the game of *boules*, nor the poultry yard of crowing cocks. In the rue Saint-Vincent our companion even pointed out a thatched cottage—the last in Paris—where Henri IV was supposed to have kept his mistresses. Finally, emerging after many detours from the rue Norvins, we caught sight of the windmills—three of them still there [...] their black sails reaching towards the clouds. Unable to contain myself any longer, I started to shout for joy.[39]

The countryside has long ago given way to the city, but the Butte Montmartre still has more of provincial tranquillity than any other part of Paris. Even today, if one steps away from the trail beaten by tourists around the Sacré-Coeur and the place du Tertre, the less frequented lanes of the Butte, with their simple shops and houses, can give a sense of something quite distinct from the cosmopolitan world below. An example is the rue de l'Abreuvoir, which in 1854 prompted Gérard de Nerval to write:

> There were two things above all which enchanted me about this little spot, sheltered by the great trees of the château des Brouillards: first, the traces of vineyard linked to the memory of St. Denis, [...] and second, the nearby water-trough* which, in the evening, is enlivened both by the spectacle of the horses and dogs being washed there and by a fountain built in the old style, where the women chat and sing while they do their washing, as though in a scene from the opening of *Werther*.[40]

The Lapin Agile

A few yards from the point at which the rue de l'Abreuvoir meets the rue des Saules stands a small cottage which was for several years the focus of the artistic life of the area. It was called then, as it is today, Le Lapin Agile. Max Jacob, Modigliani, Picasso, Mac Orlan, Apollinaire, Dorgelès all frequented it and Maurice Utrillo painted it repeatedly. The proprietor, M. Frédérique, became a figure in the Bohemian mythology of the period. The art critics who in 1912 had high praise for a painting entitled *Et le soleil se coucha sur l'Adriatique* were disconcerted to learn that it had been painted by M. Frédé's donkey, swishing its tail at the instigation of Dorgelès. In his memoirs of the time Francis Carco has left us an agreeably romantic picture of life at the Lapin. The evening would start nearby with dinner on the *terrasse* of the Restaurant Bouscara, at 2 place du Tertre:

> We would all eat at the same table, then, drawn by the lure of Frédé's place, we would go in a group to join Mac Orlan and company. And that was how we spent the night. Street-girls and ruffians with a fondness for poetry mixed with the ordinary customers at Frédé's, addressed us as 'tu', bought

---

* The site of the *abreuvoir* was no. 15, on the corner of the rue Girardon.

drinks. These characters had soft hearts and 'artistic tastes'; when one of their women dropped them for one of our group, they did not take it amiss; they left us for a while, went dancing at the Moulin de la Galette and came back with new protégées. All of them liked the casual life we led at the Lapin. And under the lights veiled with red foulards and the low painted ceiling of the main room, where Frédérique sang, who would not have succumbed, as though to a powerful drug? Neither dream nor pleasure approached the sensation. It was something else. A special kind of intoxication, a mingling of reverie and despair, indefinable, without echo. Like autumn rain that falls and stops and falls again, it caught hold of us, fondled us, enervated us. And it really did rain those nights—or else it snowed, while the drunkest of us slept stretched out on a bench, and inoffensive white mice, sly and unafraid, pattered across the chimney-piece. How to describe the atmosphere of our long vigils? It drew its essence from the haphazard setting, in which obscene clay models, a huge Christ figure in plaster, and canvases by Picasso, Utrillo and Girieud all had a place. The dense pipe-smoke added to it. And Frédérique, armed with his guitar, Mac Orlan dressed in cowboy style, the dampness of the walls, the barking dogs, the secret despair of each of us, our poverty, our youth, the time that had gone by—all these completed it.[41]

The décor of the Lapin, if not its clientèle, remains much as Carco described it, and if you walk up there in the early hours of the morning you can still, over a glass of cherries in brandy, get a flavour of the sort of cabaret that existed before the neon lights of Pigalle.

Night-life in the twenties

Already, in Carco's style, we can sense the urge to turn history into legend. And in the years following the First World War a legend was what Montmartre was to become. As a haunt of foreign tourists the Butte was bound to change its character, accommodating itself to the visitors' demands for 'art' during the daytime and entertainment in the evening. It was at the start of 1929, in the golden years of the night-club, that Evelyn Waugh stopped in Paris on his way to Monte Carlo. His account is an elegant sketch of the Montmartre of the period and its statutory round of pleasures:

I spent the night with some kind, generous, and wholly delightful Americans. They wanted to show me a place called 'Brick-Top's', which was then very popular. It was no good going to Bricky's, they said, until after twelve, so we went to Florence's first. We drank champagne because it is one of the peculiar modifications of French liberty that one can drink nothing else.

Then we went to an underground public house called the New York Bar. When we came in all the people beat on the tables with little wooden hammers, and a young Jew who was singing made a joke about the ermine coat which one of our party was wearing. We drank some more, much nastier, champagne and went to Brick-Top's, but when we got there, we found a notice on the door saying, 'Opening at four. Bricky', so we started again on our rounds.

We went to a café called *Le Fétiche*, where the waitresses wore dinner-jackets and asked the ladies in the party to dance. I was interested to see the fine, manly girl in charge of the cloakroom very deftly stealing a silk scarf from an elderly German.

We went to the Plantation, and to the Music Box, where it was so dark we could hardly see our glasses (which contained still nastier champagne), and to Sheherazade, where they brought us five different organs of lamb spitted together between onions and bay leaves, all on fire at the end and very nice to eat.

We went to Kasbek which was just like Sheherazade.

Finally, at four, we went to Brick-Top's. Brick-Top came and sat at our table. She seemed the least bogus person in Paris. It was broad daylight when we left; then we drove to the Halles and ate fine, pungent onion soup at *Le Père Tranquille*, while one of the young ladies in our party bought a bundle of leeks and ate them raw. I asked my host

if all his evenings were like this. He said, no, he made a point
of staying at home at least one night a week to play poker.[42]

The night-clubs continue to multiply, but the real atmosphere
of Montmartre, even now, has less to do with the passing
tourists than with the tenor of life in those ragged streets which
lie between the place Clichy and the boulevard de la Chapelle.
Fernande, the prostitute heroine of *Jésus-la-Caille*, has left
Montmartre and gone to live with a new lover in Belleville, to
the east; but for her this is exile. One evening, having decided
to return, she takes the métro back into Montmartre:

> Standing in one of the carriages, she saw, behind the rail-
> ings, the Canal Saint-Martin rise from the ground,* fol-
> lowed by streets and avenues which she recognised, the Gare
> de l'Est, the Gare du Nord, glimpsed in the wet, shimmering
> lights; then she reached the stop at the place Blanche and got
> off. [...] Under the bare plane trees of the boulevard de
> Clichy, by which she had so often walked up and down, she
> discerned vaguely remembered faces. Further down, a wide
> area of light, mingling with reflections from the pavement,
> indicated the place Pigalle. Fernande thought she was
> dreaming. For a long time she looked at the alluring lights,
> which dazzled the sombre sky and the façades of the nearby
> houses. [...] Everything around seemed to her miraculously
> charged with the memory of far-off days. Nothing had
> changed. Some of the girls walked casually to and fro under
> the trees; others went in the opposite direction, while young
> men in elegant silk socks and felt hats lovingly divided in the
> middle slyly insinuated themselves among the walkers. [...]
> Nights like this, the same sky, the same nostalgic smells,
> these trees, these passers-by, the whole calm, clumsy life of
> the district, every aspect of the scene combined to persuade
> her of her new happiness.[43]

Happiness may seem a strange word to associate with the
desolate prospect along the outer boulevards, and yet the
connection is one that most of the writers mentioned in these
pages would probably have understood. The bare plane trees,

---

* This is one of the places where the métro emerges to run above ground.

the wet pavements, the casual passers-by—none of them have much to do with the city we learn about in the tourist leaflets; but for a book that has tried to catch some of the images of Paris that live in our imagination, they are perhaps as good a place to end as any. Four centuries ago Montaigne knew well enough that the fascination of Paris is much more than the sum of its beauties:

I love that citie for her owne sake, and more in her only subsisting and owne being, than when it is full fraught and embellished with forraine pompe and borrowed garish ornaments. I love hir so tenderly that hir spottes, her blemishes and hir warts are deare unto me. I am no perfect French man but by this great citie, great in people, greate in regard of the felicitie of her situation, but above all, great and incomparable in varietie and diversitie of commodities; the glory of France and one of the noblest and chiefe ornaments of the world. [...] So long as she shall continue, so long shall I never want a home or a retreate to retire to and shrowd myself at all times.[44]

References

Many of the works cited have gone through numerous editions. To avoid confusion I have tried, where practicable, to identify extracts by the chapter or section of the book in which they appear rather than by page number. Translations from the French are by me unless otherwise stated.

Introduction

1 Letter to F. Scott Fitzgerald, summer 1930 (undated).
2 Marcel Proust, À la recherche du temps perdu, Du côté de chez Swann, 1913, trans. C. K. Scott Moncrieff, Swann's Way, London, 1922, Vol. II, p. 243.
3 P. G. Wodehouse, Carry On, Jeeves, 1925, ch. 6.

Chapter One

1 William Hazlitt, Notes of a Journey through France and Italy, 1826, ch. 10.
2 Eugène Sue, Les mystères de Paris, 1842–3, Pt. I, ch. 1.
3 André Breton, 'Pont-Neuf' (1950), reprinted in Poésie et autre, ed. Gérard Legrand, Paris, 1960. Translated in Yale French Studies, no. 32, 'The Surrealist Map of Love'.
4 See his Mysopogon. Vestiges of Roman Paris can still be found in the musée de Cluny and the newly opened archaeological crypt in front of Notre-Dame.
5 Edward Gibbon, The Decline and Fall of the Roman Empire, 1776, ch. 19.
6 Frances Trollope, Paris and the Parisians, 1836, Letter LII.
7 François Rabelais, The Histories of Gargantua and Pantagruel (1532–52), Bk. I, ch. 17, trans. J. M. Cohen, 1955.
8 Thomas Coryate, Coryat's Crudities, 1611, 'My Observations of Paris'.
9 Peter Abélard, The Story of My Misfortunes, ch. 6, trans. Henry Adam Bellows, 1958.
10 D. B. Wyndham Lewis, François Villon, 1928, Pt. I, ch. 3.

11 Louis-Sébastien Mercier, *Tableau de Paris*, 1781–9, ch. 270.

12 Charles Dickens, *The Uncommercial Traveller*, 1861, ch. 18.

13 Ibid., ch. 7.

14 Emile Zola, *Thérèse Raquin*, 1867, ch. 13, trans. Willard R. Trask, 1960.

15 Georges Simenon, *Pietr-le-Letton*, 1931, ch. 1, trans. Daphne Woodward, 1963.

16 Letter of 3 January 1795, quoted in John G. Alger, *Englishmen in the French Revolution*, 1889.

17 It lost this function only in 1914.

18 Letter to Mme de Circourt, 15 July 1852.

19 Letter of 16 December 1802 from Charlotte Edgeworth to her brother C. Sneyd Edgeworth.

20 Honoré de Balzac, *Oeuvres complètes*, ed. Marcel Bouteron and Henri Longnon, 1948, Vol. XIII, p. 14.

21 Ernest Hemingway, *The Sun Also Rises*, 1926, ch. 8.

22 The same building had from 1899 to 1904 been the home of Charles-Louis Philippe, author of *Bubu de Montparnasse*.

23 Quoted in George Wickes, *Americans in Paris*, 1969, ch. 10.

24 Cyril Connolly, *The Unquiet Grave*, 1944, Pt. III, 'La Clé des Chants'.

25 Ibid.

26 Théophile Gautier, *Romans et contes*, 1877, 'Le Club des Hachichins', ch. 1.

27 Francis Carco, *De Montmartre au quartier latin*, 1927, ch. 10.

28 William Cole, *A Journal of my Journey to Paris in the Year 1765*, entry for Thursday 14 October.

29 John Russell, *Paris*, London, 1960, p. 175.

30 Laurence Sterne, *A Sentimental Journey*, 1768, 'The Fragment'.

31 Robert Chasles, *Les illustres françoises*, 1713, 'Histoire de Monsieur Dupuis et de Madame de Londé'.

32 N. M. Karamzin, *Letters of a Russian Traveler, 1789–1790*, trans. Florence Jonas, New York and London, 1957, p. 235.

33 William Cole, *A Journal of my Journey to Paris in the Year 1765*, entry for Thursday 24 October.

34 Jean Rhys, *Quartet*, 1928, ch. 3.

35 Victor Hugo, *Les misérables*, 1862, Pt. V, Bk. IV, trans. Norman Denny, 1976.

36 Ibid.

37 Louis Aragon, *Les beaux quartiers*, 1936, Pt. III, ch. 10.

38 Emile Zola, *L'oeuvre*, 1886, ch. 8, trans. Thomas Walton, 1950.

Chapter Two

1 Romain Rolland, *Jean-Christophe, La foire sur la place*, trans. Gilbert Cannan, 'The Market-Place' in *John Christopher in Paris*, London, 1911, p. 132.

2 Henry James, *A Small Boy and Others*, 1913, ch. 25.

3 Ibid.

4 Honoré de Balzac, *Oeuvres complètes*, ed. Bouteron and Longnon, 1946, Vol. XVII, pp. 66–7, trans. M. A. Crawford, 1965.

5 Arsène Houssaye, *Les confessions*, 1885, Vol. I, Bk. VI.

6 Martin Lister, *A Journey to Paris in the Year 1698*, ed. R. F. Stearns, London, 1967, pp. 186–7.

7 Letter to Charles Montague, 9 August 1698, quoted in C. K. Eves, *Matthew Prior: Poet and Diplomatist*, New York, 1973.

8 Arthur Young, *Travels in France*, 1792, entry for 4 January 1790.

9 William Hazlitt, *Notes of a Journey through France and Italy*, 1826, ch. 10.

10 W. M. Thackeray, *The Paris Sketch Book*, 1840, 'An Invasion of France'.

11 Wilde had no exclusive preference for respectable hotels. Late in 1891 he was staying not far away in an hotel at 29 boulevard des Capucines. At the first of Wilde's trials Fred Atkins, an ex-billiard marker and book-maker's clerk, gave evidence that during his stay there with Wilde he had returned one night from the Moulin Rouge to find him in bed with Maurice Schwabe. The testimony gained a certain piquancy from the fact that Schwabe was the nephew by marriage of Sir Frank Lockwood, the Solicitor-General, who was to prosecute Wilde in his last trial.

12 George Orwell, *Down and Out in Paris and London*, 1933, ch. 12.

13 Léon-Paul Fargue, *Le piéton de Paris*, 1939, 'Palaces et hôtels'.

14 Letter to Ernest Chevalier, 25 June 1842.

15 Guy de Maupassant, *Bel-Ami*, 1885, Pt. I, ch. 1.

16 Francis Carco, *Nostalgie de Paris*, 1941, ch. 9.

17 Edmond and Jules de Goncourt, *Journal*, October 1857, trans. Robert Baldick, 1962.

18 Emile Zola, *La curée*, 1872 ch. 4.

19 Edmond and Jules de Goncourt, *Journal*, November 1852, trans. Robert Baldick, 1962.

20 Frances Trollope, *Paris and the Parisians*, 1836, Letter II.

21 Quoted in John Forster, *The Life of Charles Dickens*, 1872–4, Bk. VII, ch. 5.

22 Cyril Connolly, *Enemies of Promise*, 1938, ch. 21.

23 Writers in the rue de Richelieu: no. 40 is the site of the house in which Molière lived for the last few months of his life, no. 61 the site of the house in which Stendhal lived from 1822 to 1823. As to the others, Tallemant lived at no. 66 (1683–92), Thomas Paine at no. 95 (1793), Balzac intermittently at no. 108 (1837–40), and Diderot died at no. 39.

24 Quoted in John Morley, *Studies in Literature*, London, 1891, p. 95.

25 Chamfort, *Maximes, pensées, caractères et anecdotes*, ed. Jean Dagen, Paris, 1968, ch. 8, no. 496.

26 Pierre-Louis Ginguené, quoted in Emile Dousset, *Chamfort et son temps*, 1943, 'Chamfort et la prison', section 3.

27 Denis Diderot, opening lines of *Le neveu de Rameau*, 1761, trans. L. W. Tancock, 1966.

28 William Wordsworth, *The Prelude* (1805 edition), Bk. IX, ll. 53–54.

29 J. G. Lemaistre, *A Rough Sketch of Modern Paris*, 1803, Letter XI.

30 Edward Bulwer-Lytton, *Pelham*, 1828, Vol. I, ch. 19.
31 Sir Walter Scott, *Paul's Letters to his Kinsfolk*, 1816, Letter XV.
32 Théophile Gautier is the source of this anecdote. See Jean Richer, *Nerval par les témoins de sa vie*, Paris, 1970, p. 27.
33 Quoted in Pierre Gaxotte, *Paris au XVIIIe siècle*, 1968, ch. 7.
34 Quoted in John Palmer, *Molière, His Life and Works*, 1930. ch. 22.
35 William Cole, *A Journal of My Journey to Paris in the Year 1765*, entry for Thursday 21 November.
36 Nicolas-Edmé Restif de la Bretonne, *Les nuits de Paris*, 1788, 'La nuit des Halles', trans. Linda Asher and Ellen Fertig, 1964.
37 Jean Rhys, *Good Morning Midnight*, London, 1967. p. 40.
38 Francis Carco, *Nostalgie de Paris*, 1941, ch. 4.
39 Emile Zola, *Le ventre de Paris*, 1873, ch. 1, trans. E. Vizetelly, 1896.
40 Ibid.

Chapter Three

1 Jacques Hillairet, *Dictionnaire historique des rues de Paris*, Paris, 1963, Vol. I, p. 334.
2 The plaque on the right-hand side gives an outline plan of the fortress.
3 John Evelyn, *Diary*, 11 March 1651.
4 Le Petit had also killed a young Augustinian novice a few years earlier, which cannot have improved his standing with the clergy.
5 Nicolas-Edmé Restif de la Bretonne, *Les nuits de Paris*, 1788, 'Exécution aux flambeaux', trans. Linda Asher and Ellen Fertig, 1964.
6 François-René de Chateaubriand, *The Memoirs of Chateaubriand*, selected and translated by Robert Baldick, London, 1961, pp. 89–90.
7 Charles-Louis Philippe, *Bubu de Montparnasse*, 1901, trans. Laurence Vail, Paris, 1932, pp. 1–2.
8 Sir Walter Scott, *Ivanhoe*, 1819, ch. 3.
9 Martin Lister, *A Journey to Paris in the Year 1698*, ed. R. F. Stearns, London, 1967, pp. 96–7.
10 Letter to Mme de Grignan, 20 February 1671, trans. Arthur Stanley, 1946.
11 Jacques Wilhelm, *La vie quotidienne au Marais au XVIIe siècle*, Paris, 1966, pp. 47–9.
12 Letter to the marquis de Pomponne, 27 November 1664, trans. Arthur Stanley, 1946.
13 Tallemant des Réaux, *Historiettes*, 'Mesdames de Rohan'.
14 Ibid., 'La présidente Aubry, son mary, Orgeval et Senas'.
15 Ibid., 'Mesdames de Rohan'.
16 The burlesque poet Paul Scarron had died in this same house on the corner of the rue de Turenne in 1660.
17 Louis-Sébastien Mercier, *Tableau de Paris*, 1781, ch. 84, trans. Wilfrid and Emilie Jackson, 1929.
18 Letter to Lady Blessington, 27 January 1847.
19 Léon Daudet, *Paris vécu*, 1929, 'Rive droite', ch. 1.
20 Tallemant des Réaux, *Historiettes*, 'Monsieur de Sully', trans. Hamish Miles, 1925, revised F. J. Barnett, 1965.

21 De Sade's letters from the Bastille nonetheless complain bitterly about the distasteful nature of prison food 'to one accustomed to a dainty table'.

22 Charles Dickens, *A Tale of Two Cities*, Bk. III, ch. 10.

23 For further details about Latude, and other anecdotes connected with the Bastille, see F. Funck-Brentano, *Légendes et archives de la Bastille*, Paris, 1904.

24 Quoted by Funck-Brentano, op. cit., ch. 4, section 1.

25 See Funck-Brentano, op. cit., ch. 4, section 3.

26 Victor Hugo, *Les misérables*, 1862, Pt. IV, Bk. VI, trans. Norman Denny, 1976.

27 Henry Miller, *Tropic of Cancer* (1934), London, 1963, pp. 42–4.

28 W. Somerset Maugham, *The Razor's Edge*, 1944, ch. 5, section 2.

29 Georges Simenon, *Le pendu de Saint-Pholien*, 1931, ch. 3, trans. Tony White, 1963.

30 Francis Carco, *Nostalgie de Paris*, 1941, ch. 9.

31 D. B. Wyndham Lewis, *François Villon*, 1928, Pt. I, ch. 3.

32 J.-K. Huysmans, 'La rue de la Chine' in *Croquis parisiens*, 1880.

33 A rough plan marking the sites of the most notable graves can be obtained from the administrative office inside the cemetery.

34 Etienne Pivert de Senancour, 'Promenade en octobre', quoted in Pierre Citron, *La poésie de Paris dans la littérature française de Rousseau à Baudelaire*, Paris, 1961, Vol. I, p. 182.

35 Letter to his sister, Monday 6 September 1819. Balzac was living at what was then 9 rue de Lesdiguières in a building later demolished to make way for the boulevard Henri IV.

36 Honoré de Balzac, *Oeuvres complètes*, ed. Bouteron and Longnon, Paris, 1949, Vol. VI, pp. 515–6, trans. M. A. Crawford, 1951.

Chapter Four

1 D. B. Wyndham Lewis, *François Villon*, 1928, Pt. II, section 3.

2 Quoted in Jacques Hillairet, *Dictionnaire historique des rues de Paris*, Paris, 1963, Vol. II, p. 230.

3 Nicolas-Edmé Restif de la Bretonne, *Les nuits de Paris*, 1788, 'Les violateurs des sépultures', trans. Linda Asher and Ellen Fertig, 1964.

4 Ibid., 'Suite des violateurs'.

5 Elliot Paul, *A Narrow Street*, 1942, Pt. I, ch. 2.

6 See Francis Carco, *De Montmartre au quartier latin*, Paris, 1927.

7 Ernest Hemingway, *The Sun Also Rises*, 1926, ch. 8.

8 *The French Journals of Mrs Thrale and Dr Johnson*, ed. Moses Tyson and John Guppy, Manchester, 1932, pp. 204–5 (Footnote).

9 Ernest Hemingway, *A Moveable Feast*, 1964, ch. 4.

10 Stella Bowen, *Drawn from Life*, 1941, ch. 5.

11 Ernest Hemingway, 'The Snows of Kilimanjaro', 1938.

12 The location of the Pomme de Pin has caused some confusion, partly because there is a misleading inscription at 1 place de la Contrescarpe

(i.e. on the wrong side of the square), partly because there was another cabaret of the same name on the Ile de la Cité.

13 George Orwell, *Down and Out in Paris and London*, 1933, ch. 1.

14 Honoré de Balzac, *Oeuvres complètes*, ed. Bouteron and Longnon, Paris, 1949, Vol. VI, pp. 222–3, trans. M. A. Crawford, 1951.

15 W. M. Thackeray, *The Paris Sketch Book*, 1840, 'The Case of Peytel'.

16 Alfred Perlès, 'Gobelins Tapestries', reprinted in *The Left Bank Revisited*, ed. Hugh Ford, University Park (Pennsylvania) and London, 1972.

17 In the interests of getting Jake Barnes and Bill Gorton to the boulevard du Montparnasse, Hemingway extends the rue de Pot-de-Fer to join the rue Saint-Jacques, which is in reality some distance away. The two characters turn onto the boulevard de Port-Royal just opposite the hôpital Cochin where in February 1929 George Orwell had the unenviable experience, recorded in his essay 'How the Poor Die', of being treated for pneumonia. This was also the hospital to which Samuel Beckett was taken after he had been stabbed by a tramp one night on the boulevard Saint-Michel. According to James Joyce, Beckett's indignation was directed less against the tramp than against the judge in the case, who he felt should have bought him a new overcoat to replace the one damaged by the tramp's knife.

18 James Charters, *This Must Be The Place*, London, 1934, pp. 18–19.

19 Quoted in George Wickes, *Americans in Paris*, 1969, ch. 9.

20 Simone de Beauvoir, *La force de l'âge*, 1960, ch. 6, trans. Peter Green, 1962.

21 Ibid.

22 André Salmon, *Montparnasse*, 1950, ch. 4.

23 Jean Rhys, *Quartet*, 1928, ch. 15.

24 Henry Miller, *Tropic of Cancer*, (1934), London, 1963, pp. 20–21.

25 Honoré de Balzac, *Oeuvres complètes*, ed. Bouteron and Longnon, Paris, 1951, Vol. XX, p. 364.

26 Ernest Hemingway, *Green Hills of Africa*, 1935, ch. 4.

27 Gertrude Stein, *The Autobiography of Alice B. Toklas*, 1933, ch. 2.

28 John Evelyn, *Diary*, 1 April 1644.

29 W. M. Thackeray, *The Paris Sketch Book*, 1840, 'On the French School of Painting'.

30 Edmond Texier, *Tableau de Paris*, Paris, 1852, Vol. II, p. 64.

31 Alfred de Musset, *La confession d'un enfant du siècle*, 1836, Pt. II, ch. 4.

32 George Moore, *Memoirs of My Dead Life*, 1906, ch. 9.

33 Georges Perec, *Tentative d'épuisement d'un lieu parisien*, 1975, entry for Friday 18 October 1974.

34 Quoted in John Russell, *Paris*, London, 1960, p. 213.

35 Simone de Beauvoir, *La force de l'âge*, 1960, ch. 5, trans. Peter Green, 1962.

36 Daniel Halévy, *Pays parisiens*, 1932, ch. 9.

37 William Cole, *A Journal of My Journey to Paris in the Year 1765*, entry for Thursday 24 October.

38 Ibid.

39 For a literary perspective on the Restaurant Magny, see Robert Baldick,

Dinner at Magny's, London, 1971. The book recreates the atmosphere and conversation of six of the celebrated Magny dinners which were held between 1862 and 1872. They were attended by writers such as the Goncourts, Flaubert, Gautier, Turgenev and Sainte-Beuve.

40 The café Procope, at 13 rue de l'Ancienne-Comédie, was founded in 1686 by a Sicilian nobleman, Procopio dei Coltelli, who recognised the commercial possibilities of coffee at a time when it was still being sold as a novelty at the Saint-Germain fair. The Procope, with Voltaire as its patron saint, has had a distinguished literary career. It was the birthplace of the *Encyclopédie*, it served Danton and Marat at the time of the Revolution, and in the 19th century it was patronised by Hugo, Musset, George Sand, Gautier, Balzac, Verlaine, Huysmans and others.

41 André Maurois, *Prométhée, ou la vie de Balzac*, 1965, ch. 8, trans. Norman Denny, 1965.

42 Translation by Michael Hamburger in *Twenty Prose Poems of Baudelaire*, London, 1946.

43 Cyril Connolly, *The Unquiet Grave*, 1944, Pt. III, 'La Clé des Chants'.

44 Simone de Beauvoir, *La force de l'âge*, 1960, ch. 8, trans. Peter Green, 1962.

45 Ernest Hemingway, *A Moveable Feast*, 1964, ch. 4.

46 Ibid.

47 Sylvia Beach, *Shakespeare and Company*, 1959, ch. 5.

48 'La maison des amis du livre' at 7 rue de l'Odéon, where writers such as Valéry, Gide and Claudel gave readings.

49 In 1964 Shakespeare and Company was re-established at 37 rue de la Bûcherie by George Whitman, putative great-grandson of the poet. At this address it still maintains an agreeable tradition of lectures, poetry readings and literary hospitality. Among its past guests are Allen Ginsberg, Lawrence Ferlinghetti, and Alan Sillitoe.

Chapter Five

1 Henry James, *The Tragic Muse*, 1890, ch. 5.

2 Louis-Sébastien Mercier, *Le nouveau Paris*, 1798, 'De la race détronée', trans. Reay Tannahill, 1966.

3 Hilaire Belloc, *Danton: a study*, 1911, ch. 7.

4 Quoted in Norman Hampson, *Danton*, 1978, ch. 10.

5 Marcel Proust, *À la recherche du temps perdu, Du côté de chez Swann*, 1913, trans. C. K. Scott Moncrieff, *Swann's Way*, London, 1922, Vol. II, pp. 248–9.

6 Gustave Flaubert, *L'éducation sentimentale*, 1869, Pt. I, ch. 3, trans. A. Goldsmith, 1941.

7 Ibid., Pt. II, ch. 4, trans. A. Goldsmith, 1941.

8 Quoted in John Forster, *The Life of Charles Dickens*, 1872–4, Bk. VII, ch. 5.

9 Camille Selden, *The Last Days of Heinrich Heine*, trans. Clare Brune, London, 1884, p. 2.

10 Emile Zola, *Les romanciers naturalistes*, Paris, 1881, pp. 179–80.

11 Barbusse lived at no. 105 in 1908, Colette at no. 117 bis in 1903. Proust's home until 1906 was no. 45, he then moved to the ground-floor flat of 102 boulevard Haussmann, where he wrote most of *À la recherche du temps perdu* in the security of his cork-lined room.

12 Letter to John Forster, ?30 November 1846.

13 Letter to John Forster, 6 December 1846.

14 From *is* 5, Two, IX, in *Poems 1923–1954*.

15 Frances Trollope, *Paris and the Parisians*, 1836, Letter X.

16 Marcel Proust, *À la recherche du temps perdu, Du côté de chez Swann*, 1913, trans. C. K. Scott Moncrieff, *Swann's Way*, London, 1922, Vol. II, p. 282.

17 Ibid., pp. 287–8.

18 Jean-Paul Clébert, *Paris insolite*, 1952, ch. 7, section 4.

19 Léon-Paul Fargue, *Le piéton de Paris*, 1939, 'Passy-Auteuil'.

20 Quoted in Jacques Hillairet, *Dictionnaire historique des rues de Paris*, Paris, 1963, supplément, p. 132.

21 The Académie Goncourt is a literary society composed of ten writers, set up by Goncourt's will. Each year it awards the Prix Goncourt to a work of imaginative prose fiction.

22 André Gide, *Journal*, 2 June 1930, trans. Justin O'Brien, 1949.

23 Roland Barthes, 'La Tour Eiffel' (1964), trans. Richard Howard, 1979.

24 Edmond and Jules de Goncourt, *Journal*, Monday 6 May 1889, trans. Robert Baldick, 1962.

25 Ibid., Tuesday 2 July 1889.

26 William Cole, *A Journal of my Journey to Paris in the Year 1765*, entry for Friday 25 October.

27 Martin Lister, *A Journey to Paris in the Year 1698*, ed. R. F. Stearns, London, 1967, pp. 240–1.

28 Marcel Proust *À la recherche du temps perdu, Le côté de Guermantes*, 1913, trans. C. K. Scott Moncrieff, *The Guermantes Way*, London, 1925, Vol. I, pp. 31–2.

29 Henry James, *The American*, 1877, ch. 3.

30 Henry Miller, *Tropic of Cancer*. (1934), London, 1963, pp. 259–62.

31 Letter to Mrs Ruxton, 29 April 1820.

32 In 1800 Stendhal lived at no. 79 and from 1806 to 1807 at no. 69.

33 Saul Bellow, 'Old Paris', *Granta* 10, 1984.

Chapter Six

1 Edmond and Jules de Goncourt, *Journal*, Easter Sunday 28 March 1880, trans. Robert Baldick, 1962.

2 Alphonse Daudet, *Sapho*, 1884, ch. 1.

3 Ibid., ch. 3.

4 Dumas père lived at no. 79 in 1843. (In 1879 Manet had his studio in the same building.) Heine lived at no. 50, 1848–51.

5 André Gide, *Si le grain ne meurt*, 1925, Pt. I, ch. 10.

6 Daniel Halévy, *Pays parisiens*, 1932, ch. 5.

7 Emile Zola, *Nana*, 1880, ch. 8, trans. E. Vizetelly, 1884.

8 Théophile Gautier, 'Les lorettes' (1845), reprinted in *Souvenirs de théâtre, d'art et de critique*, 1883.

9 Privat d'Anglemont, *Paris inconnu*, 1861, 'Paris en villages', ch. 2.

10 W. M. Thackeray, *The Paris Sketch Book*, 1840, 'On the French School of Painting'.

11 Edmond and Jules de Goncourt, *Journal*, Wednesday 3 April 1878, trans. Robert Baldick, 1962.

12 Arnold Bennett, *Sketches for Autobiography*, ed. James Hepburn, London, 1979, p. 145.

13 Arnold Bennett, *Journals*, Vol. I, 1896–1910, London, 1932.

14 W. Somerset Maugham, *The Vagrant Mood*, 1952, 'Some Novelists I Have Known', section 5.

15 Sand enthusiasts should visit the nearby musée Renan-Scheffer at 16 rue Chaptal, where a number of rooms are devoted to her.

16 Quoted in John Forster, *The Life of Charles Dickens*, 1872–4, Bk. VII, ch. 5.

17 Alphonse Daudet, 'Tourguéneff' (1880), reprinted in *Trente ans de Paris*, 1888.

18 Daniel Halévy, *Pays parisiens*, 1932, ch. 5.

19 Alphonse Daudet, 'La fin d'un pitre et de la bohème de Murger' in *Trente ans de Paris*, 1888.

20 Ibid.

21 H. P. Hugh, 'The Two Montmartres' in *Paris Magazine*, June 1899.

22 George Moore, *Confessions of a Young Man*, 1886, ch. 7.

23 W. M. Thackeray, *The Paris Sketch Book*, 1840, 'An Invasion of France'.

24 See Louis Chevalier, *Montmartre du plaisir et du crime*, 1980, Pt. I, ch. 2.

25 Emile Zola, *L'assommoir*, 1877, ch. 1, trans. L. W. Tancock, 1970.

26 George Moore, *Confessions of a Young Man*, 1886, ch. 2.

27 Jean Rhys, *Quartet*, 1928, ch. 22.

28 Edmond and Jules de Goncourt, *Journal*, Sunday 13 March 1892, trans. Robert Baldick, 1962.

29 The source of these details is Jean-Pierre Crespelle, *La vie quotidienne à Montmartre au temps de Picasso, 1900–1910*, Paris, 1978.

30 George Moore, *Memoirs of My Dead Life*, 1906, ch. 4.

31 Not the same person as La Goulue. (Marie Pellegrin's friend La Glue was supposed to have sat for Manet's portrait of Olympe.)

32 George Moore, *Memoirs of My Dead Life*, 1906, ch. 4.

33 Jean Rhys, *Quartet*, ch. 2.

34 Francis Carco, *Jésus-la-Caille*, 1914, Pt. I, ch. 1.

35 Quoted in Louis Chevalier, *Montmartre du plaisir et du crime*, 1980, Pt. VI, ch. 1.

36 Henry Miller, *Black Spring*, 1936, 'Walking Up and Down in China'.

37 Daniel Halévy, *Pays Parisiens*, 1932, ch. 9.

38 H. P. Hugh, 'The Two Montmartres' in *Paris Magazine*, June 1899.

39 Roland Dorgelès, *Portraits sans retouche*, 1952, ch. 8.

40 Gérard de Nerval, *Promenades et souvenirs*, 1854–5, 'La Butte Mont-martre'.
41 Francis Carco, *De Montmartre au quartier latin*, Paris, 1927, ch. 9.
42 Evelyn Waugh, *When the Going was Good*, 1946, ch. 1.
43 Francis Carco, *Jésus-la-Caille*, 1914, Pt. III, ch. 5.
44 Michel de Montaigne, *Letters*, quoted in *Yale French Studies*, no. 32, 'An Early Portrait'.

Acknowledgements

Acknowledgement is due to the following for kindly giving permission to reproduce copyright material.

Bantam Books, Inc: extract from Emile Zola, *Thérèse Raquin*, translated by Willard R. Trask. Copyright © 1952 by Bantam Books, Inc.

B. T. Batsford Ltd: extract of Jean-Paul Sartre from John Russell, *Paris*. Reprinted by permission of A. D. Peters & Co Ltd.

Christian Bourgois Éditeur: extract from Georges Perec, *Tentative d'épuisement d'un lieu parisien*;

John Calder (Publishers) Ltd: three extracts from Henry Miller's *Tropic of Cancer* and one from *Black Spring*;

Jonathan Cape Ltd: extract from Baudelaire, *Twenty Prose Poems of Baudelaire*, translated by Michael Hamburger. All rights reverted to Michael Hamburger. Extracts from Ernest Hemingway, *Green Hills of Africa*, 'The Snows of Kilimanjaro' from *The First Forty-Nine Stories*, *Fiesta (The Sun Also Rises)*, and *A Moveable Feast*. Reprinted by permission of the Executors of the Ernest Hemingway estate;

Chatto & Windus: two extracts from Marcel Proust, *Du côte de chez Swann*, translated by C. K. Scott Moncrieff;

Editions Denöel: extract from Jean-Paul Clébert, *Paris insolite*;

J. M. Dent & Sons Ltd: two extracts from Gustave Flaubert, *A Sentimental Education*, translated by Anthony Goldsmith, Everyman's Library Series;

André Deutsch Ltd: four extracts from Simone de Beauvoir, *The Prime of Life*, translated by Peter Green (1962), three extracts from Jean Rhys, *Quartet* (1928), one from *Good Morning Midnight*;

Gerald Duckworth & Co Ltd; extract from Evelyn Waugh, *When the Going was Good*. Reprinted by kind permission of A. D. Peters & Co Ltd;

Eyre & Spottiswoode: extract from Arthur Stanley, *Mme de Sévigné*;

A Fayard et Cie: extract from Georges Simenon, *Le pendu de Saint-Pholien*, translated by Tony White, and one from *Pietr-le-Letton*, translated by Daphne Woodward. Reprinted by permission of Georges Simenon;

The Folio Society Ltd: three extracts from Victor Hugo, *Les misérables*, translated by Norman Denny for members of The Folio Society in 1976;

Editions Gallimard: two extracts from Léon-Paul Fargue, *Le piéton de Paris* (1939), three extracts from Francis Carco, *Nostalgie de Paris* (1952);

Granta 10: extract from Saul Bellow, *Old Paris* reprinted by kind permission of A. M. Heath

Éditions Bernard Grasset: four extracts from Daniel Halévy, *Pays parisiens*;

Hachette Literature: extract from Jacques Wilhelm, *La vie quotidienne au Marais au XVIIe siècle*;

Hamish Hamilton Ltd: extract from Robert Baldick, *The Memoirs of Chateaubriand*;

William Heinemann Ltd: extract from W. Somerset Maugham, *The Vagrant Mood*, and one from *The Razor's Edge*. Reprinted by permission of the Executors of the Estate of W. Somerset Maugham. Poem by François Villon, *Epitaph*, translated by Richard Aldington;

Éditions Robert Laffont: extract from Louis Chevalier, *Montmartre du plaisir et du crime*;

The Free Press, a division of Macmillan Publishing Inc. New York: extract from Peter Abélard, *The Story of My Misfortunes*, translated by Henry Adams Bellows 1958.

Editions Albin Michel: extract from Francis Carco, *De Montmartre au quartier latin* and two from *Jesus la Caille*;

Oxford University Press: six extracts from Robert Baldick, *Pages from the Goncourt Journal*;

Penguin Books Ltd: two extracts from Honoré de Balzac, *Old Goriot*, translated by Marian Ayton Crawford (Penguin Classics, 1951), copyright © Marian Ayton Crawford, 1951, and one from *Cousine Bette*, translated by Marian Ayton Crawford (Penguin Classics, 1965), copyright © Marian Ayton Crawford, 1965, extract from Denis Diderot, *Rameau's Nephew and d'Alembert's Dream*, translated by L. W. Tancock (Penguin Classics, 1966), copyright © L. W. Tancock, 1966, extract from François Rabelais, *Gargantua and Pantagruel*, translated by J. M. Cohen, 1955, extract from Emile Zola, *L'assommoir*, translated by L. W. Tancock (Penguin Classics, 1970), copyright © L. W. Tancock, 1970;

The Pennsylvania State University Press: extract from Alfred Perlès, 'Gobelins Tapestries' in *The Left Bank Revisited*, ed. Hugh Ford;

Random House, Inc: three extracts from Restif de la Bretonne, *Les nuits de Paris*, translated by Linda Asher and Ellen Fertig;

Martin Secker & Warburg Ltd: two extracts from George Orwell, *Down and Out in Paris and London*. Reprinted by permission of the Estate of the late Sonia Brownell Orwell;

Sheed & Ward Ltd: three extracts from D. B. Wyndham Lewis, *François Villon*.

Every effort has been made to trace copyright holders. In some cases this has proved impossible. The author and publishers of this book would be pleased to hear from any copyright holders not acknowledged.

Index

Note: Cafés, bars, brasseries, cabarets, clubs and restaurants are indexed together under cafés. Streets, squares and bridges are indexed together under Paris. As in the text, Hotel indicates a place of accommodation for travellers, hôtel a large private residence.